Landmark ENTERTAINING

Party Traditions And Favorite Recipes
From The Junior League Of Abilene

The
JUNIOR
LEAGUE OF
ABILENE

LANDMARK ENTERTAINING

The Junior League of Abilene wishes to express a very special thank you to the following individuals and businesses for their overwhelming support and contributions toward the production of this book:

Photographer: Steve Butman
Committee Photographer & Stylist: Mary Ann Fergus

Abilene Convention and Visitors Bureau	The Gilded Lily	Paramount Theatre
Abilene Preservation League	Grace Cultural Center	Philpott Florists
Antiques and Almost	Hancock Fabrics	Pier One
Boydstun Hardware, Baird	Sarah and Horace Hatfield	Melissa Scott
Silvetta Burns	Hendrick Home for Children	Sharon's Specialities
Busch Jewelers	Judi Hughes	Spano's Italian Cafe
Caldwell Music Company	Jerry Jordan	Surprises
Speck Childs	Market Street Mall, Baird	Swenson House
Lynn Dickey	Lindsey Minter	T & P Depot
Dillards	Portia Moore	Tiffany's of San Diego, Ca.
French Market Accents	Connye Owen	Waldrop's Fine Furniture
	Dian Owen	Lenore Waldrop

Published by
The Junior League of Abilene
774 Butternut Street
Abilene, Texas 79602
(915)-677-1879

©1996 The Junior League of Abilene

ISBN: 0-9611620-0-7
Library of Congress Number: 96-085128

Manufactured in the United States of America
First Printing: 1996 15,000

Designed, Edited and Manufactured by
Favorite Recipes® Press
P.O. Box 305142
Nashville, Tennessee 37230
1-800-358-0560

Book Design: David Malone, Joe Montgomery

Cover Art: *Paramount at Night* by Jerry Jordan, Taos, New Mexico
From the collection of Mr. and Mrs. Dan Fergus, Jr.

CONTENTS

*Refers to old favorites from past
Junior League of Abilene cookbooks*

The Paramount Theatre opened on May 19, 1930, at a time when people of the Big Country needed it the most. The Depression had just begun; growth in Abilene had faltered, and spirits were low. This magnificent theatre helped people forget their economic woes and transformed their dreams both on screen and on stage.

Mr. H. O. Wooten, hotel owner and real estate developer, began construction on the Paramount in 1929. It was his intent to change Abilene's cow town image

PARAMOUNT THEATRE

into one of cosmopolitan culture. The theatre was built as a memorial to the city.

Those who viewed the Paramount for the first time found the decor equally as fascinating as the latest movie on the theatre's wide screen. Drifting white clouds and points of star light twinkled against a "sky" of midnight blue. Spanish alcoves with domed castle turrets

glowed in direct lighting on either side of the Paramount's ample stage.

In the early years, the Paramount was adorned with paintings and statues from France and Italy. The interior gleamed with decorative Spanish lighting and antique Italian furnishings. Uniformed ushers gave out programs at the door, assisted patrons to their seats, and patrolled the aisles in grand fashion. The Paramount's ticket girls were some of Abilene's most beautiful and were always attractively dressed.

The theatre closed in 1979 but was saved from demolition by local preservation efforts.

A complete restoration was completed in 1987 and the theatre is now operated by a nonprofit organization. Mr. H. O. Wooten would have been proud to learn that this "Grand Old Lady of Theatre" truly has become a cultural center for classic movies and performing arts.

AFTER THE THEATRE

Sweet-and-Sour Cream Cheese Appetizer
Dijon Beef Tender OR *Tenderloin of Beef with Wine Gravy*
Pecan Rice
Brussels Sprouts with Scallions
Butter and Red Leaf Lettuce with Sunshine Dressing
Herbed Rolls
Kahlúa Pound Cake
Peach Torte   White Chocolate Cake

A black-tie atmosphere makes for an unforgettable evening. All is glitz and glitter, complete with dramatic candle lighting and colorful theatrical props. Compose your invitations on sheet music, rolled and tied with black satin ribbon. Elegant table coverings can be fashioned from tapestry or heavy brocade and set with gleaming silver or crystal candelabra. Arrange orchestra instruments in prominent places to echo the effect of your table's centerpiece.

Use a chalkboard framed in gilt molding to announce the upcoming meal and correlate each course in theatre playbill fashion. Begin with appetizers as the Overture and end with desserts as the Grande Finale. A "Playbill Who's Who" of each guest, with biographies, "past performances," and current endeavors, assists your guests in getting to know one another.

All of these ingredients are just a few ideas for a spectacular opening night, so book your ticket now and receive rave reviews.

In 1885 the T & P Depot was a two-story wooden building featuring an eating house and hotel. Early maps show that by 1902 a simpler one-story depot was built, which replaced the older, more ornate version. In 1910 the present depot was built west of the 1902 building, resulting from the efforts of local civic leaders to promote Abilene. It originally featured dormers on the roof and tower before it was remodeled.

The present depot has a tile roof, brickwork that creates a molded cornice effect, and roof cupholes. There is a gable over the North First Street entrance. This wonderful landmark has

for the citizens of Abilene.

On March 14, 1911, Teddy Roosevelt made a ninety-second speech at the depot on his way through Abilene. After rising flood waters covered the railroad tracks in 1911, the T & P Railroad determined that the tracks should be raised to the present level. Underpasses for automobiles were built in 1936 as part of the Public Works Administration program. The last passenger train left the depot in March, 1967, with only thirty-nine passengers aboard.

The restoration of the depot to its 1920s appearance was completed in 1994. This premier structure now houses the Cultural

THE T & P DEPOT

served as a gathering place for many years and holds fond memories

Affairs Council as well as the Abilene Convention and Visitors Bureau.

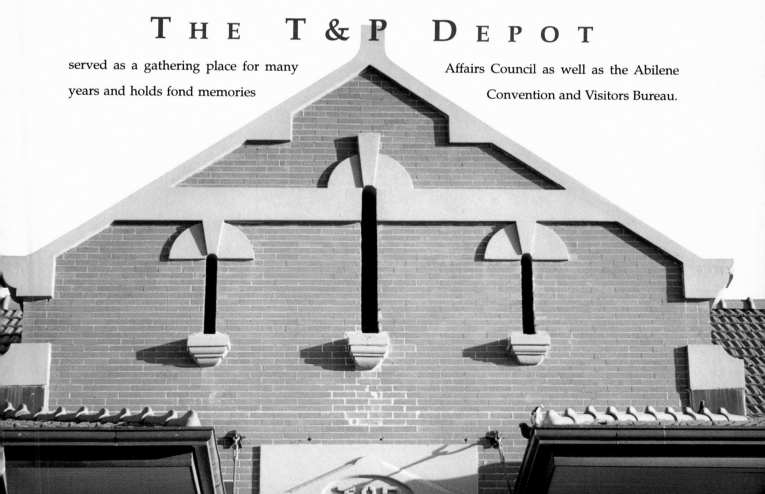

FISHERMAN'S BREAKFAST

Brunch Pizza
Breakfast Trifle
Sliced Fruit *
Smoked Salmon with Cream Cheese and Capers *
Mimosas *

Surprise the sportsmen in your family with a hearty breakfast by the waterside. Envision a peaceful picnic spread complete with tartan throws, overstuffed pillows, and the sweet serenade of bird song. A quick closet clean-out should yield a host of table decor that can be used in a variety of ways. Old-fashioned lures, bamboo poles, and other sporting gear set the theme and can be used creatively on your "table."

Consider the many possibilities for containers to hold local greenery, such as an old fishing creel or a minnow bucket. A sheer mosquito net suspended from the trees produces a wonderful expedition effect, and it may be time to break out the pith helmets and field glasses. Other "necessary" creature comforts should include linens, silver, crystal, and china. Don't let this big one get away!

Menu suggestion–recipe not included

"Every room a ceiling fan, every bed a Sealy" read the circa 1928 brochure advertising the Grace Hotel to travelers. Built by W. L. Beckham in 1909 and named after his daughter, the "Mission Revival" hotel was touted by the proprietor as the finest between Ft. Worth and San Diego. The twentieth century commercial building with its decorative stone trim was conveniently located by the train depot, making it popular with travelers. It was a welcome sight for weary travelers as they approached the City of Abilene by train. Originally planned as a three-story structure, the hotel had a fourth floor added in 1924.

Its most notable tenant was independent railroad builder Morgan Jones. The "Old Mahn," as he was referred to, had supervised construction of the tracks for the Union Pacific, Southern Pacific, Texas and Pacific, Gulf, Colorado and Santa Fe, and Ft. Worth and Denver City before building the connecting lines to the north and south of Abilene. Jones was a semipermanent tenant of the Grace Hotel from 1909 until shortly before his death in 1926.

In addition to serving as a hotel, the Grace played many other roles during its first life. It served as the headquarters for West Texas Coaches, a bus company, the Western Union office, home of the radio station KFYO, and even as a temporary location for the Taylor County

GRACE HOTEL

Courthouse. In 1947 the Grace underwent a renovation and its name was changed to The Drake. The Drake steadily declined until a boiler failure in 1972 forced its closure.

In 1986 the hotel was rescued by the Abilene Preservation League and eventually was restored as the Grace Cultural Center, which now houses the Fine Arts Museum, a Historical Museum, and a Children's Participatory Museum.

COURTYARD FIESTA

Tortilla Chips with Fiesta Green Sauce, Black Bean Salsa,
Guacamole, and Huma Salsa
Chicken Fajitas
Tex-Mex Rice
Tasty Black Beans
Avocado Salad
Lemon Ice Cream Pie with Raspberry Sauce

In West Texas, Southwestern fare is a real favorite and is used often for a variety of occasions. It is hard to find anyone who does not like "Tex-Mex" and this does not have to be an expensive meal to prepare.

Surprise your guests by delivering a small pinata with an invitation stuffed inside along with candy, small trinkets, confetti, and streamers. Bright colors should prevail at this party and are readily available by utilizing colorful fabric, crepe paper, fresh sunflowers, or other paper goods. Be creative in your music selections, ranging from Spanish bullfighting music to music by the latest Latin stars.

Fill a flat pottery bowl with colorful dried beans or rice and nestle various sized candles for a dramatic centerpiece. Cut out the crowns of inexpensive straw sombreros and set colorful potted flowers inside the cutouts. Sombreros can also double as serving pieces on a buffet. Use colorful quilts, traditional serape blankets, or any other colorful table coverings.

To further enhance the fiesta spirit, have carnations ready to pin into the ladies' hair upon their arrival and—for those who will oblige—paint the gentlemen with a bandito mustache. Visit your local import store for fun favors such as Mexican jumping beans, castanets, finger stretchers, and marionette puppets.

anch life is still a dominant feature of Texas, and Abilene is in the heart of ranch country. Situated in the southern region of the Great Plains, the area has an overabundant supply of grassland, coupled with the semiarid climate, which gives rise to the phenomenon of the West Texas ranch. What originally grew out of necessity for survival and most logical use of the land has now become a fiercely protected way of life for a privileged few.

A great mystique has evolved around the handful of ranches that remain family-owned and managed. The ranch families'

however, they all share one common "brand" of hospitality.

We salute our ranching heritage, which has a time-honored tradition of grand-scale entertaining. There is simply no substitute for the original, Texas-sized ranch gathering

HISTORIC RANCHES OF TEXAS

love of the land and preference for ranch life makes them a breed unto themselves. Indeed, it takes a special individual who can adapt to the forces of nature, the cycles of Wall Street, and the whims of government, while reading the minds of cattle and horses. The descendants of these ranch settlers are still here today—and their children's children will continue in this rich legacy for many years to come. Each ranch has its own unique personality;

that we have all come to know, love, and respect.

Pictured here is the landmark Hendrick Home for Children River Ranch, which was dedicated in 1939 by Tom and Ida Hendrick for the express purpose of fostering children. Such a gift as this immense Texas ranch, solely for the benefit of children, is demonstrative of the type of people who dwell in this land. Their genuine love for mankind is only surpassed by their generosity of spirit and kindness to others.

CHUCK WAGON BUFFET

London Broil with Tarragon Butter
Grilled Corn on the Cob OR *Mixed Grilled Vegetables**
Mandarin Orange Tossed Salad
Honey Whole Wheat Bread
Cherry Cobbler

Casual outdoor entertaining can be a true delight to your guests, and any size backyard or patio is easily turned into a "Texas Ranchette." Invitations written on brown paper sacks or faded denim swatches will reflect the rustic atmosphere of this informal, western dining theme. Start with a simple buffet-style table and build your chuck wagon effect from there.

Jars of colorful marinated vegetables, wooden bowls, strings of chile peppers and garlic are found in many kitchens and can be transformed with a small raffia tie. Set out southwestern blankets or burlap runners for table coverings. Worn boots and cowboy hats make interesting and unexpected containers for greenery and wildflowers. Ropes, spurs, branding irons, and other cowboy memorabilia will make your guests feel as if they were home on the range.

Brush up on your cowboy poetry with your best southern drawl and entertain with pearls of wisdom during dessert. Bales of hay double as extra seating, or just throw an old-fashioned picnic quilt on the ground. A game of horseshoes tops off the effect, and the guests can take home jars of homemade jams or pickled vegetables topped with calico trim.

*Menu suggestion–recipe not included

The George W. McDaniel House, located at 774 Butternut, is an outstanding example of a Prairie-influenced residence and has been listed on the National Register for its architectural merits. Now the headquarters for the Abilene Junior League, the McDaniel House is virtually unaltered and retains its historic integrity and character.

During the 1920s, many residential period, but Prairie-influenced houses were built by some of Abilene's most prosperous citizens. This particular house is representative of that trend.

George W. McDaniel, for whom the structure was built, owned a hardware and grocery store at South Second and Chestnut Streets and benefitted from the 1920s economic boom. This historical house was

JUNIOR LEAGUE
OF ABILENE

structures were built in Abilene as the local construction industry experienced one of its most profitable periods. Citizens of Abilene enjoyed community-wide prosperity as the city consolidated its position as the financial hub of West Texas. With the oil boom, many people moved to—or traded with—Abilene, which grew in importance during the decade. Bungalows were the most common houses built in that

designed as a two-story wood frame dwelling with brick veneer. A composition shingled hipped roof supported on massive piers forms a deep three-bay porch that stretches entirely across the east side of the house. These elements, with the horizontal emphasis when viewed from the front, place this structure in the Prairie School of architecture.

MOTHER-DAUGHTER TEA

Strawberries in a Cloud

Chocolate Cookies

Lone Star Lemon Bars

Swedish Wafers

Filled Cream Cheese Foldovers

Mocha Punch

Texas Tea

Favorite recipes from our past Junior League cookbooks are featured at this well loved gathering. There is no age limit for this beautiful party; tea time can be enjoyed by everyone—from toddlers to great-grandmothers. For invitations, think Victorian with antique Raphael angels and lace. Live chamber music or a harpist is appropriate and will make a strong visual statement. Flowers, formal table linens, and your finest silver are able to come out of hiding to embellish your table in great splendor.

Alternate ideas for table decor could feature whimsical hat stands with antique hats, stacked hatboxes, strings of faux pearls, and yards of satin ribbon. While the mothers visit, the younger guests can entertain themselves in a separate craft area. Tulle, silk flowers, lace and other decorations provided by the hostess spark fabulous millinery creations and embellished gloves. After all, a proper young lady is never seen without her hat and gloves.

For Mother's Day tea, our little darlings can create prized mementos for Mom. Delicate drawstring bags stuffed with sachet and tied with satin ribbon, homemade greeting cards trimmed with dried flowers, and a frame made of buttons are just a few of many enchanting ideas. With just a little effort, a formal tea such as this will be long remembered and cherished by mothers and daughters of all ages.

The first swimming pool in Abilene, located at 1202 Elmwood, will always be anchored in the memories of several longtime Abilene residents. So many good times and memories were made in those first years that it is difficult to find anyone who does not reminisce with a smile and a giggle. The pool was even used by the Abilene Fire Department for swimming and lifesaving classes.

In 1928, when the pool was initially constructed, there were no filtration nor

McDaniel Pool

chlorination systems, as these were unheard of in those times. Instead, an ingenious flow-through pump system was devised that allowed the pool to be filled from two wells, both still operational on the property, and then drained every few days on an as-needed basis. Draining was accomplished through a number of pipes running out to various areas of the magnificent lawn and garden. An early-day irrigation system!

The pool was lovingly restored in 1986 by Ms. Dian Owen, the present owner and resident of this historical estate. At the time of restoration, Ms. Owen determined that the pool should remain raised above the ground, utilizing the ground support and brick retaining walls for lateral support. The steps leading up to the pool on the west side are also part of the original structure and are fabricated with a unique round-edged brick, which is no longer made. This same type of brick can be found throughout the grounds of the estate and, wherever possible, the bricks have been carefully preserved in the landscaping and boundary fences.

The pool remains fully operational, and on a hot Texas day the sound of riotous laughter from children can still be heard as it is enjoyed by new generations of the estate's legacy.

POOLSIDE ELEGANCE

Lamb Shish Kabobs with White Rice
Strawberry Spinach Salad OR
Fruit Salad * *with Poppy Seed Dressing*
Croissants
Leffel's Kahlúa Almond Fudge Ice Cream
Ginger Almond Tea

With a little imagination and a few hours of summer twilight, a backyard swimming pool can be transformed into a mysterious blue lagoon. A warm, sultry evening filled with good friends and good food is a welcome change of pace.

Set the mood with your invitations by affixing petite dried flowers to a thick, paneled card. Drop scented faux flower petals into the envelope to invoke a romantic mood. Heavy white linen, Battenberg lace, or crisp floral chintz can serve as table coverings. Seashells and fresh-cut bouquets in clear vases work well as casually elegant centerpieces. Glitter and fruit in the water of the clear vases renders an intriguing effect.

Hurricane glasses anchored with sand can house gleaming white candles. Seashells scattered around the table contribute to the theme. Appropriate music rounds out the setting and may range from light classical to steel drum.

For added drama, mount long-burning candles with greenery and flowers on buoyant material and float them in the pool. Glittered shells wrapped in sheer netting make a fine cache for party favors.

Menu suggestion—recipe not included

One of the few grand old homes that still remain in Abilene, the Swenson House was built by William and Shirley Swenson as their family country home circa 1910. This noteworthy Prairie-style structure boasts a remarkable example of a Spanish Colonial Revival interior, which dominates the grand entry hall and staircase. Leaded stained glass windows around the front door are set high into the ceiling of the entry and are a natural accompaniment to finely carved, mahogany-stained balustrades. The second floor's full mezzanine echoes the first floor's dark Spanish design and gives the entire structure superb balance and a great warmth.

The W. G. Swenson family was one of Abilene's original leading families who first settled Abilene and were instrumental in its growth and development. The Abilene Preservation League now owns the house and maintains it on a full-time basis as a House Museum. The Abilene Preservation League is a local nonprofit organization dedicated to the protection of historically and architecturally significant buildings.

SWENSON HOUSE

HOLIDAY CELEBRATION

Cheese Ring with Raspberry Sauce

Stuffed Pork Roast

Glazed Carrots with Bacon and Onion

Corn and Rice

Frozen Cranberry Salad

Cardamom Bread

Kahlúa Pecan Pie

Pumpkin Cheesecake with Cranberry Glaze

Chocolate-Covered Caramels

A "Charles Dickens' Christmas" is a classic holiday expression for any home. You will be surprised at the amount of greenery you can gather from your own area, with the decorating results being much more satisfying than if you use store-bought items.

Traditional evergreens mixed with fresh fruits are a particular enhancement to a holiday table set with your favorite china. Fill glass hurricanes with lemons, limes, and handfuls of nuts. Write your invitations (or even place cards) on ornaments with a metallic paint pen.

Position carolers at the entryway to coax guests into a sing-along by handing out copies of music. Golden angels fashioned out of pears and ribbon for wings herald tidings at each place and make heavenly party favors. After-dinner entertainment might include a game of charades using only Christmas words.

The holidays offer a timeless theme for entertaining, and your guests will no doubt feel the warmth and love of the season when you put yourself into the experience with hand-fashioned creativity.

PARTY POTPOURRI

Entertaining can be on a grand scale or a simple, casual affair. Coming together to enjoy good company and to take a break from today's fast-pace lifestyle doesn't have to be a burden and should mean a special memory for host and guest alike.

Whether your party is a celebration or a regular gathering of friends, adding humor, intrigue, or a bit of a challenge through the theme, games, or icebreakers can make the event even more successful.

Instead of the usual celebrations and dinner parties, try theme parties centered around games and activities or perhaps around the menu. Supper clubs are always a favorite and a wonderful opportunity for you to try the unconventional. Host a Limerick Party where everyone is given the beginning of a limerick and asked to create an original ending; or finish a jigsaw puzzle, play Bunko, or bridge. A Mystery Party with guests searching for clues to solve the case is fun and makes for whimsical interaction among friends. Try giving each guest a bag containing a mystery item. The object of this icebreaker is for each person to guess what the secret item is by touching, feeling, or smelling the bag.

Playing games or learning facts about each other can be an amusing way for your guests to get to know each other better. And who knows, you may make a new best friend. Whether it be bridge clubs, supper clubs, baby showers, graduation parties, or debutante parties, use your imagination and make your party enjoyable, entertaining, and memorable for everyone.

MENUS

WEST TEXAS FAIR BLUE RIBBON BARBECUE
Brisket
Best Baked Beans or *Cuban Black Beans*
Napa Cabbage Salad or *Marinated Vegetable Salad*
Icebox Dinner Rolls
Four-Berry Cobbler

AFTER THE HUNT
Cheese Bites
Grilled Quail with Currant Sauce or *Quail Stuffed with Jalapeños*
Baked Mushrooms
Cauliflower and Wild Rice
Mardi Gras Salad
Apple Pie with Rum Butter Sauce

LADIES LUNCHEON
Turkey Cranberry Croissants
Broccoli Salad with Raisins or *Fruit Salad with Orange Almond Dressing*
Autumn Apple Cake

DINNER UNDER THE STARS
Barbequed Chicken with Honey Mustard Glaze
New Potato Casserole
Asparagus Bundles with Hazelnut Dressing
Banana Pudding Supreme
Summertime Iced Tea

FOOTBALL FEAST
Taco Soup
Hot Croissant Sandwiches with *Sweet Hot Mustard*
Black-Eyed Pea Corn Bread
Caramel Brownies
White Chocolate Chip Cookies
Cornflake Crispies   *Candied Pecans*

Menus

Father's Day Brunch
Roulade of Cheese Soufflé or *Brunch Enchiladas*
Fresh Fruit Salad
Sausage Muffins or *Pumpkin Muffins* or *Orange Crunch Muffins*
Bavarian Apple Torte
Spiced Tea

Sweetheart Dinner
Coconut Shrimp
Grilled Stuffed Beef Tenderloin with Bordelaise Sauce
Herbed Baked Potatoes   Asparagus Parmesan
Hearts of Palm Salad with Watercress Vinaigrette
Velvet Cream Biscuits
Strawberry Cake with Strawberry Cream Cheese Frosting
Flavored Coffee

Baby Shower Luncheon
Chicken Salad with Artichokes or *Hot Croissant Sandwiches*
Tossed Salad with Raspberry Vinaigrette
Poppy Seed Gems or *Zucchini Bread*
Strawberries Romanoff or *Strawberry Frozen Dessert*

Bridal Luncheon
Chicken in Pastry
Splendid Raspberry Spinach
Yeast Biscuits
Easy English Trifle

New Year's Eve Cocktail Party
New Year's Black-Eyed Pea Dip   Crab Cream Cheese Appetizer
Hot Artichoke Dip   Mushroom Caps   Savory Cheese Ball   Vegetable Pizza
Crème de Menthe Squares   Almond Cream Confections
Apricot Brandy Pound Cake
Apricot Brandy Slush   Hot Buttered Rum   Peachys

APPETIZERS

APPETIZERS

Antipasto, 37

Asparagus Cream Cheese Sandwiches, 37

Cucumber Sandwiches, 38

Brie Crisps, 38

Cheese Bites, 39

Baked Monterey Jack Slices, 39

Mushroom Caps, 39

Roasted Pecans, 40

Hot and Spicy Pecans, 40

Candied Pecans, 40

Coconut Shrimp, 41

Spicy Shrimp, 41

Vegetable Pizza, 42

Baked Party Brie, 42

Caramelized Brie with Pecans, 43

Cheese Ring with Raspberry Sauce, 43

Savory Cheese Ball, 44

Crab Cream Cheese Appetizer, 44

Sweet-and-Sour Cream Cheese Appetizer, 44

Elephant Garlic Spread, 45

Hot Artichoke Dip, 45

New Year's Black-Eyed Pea Dip, 46

Black Bean Salsa, 46

Fiesta Green Sauce, 47

Guacamole, 47

Huma Salsa, 47

Jalapeño Cream Cheese Dip, 48

Spinach Dip Florentine, 48

ANTIPASTO

Ingredients
1 cup chopped onion
1 garlic clove, minced
1 cup vegetable oil
1 (8-ounce) can tomato paste
1 bunch celery, finely chopped
1 pound carrots, finely chopped
8 ounces fresh mushrooms, finely chopped
2 bunches green onions, finely chopped
2 green bell peppers, finely chopped
3 zucchini, finely chopped
3 yellow squash, finely chopped
1 head cauliflower, finely chopped
1 (16-ounce) jar banana pepper rings
1 (8-ounce) can artichoke hearts, drained, chopped
1 (16-ounce) jar dill pickles, drained, chopped
1 (6-ounce) can pitted black olives, drained, chopped
1 (8-ounce) can hearts of palm, drained, chopped
1 (8-ounce) jar picante sauce
Salt and pepper to taste
Oregano to taste
Grated Parmesan cheese to taste

METHOD OF PREPARATION

Sauté the onion and garlic in the oil in a sauce-pan until tender. Stir in the tomato paste. Remove from heat.

Add the celery, carrots, mushrooms, green onions, green peppers, zucchini, yellow squash, cauliflower, undrained pepper rings, artichokes, dill pickles, olives and hearts of palm, tossing to mix. May add red wine or vinegar if additional liquid is desired. Stir in the picante sauce, salt, pepper and oregano. Sprinkle with Parmesan cheese.

Chill, covered, for 8 to 10 hours. Serve with tortilla chips or crackers.

Note: May store in the refrigerator for up to 3 weeks.

MAKES 12 CUPS

ASPARAGUS CREAM CHEESE SANDWICHES

Ingredients
12 ounces cream cheese, softened
1 (16-ounce) can asparagus tips, drained, chopped
2 hard-cooked eggs, chopped
Dash of Tabasco sauce
Lemon juice to taste
Lemon pepper to taste
Seasoned salt to taste
1 loaf (about) extra-thin sandwich bread slices
Melted butter
Grated Parmesan cheese to taste

METHOD OF PREPARATION

Combine the cream cheese, asparagus, eggs, Tabasco sauce, lemon juice, lemon pepper and seasoned salt in a bowl, stirring until mixed.

Trim the crusts from the bread. Spread the cream cheese mixture on half the bread slices; top with the remaining bread. Cut each sandwich into fingers or triangles. Dip each portion in butter; roll in Parmesan cheese.

Arrange the sandwiches on a baking sheet. Broil until brown on both sides, turning once.

Note: Sandwiches may be frozen for future use before baking. They make a great accompaniment to soup or salad.

MAKES 48 SANDWICHES

CUCUMBER SANDWICHES

Ingredients
1 cucumber
8 ounces cream cheese, softened
3 tablespoons mayonnaise
1/2 teaspoon chopped chives
1/2 teaspoon paprika
Dash of cayenne
Dash of onion salt
18 to 20 slices (about) extra-thin sandwich bread

METHOD OF PREPARATION

Seed and coarsely grate the cucumber. Drain in a colander.

Combine the cucumber, cream cheese, mayonnaise, chives, paprika, cayenne and onion salt in a bowl and mix well. Chill, covered, for 1 hour.

Trim the crusts from the bread. Spread the cucumber mixture on half the bread; top with the remaining bread. Cut each sandwich into quarters.

MAKES 36 TO 40 APPETIZERS

BRIE CRISPS

Ingredients
4 ounces Brie cheese, softened
1/2 cup butter, softened
2/3 cup flour
1/4 teaspoon cayenne, or to taste
1/8 teaspoon salt
Paprika to taste

METHOD OF PREPARATION

Remove the rind from the cheese. Combine the cheese and butter in a food processor container. Process until creamy. Add the flour, cayenne and salt.

Process until the mixture almost forms a ball. Shape into a roll 1 to 1 1/2 inches in diameter. Chill, wrapped in plastic wrap, for 8 to 10 hours.

Cut the roll into 1/4-inch slices. Place 2 inches apart on a baking sheet.

Bake at 400 degrees for 10 to 12 minutes or until the edges are brown. Remove to a wire rack to cool. Sprinkle with paprika.

MAKES 16 TO 24 APPETIZERS

CHEESE BITES

Ingredients
2 cups butter, softened
4 (5-ounce) jars Old English cheese spread
1 1/2 teaspoons Worcestershire sauce
1 teaspoon Tabasco sauce
1 teaspoon onion powder
Cayenne to taste
3 loaves Pepperidge Farm thinly sliced sandwich bread
Dillweed to taste

METHOD OF PREPARATION
Beat the butter, cheese spread, Worcestershire sauce, Tabasco sauce, onion powder and cayenne in a mixer bowl until of the consistency of frosting, scraping the bowl occasionally.

Stack 3 bread slices; trim the crusts.

Spread some of the cheese mixture between the bread slices. Cut the stack into quarters. Spread some of the cheese mixture over the top and sides of the quarters. Place on a baking sheet. Repeat the process with the remaining bread slices and cheese mixture.

Freeze until firm. Remove from the freezer. Wrap between sheets of waxed paper. Store in the freezer.

Place frozen cheese bites on a baking sheet. Bake at 350 degrees for 15 to 20 minutes or until light brown. Sprinkle with additional cayenne and dillweed.

MAKES 72 APPETIZERS

BAKED MONTEREY JACK SLICES

Ingredients
1 pound Monterey Jack cheese

METHOD OF PREPARATION
Cut the cheese into 1/4-inch slices. Cut each slice into a circle 1 1/2 inches in diameter or a 1 1/2-inch square.

Place 3 inches apart on a parchment-lined baking sheet or a nonstick baking sheet.

Bake at 400 degrees for 10 minutes.

Let stand until cool. Store in an airtight container.

Variation: Sprinkle the cheese slices with cayenne, sesame seeds, caraway seeds, garlic powder or sliced almonds before baking.

MAKES 36 TO 48 APPETIZERS

MUSHROOM CAPS

Ingredients
2 (16-ounce) packages fresh mushrooms
1 cup shredded mozzarella cheese
1 cup shredded longhorn or Colby cheese
1 envelope onion soup mix
8 ounces sausage

METHOD OF PREPARATION
Remove stems from the mushrooms and discard.

Combine the mozzarella cheese, longhorn cheese, soup mix and sausage in a bowl and mix well. Shape the mixture into balls and place in the mushrooms caps. Place on a baking sheet.

Bake at 350 degrees for 30 minutes or until the sausage is cooked through and brown.

MAKES 20 TO 25 APPETIZERS

ROASTED PECANS

Ingredients
1 to 1½ cups pecan halves
2 tablespoons melted butter or margarine
1 teaspoon salt

METHOD OF PREPARATION
Combine the pecans, butter and salt in a bowl, stirring to coat. Spread in a baking pan.

Bake at 350 degrees for 15 minutes, stirring frequently.

SERVES 8 TO 10

HOT AND SPICY PECANS

Ingredients
½ cup butter
¼ cup Worcestershire sauce
1 tablespoon garlic powder
1 tablespoon cayenne
1 tablespoon black pepper
2 teaspoons salt
3 to 4 cups pecan halves

METHOD OF PREPARATION
Heat the butter in a saucepan until melted. Stir in the Worcestershire sauce, garlic powder, cayenne, black pepper and salt. Remove from heat.

Add the pecans to the butter mixture. Stir for 5 minutes or until coated. Spread the pecans in a single layer on a baking sheet.

Bake at 350 degrees for 15 minutes.

SERVES 24 TO 32

CANDIED PECANS

Ingredients
1 cup sugar
1 teaspoon salt
1 teaspoon cinnamon
1 egg white, at room temperature
1 tablespoon water
1 pound pecan halves

METHOD OF PREPARATION
Combine the sugar, salt and cinnamon in a bowl and mix well.

Beat the egg white and water in a mixer bowl until frothy but not stiff. Add the pecans, stirring until coated. Add the sugar mixture, stirring until the pecans are coated.

Spread the pecans in a single layer on an ungreased baking sheet. Bake at 300 degrees for 15 minutes; stir. Bake for 15 minutes longer. Stir the pecans to separate.

Let stand until cool. Store in an airtight container.

Note: May freeze the pecans for future use.

SERVES 16 TO 24

COCONUT SHRIMP

Ingredients

1/2 cup flour
1 teaspoon dry mustard
1 teaspoon salt
2 eggs
1 cup cream of coconut
1 cup (or more) flaked coconut
2/3 cup bread crumbs or cracker crumbs
1 pound large peeled shrimp with tails
Vegetable oil for deep-frying

METHOD OF PREPARATION

Combine the flour, dry mustard and salt in a bowl and mix well.

Beat the eggs in a mixer bowl until frothy. Add the cream of coconut, stirring until blended.

Combine the coconut and bread crumbs in a bowl and mix well.

Coat the shrimp with the flour mixture. Dip in the egg mixture and coat with the coconut mixture. Place the shrimp on a baking sheet.

Chill until just before serving time.

Heat the oil in a deep fryer to 375 degrees. Fry the shrimp in the hot oil for 1 to 2 minutes or until light golden brown. Drain on paper towels.

SERVES 4 TO 6

SPICY SHRIMP

Ingredients

1 tablespoon olive oil
2 tablespoons unsalted butter
2 tablespoons finely minced shallots
1 tablespoon finely minced garlic
1 3/4 pounds large shrimp, peeled
Salt and pepper to taste
2 tablespoons (or more) lemon juice
2 tablespoons finely chopped fresh dillweed

METHOD OF PREPARATION

Heat the olive oil and butter in a skillet over low heat until the butter melts. Add the shallots and garlic.

Sauté for 2 minutes; do not brown. Add the shrimp. Increase the heat slightly.

Cook for 3 minutes or until the shrimp turn pink, stirring frequently. Season with salt and pepper; toss.

Spoon the shrimp mixture into a bowl. Stir in the lemon juice and dillweed.

Chill, covered, for 3 to 4 hours. Adjust the seasonings.

Note: Serve as a first course or thread onto bamboo skewers and serve as an appetizer.

SERVES 4 TO 6 AS FIRST COURSE
SERVES 10 AS APPETIZER

VEGETABLE PIZZA

Ingredients
2 (8-count) cans crescent rolls
16 ounces cream cheese, softened
2/3 cup mayonnaise
1 teaspoon dillweed
1/2 teaspoon onion powder or grated onion
1/4 teaspoon garlic powder
1 1/2 cups grated carrots
1 1/2 cups chopped celery
1/2 cup chopped olives

METHOD OF PREPARATION

Unroll the crescent roll dough rectangles onto an 11x17-inch baking sheet, pressing edges and perforations to seal.

Bake at 375 degrees for 9 to 12 minutes or until brown. Let stand until cool.

Beat the cream cheese, mayonnaise, dillweed, onion powder and garlic powder in a mixer bowl until blended. Spread over the baked layer. Sprinkle with the carrots, celery and olives.

Chill until serving time. Cut into squares.

Variation: Top with your favorite vegetables to vary taste and color.

SERVES 15

BAKED PARTY BRIE

Ingredients
1 (16-ounce) package frozen puff pastry
1 (8-inch) round Brie cheese
1 tablespoon melted butter
1 tablespoon brown sugar
1 egg yolk
1 tablespoon water

METHOD OF PREPARATION

Thaw the puff pastry slightly at room temperature. Place the puff pastry on a lightly floured surface. Roll the pastry with a floured rolling pin. Cut 2 rounds slightly larger than the Brie round. Cut strips long enough to wrap the Brie.

Remove the top rind of the Brie. Place 1 of the 2 rounds of puff pastry on an ungreased baking sheet. Place the Brie on top of the round. Spread the top with a mixture of the butter and brown sugar. Place the remaining puff pastry round over the top to cover, pinching the top and bottom rounds together to seal. Wrap the side of the Brie with the strips to cover and seal the seam. Brush with a mixture of the egg yolk and water. Score the top with a sharp knife.

Bake at 400 degrees for 10 minutes; reduce oven temperature to 325 degrees.

Bake for 10 to 15 minutes longer or until golden brown. Serve hot or allow to cool. Serve with ginger crackers. Garnish with fruit.

Note: Use extra pastry cuttings to create leaves to affix to the top of the Brie.

SERVES 6 TO 8

CARAMELIZED BRIE WITH PECANS

Ingredients
1 (1-pound) round Brie cheese
1 cup chopped pecans
1 cup packed brown sugar
3 to 4 tablespoons Cognac

METHOD OF PREPARATION
Remove the rind from the cheese.

Place the Brie in a pie plate. Sprinkle with the pecans; spread the brown sugar over the top. Drizzle with the Cognac.

Bake at 300 degrees for 8 to 10 minutes or until the cheese is bubbly.

Serve with unsalted crackers.

SERVES 12 TO16

CHEESE RING WITH RASPBERRY SAUCE

Ingredients
1 cup mayonnaise
1/4 teaspoon (about) red pepper
1/4 teaspoon (about) black pepper
1 cup grated onion
1 cup chopped pecans
1 1/4 pounds shredded Cheddar cheese
1 jar raspberry preserves

METHOD OF PREPARATION
Line a bundt pan or ring mold with plastic wrap.

Combine the mayonnaise, red pepper and black pepper in a bowl and mix well. Add the onion, pecans and cheese, stirring until mixed. Spoon into the prepared bundt pan; press firmly with a spatula.

Chill, covered, for 8 to 10 hours. Invert onto a serving plate. Spoon the preserves into a small bowl and place in the center of the ring or spoon the preserves into the ring. Surround the ring with assorted party crackers.

Note: Surround the ring with parsley to resemble a wreath during the Christmas holidays.

SERVES 24

SAVORY CHEESE BALL

Ingredients

16 ounces cream cheese, softened
10 ounces shredded sharp Cheddar cheese, softened
1/2 cup sliced green olives, drained
2 tablespoons chopped green bell pepper
2 tablespoons chopped green onions
2 teaspoons Worcestershire sauce
1 teaspoon garlic powder
1 teaspoon lemon juice
Chopped pecans

METHOD OF PREPARATION

Combine the cream cheese and Cheddar cheese in a bowl, mixing until blended. Add the olives, green pepper, green onions, Worcestershire sauce, garlic powder and lemon juice and mix well.

Shape the cheese mixture into a ball. Wrap tightly in plastic wrap.

Chill until firm. Roll the cheese ball in chopped pecans.

Serve with assorted party crackers.
SERVES 30

CRAB CREAM CHEESE APPETIZER

Ingredients

16 ounces cream cheese, softened
12 ounces crab meat
2 scallions, chopped
2 dashes of Worcestershire sauce

METHOD OF PREPARATION

Combine the cream cheese, crab meat, scallions and Worcestershire sauce in a bowl and mix well. Serve with assorted party crackers.
SERVES 30

SWEET-AND-SOUR CREAM CHEESE APPETIZER

Ingredients

8 ounces cream cheese, cubed
1 1/2 cups catsup
1 cup honey
1/2 cup finely chopped onion
1/4 cup lemon juice
2 tablespoons vinegar
2 tablespoons Worcestershire sauce
1 tablespoon mustard
1/2 teaspoon salt
1/2 teaspoon pepper
1/4 teaspoon garlic powder
8 ounces cream cheese, softened

METHOD OF PREPARATION

Combine 8 ounces cream cheese, catsup, honey, onion, lemon juice, vinegar, Worcestershire sauce, mustard, salt, pepper and garlic powder in a saucepan. Cook over low heat for 10 minutes, stirring frequently. Remove from heat.

Chill, covered, until serving time.

Place 8 ounces cream cheese on a serving plate. Spoon 1/2 cup or more of the chilled sauce over the cream cheese. Serve with assorted party crackers. The cream cheese mixture may be stored in the refrigerator for months.

Note: Serve any of the following over cream cheese for a quick and easy appetizer: jalapeño jelly; cocktail sauce topped with crab meat; Pickapeppa, Jezebel or picante sauce; toasted almonds and chutney; or a coating of coarsely ground black pepper.
SERVES 10 TO 12

ELEPHANT GARLIC SPREAD

Ingredients

2 unpeeled elephant garlic cloves
1 (3-ounce) package sun-dried tomatoes
1/2 cup olive oil
3 tablespoons chopped fresh basil
1/4 teaspoon pepper
Crusty French bread, sliced, toasted

METHOD OF PREPARATION

Place the unpeeled garlic on a baking sheet. Roast at 325 degrees for 1 hour or until soft. Let stand for 5 minutes. Remove the skins.

Pour boiling water to cover over the sun-dried tomatoes in a bowl. Let stand for 20 minutes and drain the tomatoes.

Process the sun-dried tomatoes, olive oil, basil and pepper in a blender or food processor until smooth. Add the garlic.

Process until blended. Spread on toasted French bread slices.

Garnish with sprigs of fresh basil.

Note: Use in place of butter or margarine as a sandwich spread.

SERVES 10 TO 12

HOT ARTICHOKE DIP

Ingredients

1 (10-ounce) can artichoke hearts, drained
1 cup mayonnaise
1 cup grated Parmesan cheese
1/8 teaspoon garlic salt
5 to 6 drops of Worcestershire sauce
1 to 2 drops of Tabasco sauce

METHOD OF PREPARATION

Chop the artichokes and pat dry.

Combine the artichokes, mayonnaise and cheese in a bowl and mix well. Stir in the garlic salt, Worcestershire sauce and Tabasco sauce.

Spoon into a greased 6x6-inch baking dish.

Bake at 350 degrees until bubbly. Serve with toast points, chips or assorted party crackers.

MAKES 2 1/2 CUPS

New Year's Black-Eyed Pea Dip

Ingredients

8 ounces dried black-eyed peas
2 cups water
1/4 teaspoon salt
Chopped ham or bacon to taste
Chopped jalapeños to taste
1/2 teaspoon red food coloring (optional)
1 (4-ounce) can chopped green chiles
1 cup tomato juice
1/2 cup chopped onion
1/8 to 1/4 teaspoon garlic powder
1 (8-ounce) jar Cheez Whiz
Tabasco sauce to taste

Method of Preparation

Sort and rinse the peas. Combine the peas with enough water to cover in a bowl. Let stand for 8 to 10 hours; drain.

Combine the peas and 2 cups water in a heavy saucepan. Bring to a boil; reduce heat.

Simmer for 30 minutes. Stir in the salt, ham or bacon and jalapeños.

Simmer for 30 minutes longer. Stir in the red food coloring. Drain, reserving the liquid.

Process the peas, undrained chiles, tomato juice, onion and garlic powder in a blender or food processor until puréed. May add some of the reserved liquid for desired consistency. Spoon into a double boiler. Stir in the Cheez Whiz and Tabasco sauce.

Cook over boiling water over medium heat until the cheese melts, stirring constantly. Serve warm with corn chips or tortilla chips.

Variation: May substitute two 16-ounce cans black-eyed peas with jalapeños cooked with ham or bacon for the dried peas.

Serves 10 to 12

Black Bean Salsa

Ingredients

2 (15-ounce) cans black beans, rinsed, drained
1 (17-ounce) can whole kernel corn, drained
2 large tomatoes, seeded, chopped
1/2 large avocado, chopped
1/2 purple onion, chopped
3 to 4 tablespoons lime juice
2 to 4 tablespoons chopped fresh cilantro
2 tablespoons olive oil
1 tablespoon red wine vinegar
1 teaspoon salt
1/2 teaspoon pepper
Sliced avocado (optional)
Chopped fresh cilantro (optional)

Method of Preparation

Combine the black beans, corn, tomatoes, 1/2 avocado, onion, lime juice, 2 to 4 tablespoons cilantro, olive oil, wine vinegar, salt and pepper in a bowl and mix well.

Chill, covered, until serving time.

Top with avocado slices and chopped fresh cilantro just before serving. Serve with tortilla chips.

Makes 6 Cups

Fiesta Green Sauce

Ingredients

3 medium green tomatoes, coarsely chopped
4 tomatillos, chopped
1 to 2 jalapeños, coarsely chopped
3 small garlic cloves
3 medium avocados, sliced
4 sprigs of cilantro
1 teaspoon salt
1½ cups nonfat sour cream

Method of Preparation

Combine the tomatoes, tomatillos, jalapeños and garlic in a saucepan. Bring to a boil; reduce heat.

Simmer for 10 to 15 minutes or until the tomatoes are tender, stirring frequently. Cool slightly.

Process the tomato mixture, avocados, cilantro and salt in batches in a food processor until smooth.

Combine the tomato mixture and sour cream in a bowl and mix well.

Chill, covered with plastic wrap, until serving time. Serve with chips.

Note: Tomatillos, also known as Mexican green tomatoes, resemble small green tomatoes except for their thin parchmentlike husks, which must be removed before using. They are popular in Mexican and Southwest cuisine.

Makes 4 to 5 Cups

Guacamole

Ingredients

5 avocados, mashed
2 medium tomatoes, chopped
3 tablespoons vegetable oil
1 teaspoon salt
1 teaspoon garlic powder
1 teaspoon white pepper
Juice of 1 lemon
Lettuce leaves

Method of Preparation

Combine the avocados, tomatoes, oil, salt, garlic powder, white pepper and lemon juice in a bowl and mix well.

Spoon onto a lettuce-lined serving platter. Garnish with sprigs of cilantro or parsley.

Serves 6 to 8

Huma Salsa

Ingredients

2 (24-ounce) jars thick and chunky salsa
3/4 (6-ounce) package slivered almonds, or to taste
8 medium avocados, coarsely chopped
4 tomatoes, chopped
4 green onions with tops, chopped
2 tablespoons finely chopped fresh cilantro

Method of Preparation

Combine the salsa, almonds, avocados, tomatoes, green onions and cilantro in a bowl and mix well.

Chill, covered, for 2 to 3 hours. Serve with tortilla chips.

Variation: May substitute 1 tablespoon dried cilantro for the fresh cilantro.

Serves 20

Jalapeno Cream Cheese Dip

Ingredients
1/4 cup cold milk
1 jalapeño, seeded, sliced
1 tablespoon chopped green chiles
1 scallion, chopped
8 ounces cream cheese, chopped
6 ounces shredded Cheddar cheese
Dash of Tabasco sauce
Dash of Worcestershire sauce
Salt and cayenne to taste

Method of Preparation

Combine the milk, jalapeño, green chiles and scallion in a blender container. Process until puréed.

Add the cream cheese, Cheddar cheese, Tabasco sauce, Worcestershire sauce, salt and cayenne.

Process until blended. Chill, covered, for 1 hour or longer before serving.

Serve with assorted party crackers or chips.

Makes 2 Cups

Spinach Dip Florentine

For the dip
1 (10-ounce) package frozen chopped spinach, thawed, drained
3 ounces cream cheese, softened
1/2 cup sour cream
2 tablespoons minced green onions
2 teaspoons prepared horseradish
1 to 2 jalapeños, seeded, chopped
1/2 teaspoon salt
1/4 teaspoon ground pepper
1/2 cup shredded sharp Cheddar cheese
1/2 cup shredded Monterey Jack cheese
1 (6-ounce) jar marinated artichoke hearts, drained, chopped

For the tortilla wedges
12 large flour tortillas
Vegetable oil for deep-frying

To Prepare the Dip

Squeeze the moisture from the spinach. Combine the spinach, cream cheese, sour cream, green onions, horseradish, jalapeños, salt and pepper in a bowl and mix well. Stir in 1/4 cup of the Cheddar cheese and 1/4 cup of the Monterey Jack cheese. Spoon into a greased 9-inch pie plate. Arrange the chopped artichokes around the edge of the pie plate.

Bake at 350 degrees for 15 to 20 minutes. Sprinkle with the remaining cheese.

Bake for 5 minutes longer or until bubbly. Serve with warm tortilla wedges.

Makes About 3 Cups

To Prepare the Tortilla Wedges

Cut each tortilla into 8 wedges.

Pour the oil into a 10-inch skillet to a depth of 1/2 inch. Heat to 350 degrees.

Fry the tortilla wedges 2 at a time in the hot oil for 10 seconds on each side or until light brown. Drain on paper towels.

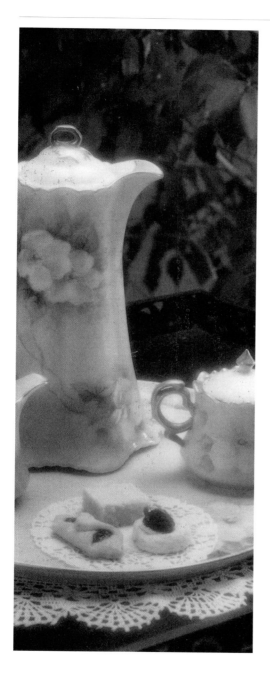

BEVERAGES

Berry Banana Smoothie, 51

Coffee Banana Smoothie, 51

Creamy Orange Cooler, 51

Hot Buttered Rum, 51

Peachys, 52

Ginger Almond Tea, 52

Spiced Tea Mix, 52

Summertime Iced Tea, 52

Texas Tea, 53

Apricot Brandy Slush, 53

Banana Slush Punch, 54

Hot Chocolate Mix, 54

Bride's Punch, 54

Burgundy Apple Punch, 55

Lemon Champagne Punch, 55

Mocha Punch, 56

Sparkling Citrus Blend, 56

Sparkling Slush Punch, 56

Sunset Punch, 56

BERRY BANANA SMOOTHIE

Ingredients
1 cup orange juice
1 small banana, sliced, frozen
1/4 cup fresh or frozen assorted berries
3 tablespoons low-fat vanilla yogurt
Sliced fresh strawberries (optional)

METHOD OF PREPARATION

Process the orange juice, banana, berries and yogurt in a blender until smooth.

Pour into tall glasses. Garnish with sliced fresh strawberries.

Note: Create this drink using a mixture of strawberries, blackberries and/or raspberries or an assortment of your favorite berries.

SERVES 2

COFFEE BANANA SMOOTHIE

Ingredients
1 1/2 cups skim milk
1 cup low-fat coffee yogurt
2 small bananas, sliced, frozen
1/4 teaspoon cinnamon
Dash of nutmeg
Sliced banana (optional)
Sprigs of fresh mint (optional)

METHOD OF PREPARATION

Process the skim milk, yogurt, frozen banana slices, cinnamon and nutmeg in a blender until smooth.

Pour into glasses. Garnish with sliced banana and sprigs of fresh mint.

SERVES 2

CREAMY ORANGE COOLER

Ingredients
1 cup 2% milk
1 cup water
1 (6-ounce) can frozen orange juice concentrate
1 small orange, seeded, chopped
1/2 teaspoon vanilla extract
10 ice cubes

METHOD OF PREPARATION

Process the 2% milk, water, orange juice concentrate, orange, vanilla and ice cubes in a blender until smooth.

Pour into glasses. Serve immediately.

SERVES 6

HOT BUTTERED RUM

Ingredients
2 cups butter, softened
1 (16-ounce) package light brown sugar
1 (16-ounce) package confectioners' sugar
2 teaspoons cinnamon
2 teaspoons nutmeg
1 quart vanilla ice cream, softened
25 ounces light rum
25 cinnamon sticks
Whipped cream

METHOD OF PREPARATION

Combine the butter, brown sugar, confectioners' sugar, cinnamon and nutmeg in a mixer bowl.

Beat until light and fluffy, scraping the bowl occasionally. Add the ice cream, stirring until blended. Spoon into a 2 1/2-quart freezer container. Freeze until firm.

Thaw the frozen mixture slightly. Combine 3 tablespoons of the frozen mixture and 1 ounce of light rum in a mug. Add enough boiling water to fill the mug and mix well. Place 1 cinnamon stick in each serving and top with whipped cream.

SERVES 25

PEACHYS

Ingredients
1 quart fresh peaches, peeled, chopped
1 (6-ounce) can frozen lemonade concentrate
5 ounces vodka
2 tablespoons sugar
Ice cubes

METHOD OF PREPARATION
Combine the peaches, lemonade concentrate, vodka and sugar in a blender container. Add just enough ice cubes to fill the blender container.

Process at high speed for 1 minute or until smooth. Pour into glasses.

SERVES 4 TO 6

GINGER ALMOND TEA

Ingredients
1 cup boiling water
5 tea bags
1 1/2 cups sugar
4 cups water
3/4 cup lemon juice
1 tablespoon vanilla extract
1 teaspoon almond extract
1 quart ginger ale, chilled

METHOD OF PREPARATION
Pour the boiling water over the tea bags in a heat-proof container. Steep, covered, for 5 minutes.

Remove the tea bags, squeezing gently. Add the sugar, stirring until dissolved. Stir in the water, lemon juice and flavorings.

Add the ginger ale just before serving and mix well. Pour over ice in glasses.

SERVES 12

SPICED TEA MIX

Ingredients
2 1/2 cups sugar
2 cups orange instant breakfast drink mix
6 ounces lemonade mix
2/3 cup instant tea
1 teaspoon ground cloves
1 teaspoon cinnamon

METHOD OF PREPARATION
Combine the sugar, orange drink mix, lemonade mix, tea powder, cloves and cinnamon in a bowl and mix well.

Combine 3 heaping tablespoons of the tea mixture with 1 cup boiling water in a mug for each serving.

Store remaining tea mixture in an airtight container.

MAKES ABOUT 6 CUPS

SUMMERTIME ICED TEA

Ingredients
6 cups boiling water
4 family-size tea bags
1 1/2 cups sugar
1 (6-ounce) can frozen limeade concentrate
1 (6-ounce) can frozen lemonade concentrate
Lime and/or lemon slices (optional)
Sprigs of fresh mint (optional)

METHOD OF PREPARATION
Pour the boiling water over the tea bags in a 1-gallon heatproof container. Steep for 20 minutes. Discard the tea bags.

Stir in the sugar, limeade concentrate and lemonade concentrate. Add enough water to fill the container and mix well.

Pour over ice in glasses. Top each serving with a slice of lime and/or lemon and a sprig of mint.

Variation: Substitute frozen orange juice concentrate for the frozen limeade concentrate.

SERVES 16

Texas Tea

Ingredients
2 cups boiling water
3 tea bags
8 cups water
1 1/2 cups (or less) sugar
1 lemon, sliced
Juice of 3 lemons
Juice of 2 oranges
2 teaspoons almond extract
1 teaspoon vanilla extract
Thinly sliced orange (optional)
Thinly sliced lemon (optional)
Sprigs of fresh mint (optional)

Method of Preparation
Pour 2 cups boiling water over the tea bags. Steep for 20 minutes. Discard the tea bags.

Bring 8 cups water, sugar and 1 sliced lemon to a boil in a saucepan.

Boil for 5 minutes. Stir in the tea, lemon juice, orange juice and flavorings. Simmer until heated through.

Serve hot in mugs with orange slices, or serve over ice with lemon slices and sprigs of mint.

Serves 10

Apricot Brandy Slush

Ingredients
9 cups boiling water
4 tea bags
2 cups sugar
1 (12-ounce) can frozen orange juice concentrate, thawed
1 (12-ounce) can frozen lemonade concentrate, thawed
2 cups apricot brandy
4 (10-ounce) bottles ginger ale

Method of Preparation
Pour 2 cups of the boiling water over the tea bags in a heatproof container. Steep, covered, for 5 minutes. Remove the tea bags, squeezing gently.

Combine the remaining 7 cups boiling water and sugar in a bowl, stirring until the sugar dissolves. Add the orange juice concentrate, lemonade concentrate and apricot brandy and mix well.

Pour the mixture into two 1-gallon heavy-duty sealable plastic bags. Freeze until firm.

Remove the plastic bags from the freezer 30 minutes before serving. Place the contents of the bags in a serving container; break into chunks. Add the ginger ale, stirring until slushy. Pour into glasses or ladle into punch cups.

Note: Use 2 bottles of ginger ale per 1 bag of frozen mixture.

Serves 19

BANANA SLUSH PUNCH

Ingredients
6 cups water
4 cups sugar
6 bananas
1 (46-ounce) can pineapple juice
2 (12-ounce) cans frozen orange juice concentrate
1 (12-ounce) can frozen lemonade concentrate
7 (28-ounce) bottles lemon-lime soda

METHOD OF PREPARATION
Combine the water and sugar in a saucepan. Simmer until the sugar dissolves, stirring frequently. Remove from heat.

Press the bananas through a sieve. Combine the bananas, pineapple juice, orange juice concentrate, lemonade concentrate and sugar mixture in a large freezer container and mix well. Freeze until firm.

Remove the frozen mixture from the freezer 2 hours before serving. Place in a punch bowl. Add the lemon-lime soda and mix well. Ladle into punch cups.

Note: Works well to divide the punch into 7 containers before freezing.

SERVES 72

HOT CHOCOLATE MIX

Ingredients
1 (8-quart) container nonfat dry milk
1 (1-pound) package confectioners' sugar
1 (16-ounce) jar non-dairy coffee creamer
1 (2-pound) can chocolate drink mix

METHOD OF PREPARATION
Combine the nonfat dry milk, confectioners' sugar, coffee creamer and chocolate drink mix in a bowl and mix well.

Combine 2 coffee scoops of the chocolate mixture with 1 cup of boiling water in a mug for each serving.

Store the chocolate mixture in an airtight container.

MAKES ABOUT 27 CUPS

BRIDE'S PUNCH

Ingredients
2 (6-ounce) cans frozen orange juice concentrate
1 (6-ounce) can frozen lemonade concentrate
1 (12-ounce) can apricot nectar
2 (6-ounce) cans pineapple juice
1 cup apricot brandy
7 cups club soda
2 to 3 bottles Champagne

METHOD OF PREPARATION
Combine the orange juice concentrate, lemonade concentrate, apricot nectar, pineapple juice and apricot brandy in a punch bowl and mix well.

Add the club soda and Champagne just before serving and mix well. Ladle into punch cups.

SERVES 24 TO 30

BURGUNDY APPLE PUNCH

Ingredients
1 (32-ounce) bottle apple juice, chilled
2 tablespoons lemon juice
1 cup sugar
1 quart ginger ale, chilled
2 (1.5-liter) bottles red burgundy, chilled
Ice ring

METHOD OF PREPARATION
Combine the apple juice, lemon juice and sugar in a punch bowl, stirring until the sugar dissolves. Stir in the ginger ale and wine.

Place the ice ring in the punch bowl. Ladle the punch into punch cups.

Note: When preparing an ice ring, boil the water to be used in order to prevent clouding. Allow the ice ring to partially freeze and add drained fruit, lemon slices or whatever is desired. Then freeze until firm.

Variation: Substitute your favorite red wine for the burgundy.

SERVES 35

LEMON CHAMPAGNE PUNCH

For the strawberry ice ring
Whole strawberries

For the punch
1 (46-ounce) can unsweetened pineapple juice, chilled
1 (12-ounce) can frozen lemonade concentrate, thawed
1 (750-milliliter) bottle Rhine wine, chilled
2 (750-milliliter) bottles Champagne, chilled

TO PREPARE THE STRAWBERRY ICE RING
Fill a 6-cup mold 2/3 full with water. Freeze until set. Arrange the strawberries on top. Freeze for 30 minutes longer. Add enough water gradually to fill the mold. Freeze until firm.

TO PREPARE THE PUNCH
Combine the pineapple juice, lemonade concentrate and wine in a punch bowl and mix well. Place the ice ring in the punch bowl.

Stir in the Champagne. Ladle into punch cups immediately.

SERVES 17

Mocha Punch

Ingredients
1 quart cold strong coffee
1 quart chocolate ice cream
1 quart vanilla ice cream
1 cup whipping cream
1/2 cup sugar
1/2 teaspoon vanilla extract
1/4 teaspoon almond extract
1/4 teaspoon salt
1/2 teaspoon nutmeg
1/4 teaspoon cinnamon (optional)

Method of Preparation
Pour the cold coffee into a punch bowl. Stir in 1-inch chunks of the ice cream.

Beat the whipping cream in a mixer bowl until soft peaks form. Add the sugar, flavorings and salt and mix well. Fold into the coffee mixture. Sprinkle with nutmeg and cinnamon.

Ladle into punch cups. Serve immediately.

Serves 35

Sparkling Citrus Blend

Ingredients
2 cups orange juice, chilled
2 cups club soda, chilled
1 cup grapefruit juice, chilled
1/2 cup ginger ale, chilled
2 tablespoons lemon juice, chilled

Method of Preparation
Combine the orange juice, club soda, grapefruit juice, ginger ale and lemon juice in a pitcher and mix well.

Pour over ice into glasses.

Note: A great beverage to serve at breakfast or brunch.

Serves 6

Sparkling Slush Punch

Ingredients
4 (3-ounce) packages cherry or strawberry gelatin
4 cups boiling water
4 cups sugar
4 cups water
2 (46-ounce) cans pineapple juice
2 cups lemon juice
2 (2-liter) bottles ginger ale

Method of Preparation
Dissolve the gelatin in 4 cups boiling water in a bowl and mix well.

Bring the sugar and 4 cups water to a boil in a saucepan. Boil until the sugar dissolves. Stir into the gelatin mixture. Let stand until cool.

Stir the pineapple juice and lemon juice into the gelatin mixture. Pour into a freezer container. Freeze until firm.

Let the frozen mixture stand at room temperature for 30 to 45 minutes before serving. Place in a punch bowl. Add the ginger ale and mix well. Ladle into punch cups.

Serves 100

Sunset Punch

Ingredients
1 quart orange juice
1 quart diet 7-Up or regular 7-Up
2 cups grape juice
2 cups apple juice
2 cups club soda

Method of Preparation
Combine the orange juice, 7-Up, grape juice, apple juice and club soda in a large container and mix well.

Pour over ice in glasses.

Serves 18

SALADS

SALADS

Cherry Fluff Salad, 59

Holiday Cherry Salad, 59

Frozen Cranberry Salad, 60

Fruit Salad with Orange Almond Dressing, 60

Grapefruit and Avocado Salad, 61

Strawberry Pretzel Salad, 61

Chicken Salad with Grapes, 62

Chicken Salad with Artichokes, 62

Chicken Salad Supreme, 63

Avocado Salad, 63

Broccoli Salad with Raisins, 64

Napa Cabbage Salad, 64

White Corn and Vegetable Cilantro Salad, 65

Green Bean, Walnut and Feta Salad, 65

Green Salad with Feta, 66

Mandarin Orange Tossed Salad, 66

Hearts of Palm Salad with Watercress Vinaigrette, 67

Mardi Gras Salad, 67

Tossed Salad with Raspberry Vinaigrette, 68

New Potato Salad, 68

Sesame Seed Salad, 69

Splendid Raspberry Spinach, 69

Strawberry Spinach Salad with Poppy Seed Dressing, 70

Poppy Seed Dressing, 70

Tomatoes Vinaigrette, 70

Marinated Vegetable Salad, 71

Garden Antipasto Salad, 71

Tabouli, 72

Sunshine Dressing, 72

CHERRY FLUFF SALAD

Ingredients

1 (14-ounce) can sweetened condensed milk
9 ounces whipped topping
1 (21-ounce) can cherry pie filling
1 (11-ounce) can mandarin oranges, drained
1 (9-ounce) can crushed pineapple, drained
2 cups miniature marshmallows
1/2 cup chopped pecans

METHOD OF PREPARATION

Combine the condensed milk and whipped topping in a mixer bowl. Beat until blended.

Stir in the cherry pie filling, mandarin oranges, pineapple, marshmallows and pecans. Spoon into a mold or shallow dish.

Chill, covered, until set.

Note: The festive colors of this salad make it a great addition to holiday dinners and salad suppers.

SERVES 12 TO 15

HOLIDAY CHERRY SALAD

Ingredients

2 (3-ounce) packages cherry gelatin
1 cup hot water
1 (20-ounce) can pitted cherries
1 cup sugar
1 (20-ounce) can crushed pineapple
1 cup chopped pecans
Juice of 1 lemon
1 tablespoon red food coloring

METHOD OF PREPARATION

Combine the gelatin and hot water in a bowl, stirring until the gelatin dissolves.

Combine the cherries and sugar in a saucepan. Cook for 5 minutes, stirring occasionally. Let stand until cool.

Stir the cherries, pineapple, pecans, lemon juice and red food coloring into the gelatin. Pour into a mold or shallow dish.

Chill for 4 hours or until set.

SERVES 12 TO 15

FROZEN CRANBERRY SALAD

Ingredients
8 ounces cream cheese, softened
1/2 cup sugar
1 (16-ounce) can whole cranberry sauce
1 (8-ounce) can crushed pineapple, drained
2 bananas, finely chopped
3/4 cup chopped pecans
8 ounces whipped topping

METHOD OF PREPARATION

Combine the cream cheese and sugar in a mixer bowl. Beat until creamy.

Stir in the cranberry sauce, pineapple, bananas and pecans. Fold in the whipped topping. Spoon into an 8x12-inch dish.

Freeze until set. Let stand at room temperature for 30 minutes before serving.

Note: A versatile salad, this cranberry dish can be served as a cool refresher in the summertime or with a meal at holidays.

SERVES 12

FRUIT SALAD WITH ORANGE ALMOND DRESSING

For the orange almond dressing
1 cup sour cream
1/2 cup mayonnaise
1/4 cup chopped almonds, toasted
2 tablespoons lemon juice
2 teaspoons grated orange peel

For the salad
1 head leaf lettuce, separated into leaves
2 cups fresh pineapple chunks
1 cup sliced strawberries
Sections of 1 orange
1 peach, sliced
1/2 cantaloupe, cut into chunks
1 cup grapes
1/2 cup whole almonds, toasted

TO PREPARE THE ORANGE ALMOND DRESSING

Combine the sour cream, mayonnaise, almonds, lemon juice and orange peel in a 1-quart bowl and mix well.

Chill, covered, until serving time.

TO PREPARE THE SALAD

Line a large salad bowl with the lettuce leaves. Arrange the pineapple, strawberries, orange sections, peach slices, cantaloupe and grapes in the bowl. Sprinkle with the almonds.

Serve with the orange almond dressing.

SERVES 6 TO 8

Grapefruit and Avocado Salad

Ingredients
1¹/3 cups grapefruit juice
¹/4 cup mild olive oil
¹/2 teaspoon salt
2 heads Bibb lettuce or butter lettuce, separated into leaves
2 bunches watercress, trimmed
Sections of 3 pink grapefruit
4 ripe avocados, thinly sliced lengthwise
Pepper to taste
Finely chopped chives

Method of Preparation
Whisk the grapefruit juice, olive oil and salt in a bowl.

Line 8 salad plates with the lettuce. Top with the watercress.

Arrange the grapefruit sections and avocado slices alternately in a pinwheel fashion on the lettuce-lined plates.

Drizzle with the grapefruit juice mixture and sprinkle with pepper. Top with chives.

Serves 8

Strawberry Pretzel Salad

Ingredients
2 cups crushed pretzels
6 tablespoons melted butter
3 tablespoons sugar
8 ounces cream cheese, softened
3/4 cup sugar
8 ounces whipped topping
1 (6-ounce) package strawberry gelatin
2 cups boiling water
2 (10-ounce) packages frozen strawberries, partially thawed
1 (8-ounce) can crushed pineapple

Method of Preparation
Combine the pretzels, butter and 3 tablespoons sugar in a bowl and mix well. Press into a 9x13-inch baking dish.

Bake at 400 degrees for 10 minutes. Let stand until cool.

Beat the cream cheese and 3/4 cup sugar in a mixer bowl until light and fluffy. Fold in the whipped topping. Spread over the baked layer.

Combine the gelatin and boiling water in a bowl, stirring until the gelatin dissolves. Stir in the strawberries and pineapple. Spoon over the prepared layers.

Chill until set. Cut into squares to serve.

Serves 12 to 15

CHICKEN SALAD WITH GRAPES

For the dressing
¹/₂ cup mayonnaise
¹/₄ cup minced green onions
3 tablespoons buttermilk
2 tablespoons minced fresh dillweed, or
1 teaspoon dried dillweed
¹/₄ teaspoon pepper

For the salad
1 pound boneless skinless chicken breasts
1 cup white wine
1 large sprig of fresh dillweed or dash of dried dillweed
¹/₈ teaspoon pepper
Salt to taste
1¹/₂ cups red or green grapes
1 cup thinly sliced celery
Pepper to taste
Bibb lettuce leaves
¹/₂ cup pecans pieces, toasted
Sprigs of dillweed

TO PREPARE THE DRESSING

Whisk the mayonnaise, green onions, buttermilk, dillweed and pepper in a bowl until mixed.

Chill, covered, in the refrigerator. May be prepared 1 day in advance.

TO PREPARE THE SALAD

Rinse the chicken and pat dry.

Arrange the chicken in a medium heavy skillet. Add the wine, 1 sprig of dillweed, ¹/₈ teaspoon pepper and salt. Add water if needed to cover the chicken.

Simmer for 11 minutes or until the chicken is cooked through, turning once. Remove the chicken to a platter. Let stand until cool. Cut into ¹/₂-inch pieces. Combine with the grapes and celery in a bowl. Add just enough dressing to coat and mix well. Season with salt and pepper to taste.

Chill, covered, for 20 minutes to 3 hours to enhance the flavor.

Spoon the chicken salad onto lettuce-lined plates. Sprinkle with the pecans; top with sprigs of dillweed. Serve with the remaining dressing.

SERVES 4

CHICKEN SALAD WITH ARTICHOKES

Ingredients
2 (6-ounce) jars marinated artichoke hearts
1 (7-ounce) package chicken rice and vermicelli mix
2¹/₂ cups chopped cooked chicken
1 (6-ounce) can sliced water chestnuts, drained, chopped
1 (3-ounce) jar pimento-stuffed olives, drained, sliced
1 cup chopped green onions
1 cup low-fat mayonnaise
1¹/₂ tablespoons curry powder
1 teaspoon pepper
Lettuce leaves or red cabbage leaves

METHOD OF PREPARATION

Drain the artichokes, reserving the marinade; coarsely chop.

Cook the rice using package directions. Stir in the reserved marinade. Let stand until cool.

Combine the artichokes, rice mixture, chicken, water chestnuts, olives and green onions in a bowl and mix well. Stir in a mixture of the mayonnaise, curry powder and pepper.

Chill, covered, for 1 to 2 hours. Serve on lettuce-lined plates.

Note: This is a wonderful "make-ahead" chicken salad.

SERVES 8 TO 10

CHICKEN SALAD SUPREME

Ingredients

2¹/2 cups chopped cooked chicken, chilled
1 cup sliced green grapes
1 cup finely chopped celery
¹/2 cup finely chopped almonds, toasted
2 tablespoons minced parsley
1 cup mayonnaise
¹/2 cup whipping cream, whipped
1 teaspoon salt
Lettuce cups
Pimento-stuffed olives or black olives

METHOD OF PREPARATION

Combine the chicken, grapes, celery, almonds and parsley in a bowl and mix well.

Stir in a mixture of the mayonnaise, whipping cream and salt.

Spoon into lettuce cups. Top with olives.

SERVES 6 TO 8

AVOCADO SALAD

Ingredients

2 avocados
6 green onions with tops, thinly sliced
Juice of 2 lemons
³/4 cup vegetable oil
2 teaspoons Beau Monde seasoning
¹/4 cup grated Parmesan cheese
1 head romaine, separated into leaves
Parmesan cheese to taste

METHOD OF PREPARATION

Cut the avocados into ¹/2-inch pieces.

Layer the avocados, green onions, lemon juice, oil, Beau Monde seasoning and Parmesan cheese in a salad bowl. Top with the romaine.

Chill, covered with plastic wrap, for 2 to 10 hours.

Toss just before serving. Sprinkle with additional Parmesan cheese.

SERVES 8 TO 10

BROCCOLI SALAD WITH RAISINS

Ingredients
4 cups chopped broccoli
1 cup raisins
1 cup sunflower seeds
10 slices crisp-fried bacon, crumbled
1/3 cup chopped red onion
1/4 cup mayonnaise-type salad dressing
1/4 cup sugar
1 tablespoon vinegar

METHOD OF PREPARATION
Combine the broccoli, raisins, sunflower seeds, bacon and red onion in a bowl and mix well.

Combine the salad dressing, sugar and vinegar in a bowl. Add to the broccoli salad, stirring to mix well.

Chill, covered, until serving time.

SERVES 8 TO 10

NAPA CABBAGE SALAD

Ingredients
1 Napa cabbage, sliced crosswise
2 bunches green onions, chopped
2 (3-ounce) packages ramen noodles, crushed
1/4 cup butter
3/4 cup vegetable oil
1/2 cup sugar
1/4 cup white vinegar
2 tablespoons soy sauce
1 large bottle sesame seeds
1 cup sliced almonds

METHOD OF PREPARATION
Toss the cabbage and green onions together in a bowl. Chill, covered, in the refrigerator.

Sauté the ramen noodles in the butter in a skillet until brown.

Bring the oil, sugar, white vinegar and soy sauce to a boil in a saucepan. Boil for 1 minute, stirring occasionally.

Mix the noodles, sesame seeds and almonds with the cabbage mixture just before serving. Add the dressing, tossing to coat.

SERVES 10 TO 12

White Corn and Vegetable Cilantro Salad

Ingredients
1 (11-ounce) can Shoe Peg or white corn, drained
1/2 cup chopped red onion
1 tomato, peeled, chopped
1/2 green bell pepper, chopped
1/2 red bell pepper, chopped
1/2 cucumber, chopped (optional)
10 to 15 black olives, sliced
3 green onions, chopped
1 jalapeño, chopped, or to taste
2 tablespoons sour cream
1 1/2 tablespoons chopped fresh cilantro
Juice of 1 lime
Seasoned salt and pepper to taste

Method of Preparation
Combine the corn, red onion, tomato, green pepper, red pepper, cucumber, olives, green onions, jalapeño, sour cream, cilantro, lime juice, seasoned salt and pepper in a bowl and mix well.

Chill, covered, until serving time.

Spoon into a salad bowl or onto a lettuce-lined serving platter.

Note: The flavor of this salad is enhanced if prepared 1 day in advance. May also serve as a dip with blue corn chips.

Serves 4 to 6

Green Bean, Walnut and Feta Salad

For the marinade
3/4 cup olive oil
1/2 cup loosely packed fresh mint leaves
1/4 cup balsamic vinegar
3/4 teaspoon salt
1 garlic clove, minced

For the salad
1 to 2 pounds fresh green beans, sliced
Salt to taste
1/2 to 1 cup chopped walnuts
1/2 to 1 cup chopped red onion
1 cup crumbled feta cheese
1/4 teaspoon pepper

To Prepare the Marinade
Process the olive oil, mint, balsamic vinegar, salt and garlic in a blender until puréed.

To Prepare the Salad
Combine the green beans and salt with enough water to cover in a saucepan.

Cook for 10 minutes or until tender-crisp; drain. Cool in ice water in a bowl for 5 minutes. Drain and pat dry.

Pour the marinade over the green beans in a bowl, tossing to coat.

Marinate, covered, in the refrigerator for 8 to 10 hours, tossing occasionally.

Spoon the salad into a serving bowl. Sprinkle with the walnuts, red onion, feta cheese and pepper.

Note: The salad may be assembled up to 3 hours in advance. Sprinkle with the pepper just before serving.

Variation: Substitute red wine vinegar for the balsamic vinegar and tomato and basil feta cheese for the feta cheese. For a lighter marinade, marinate the beans in white wine vinegar.

Serves 8 to 10

GREEN SALAD WITH FETA

Ingredients
3 heads assorted lettuces
1/2 cup pine nuts, toasted
1/4 cup olive oil
2 tablespoons vinegar
2 ounces feta cheese, crumbled

METHOD OF PREPARATION
Tear the lettuce into bite-size pieces. Place in a sealable plastic bag. Chill in the refrigerator.

Combine the lettuce and pine nuts in a bowl and mix well. Drizzle with a mixture of the olive oil and vinegar, tossing to coat. Top with the feta cheese just before serving.

Note: Use a combination of 3 of your favorite varieties of lettuce, such as Bibb, romaine and leaf lettuce to create this salad.

Variation: Substitute toasted sesame seeds for the toasted pine nuts.

SERVES 10 TO 12

MANDARIN ORANGE TOSSED SALAD

For the dressing
2 tablespoons tarragon vinegar
2 tablespoons sugar
1/2 teaspoon salt
1/4 teaspoon Tabasco sauce
Dash of pepper
1/4 cup vegetable oil

For the salad
1/4 cup blanched slivered almonds
1 tablespoon plus 1 teaspoon sugar
1/2 to 1 head lettuce, torn into bite-size pieces
1 (11-ounce) can mandarin oranges, drained
1 cup chopped celery
2 bunches green onion tops, chopped
2 cups grapefruit sections, drained, sliced (optional)
3 avocados, sliced (optional)
16 black olives, sliced (optional)
1 tablespoon chopped fresh parsley (optional)

TO PREPARE THE DRESSING
Combine the tarragon vinegar, sugar, salt, Tabasco sauce and pepper in a bowl and mix well. Add the oil in a fine stream, stirring constantly until blended.

TO PREPARE THE SALAD
Combine the almonds and sugar in a skillet. Cook over medium heat until the almonds are brown and coated, stirring constantly. Let stand until cool.

Toss the almonds, lettuce, mandarin oranges, celery, green onion tops, grapefruit sections, avocados, black olives and parsley in a salad bowl. Drizzle with the dressing, tossing to coat.

Variation: Substitute malt vinegar for the tarragon vinegar, delete the Tabasco sauce and pepper and add 1/8 teaspoon almond extract to the dressing.

SERVES 6 TO 8

HEARTS OF PALM SALAD WITH WATERCRESS VINAIGRETTE

For the watercress vinaigrette
14 tablespoons olive oil or vegetable oil
1/3 cup Champagne vinegar
1 tablespoon sugar
1 teaspoon salt
1 teaspoon paprika
Ground pepper to taste
1 to 1 1/2 cups fresh watercress leaves

For the salad
1 (16-ounce) can hearts of palm, drained
12 butter lettuce leaves
10 radicchio leaves
1 to 2 large tomatoes, cut into wedges
5 sprigs of parsley
1/4 to 1/2 cup pine nuts, toasted (optional)

TO PREPARE THE WATERCRESS VINAIGRETTE
Process the olive oil, Champagne vinegar, sugar, salt, paprika and pepper in a blender until smooth. Add the watercress leaves.

Process just until mixed; do not purée.

TO PREPARE THE SALAD
Cut the hearts of palm diagonally into 1-inch slices.

Line 5 to 6 salad plates with the lettuce, alternating the red and green leaves. Arrange 5 to 6 hearts of palm slices down the center of the lettuce on each salad plate; flank the hearts of palm with the tomato wedges. Add the parsley and sprinkle each salad with 1 teaspoon or more of the pine nuts.

Drizzle each salad with the watercress vinaigrette just before serving.

Note: May store the watercress vinaigrette in the refrigerator for 2 to 3 weeks.

SERVES 5 TO 6

MARDI GRAS SALAD

For the dressing
1/2 cup cider vinegar
1/4 cup sugar
2 teaspoons dried minced onion
1 teaspoon dry mustard
1 teaspoon salt
2/3 cup vegetable oil

For the salad
1 head lettuce, separated into leaves
2 (11-ounce) cans mandarin oranges, drained
1 (10-ounce) package fresh spinach
8 ounces fresh mushrooms, sliced
10 slices crisp-fried bacon, crumbled
1/2 finely chopped red onion
3 hard-cooked eggs, sliced
1/2 cup chopped pecans

TO PREPARE THE DRESSING
Combine the vinegar, sugar, onion, dry mustard and salt in a bowl and mix well. Add the oil in a fine stream, whisking constantly until mixed.

TO PREPARE THE SALAD
Combine the lettuce, mandarin oranges, spinach, mushrooms, bacon, red onion, eggs and pecans in a salad bowl and mix well.

Add the dressing just before serving, tossing to coat.

SERVES 8 TO 10

TOSSED SALAD WITH RASPBERRY VINAIGRETTE

For the raspberry vinaigrette
1 cup vegetable oil
1/2 cup raspberry vinegar
1/2 cup sugar
1 tablespoon (scant) Dijon mustard
1 teaspoon salt

For the salad
1 head lettuce, separated into leaves
1 apple, sliced
Grapes to taste
Chopped green onions to taste
Chopped peanuts (optional)
Chopped almonds (optional)

TO PREPARE THE RASPBERRY VINAIGRETTE
Process the oil, raspberry vinegar, sugar, Dijon mustard and salt in a blender until smooth.

TO PREPARE THE SALAD
Combine the lettuce, apple, grapes and green onions in a salad bowl and mix well. Add the vinaigrette, tossing to coat. Sprinkle with peanuts or almonds.

Variation: Substitute 1 pear and raisins for the apple and grapes.

SERVES 6 TO 8

NEW POTATO SALAD

Ingredients
3 pounds unpeeled new potatoes
1/3 cup finely chopped purple onion
1/3 cup olive oil
1/3 cup red wine vinegar
1/4 cup stone-ground mustard
2 teaspoons sugar
1/2 teaspoon salt
1/2 teaspoon freshly ground pepper
8 ounces thick-sliced bacon, crisp-fried, crumbled
1 cup chopped fresh parsley
Lettuce leaves

METHOD OF PREPARATION
Combine the new potatoes with enough water to cover in a saucepan. Bring to a boil.

Boil, covered, for 15 minutes or until tender; drain. Cool slightly.

Cut the potatoes into 1/4-inch slices. Combine the potatoes and purple onion in a bowl and toss.

Combine the olive oil, wine vinegar and mustard in a bowl and mix well. Stir in the sugar, salt and pepper. Add the bacon and parsley and mix well.

Add the bacon mixture to the potato mixture and mix. Spoon the salad onto a lettuce-lined serving platter.

SERVES 12 TO 15

SESAME SEED SALAD

For the croutons
4 to 8 slices bread, cubed
2 to 4 tablespoons margarine
Chopped garlic
2 to 3 tablespoons sesame seeds

For the dressing
2 tablespoons white wine vinegar
1 teaspoon parsley flakes
1/2 teaspoon Beau Monde seasoning
1/2 teaspoon summer savory
2 tablespoons vegetable oil
1 teaspoon MSG (optional)
Salt and pepper to taste

For the salad
Mixed lettuce greens

TO PREPARE THE CROUTONS
Sauté the bread in the margarine in a skillet. Add the garlic and sesame seeds and mix well.

Cook until the croutons are brown, turning frequently.

TO PREPARE THE DRESSING
Whisk the wine vinegar, parsley flakes, Beau Monde seasoning and summer savory together in a bowl. Add the oil in a fine stream, whisking constantly until mixed. Stir in the MSG, salt and pepper.

TO PREPARE THE SALAD
Toss the lettuce greens with the dressing in a salad bowl just before serving. Top with the croutons.

Note: This salad is good in the winter when tomatoes are not flavorful.

SERVES 4 TO 6

SPLENDID RASPBERRY SPINACH

For the dressing
2 tablespoons raspberry vinegar
2 tablespoons raspberry jam
1/3 cup vegetable oil

For the salad
8 cups spinach, trimmed, torn into bite-size pieces
1 cup fresh raspberries
3/4 cup coarsely chopped macadamia nuts
3 kiwifruit, sliced

TO PREPARE THE DRESSING
Process the raspberry vinegar and jam in a blender until mixed. Add the oil in a fine stream, processing constantly until blended.

TO PREPARE THE SALAD
Combine the spinach, 1/2 of the raspberries, 1/2 of the macadamia nuts and 1/2 of the kiwifruit with the dressing in a bowl, tossing to coat. Spoon onto a serving platter. Top with the remaining raspberries, macadamia nuts and kiwifruit.

Serve immediately.

SERVES 8

STRAWBERRY SPINACH SALAD WITH POPPY SEED DRESSING

Ingredients
1 pound fresh spinach, trimmed, torn into bite-size pieces
1/4 cup slivered almonds
1 pint fresh strawberries, sliced lengthwise
Poppy Seed Dressing (see below)

METHOD OF PREPARATION
Place the spinach in a sealable plastic bag. Chill in the refrigerator.

Arrange the almonds on a baking sheet. Toast at 350 degrees until light brown. Let cool.

Place the spinach in individual salad bowls. Top with the strawberries; sprinkle with the almonds. Drizzle with Poppy Seed Dressing.
SERVES 8 TO 10

POPPY SEED DRESSING

Ingredients
1 1/2 cups sugar
2/3 cup vinegar
2 teaspoons dry mustard
2 teaspoons salt
3 tablespoons onion juice
2 cups vegetable oil
3 tablespoons poppy seeds

METHOD OF PREPARATION
Combine the sugar, vinegar, dry mustard and salt in a blender container.

Process at medium speed until smooth. Add the onion juice.

Process until blended. Add the oil in a fine stream, processing constantly until thickened; do not use olive oil. If the dressing separates, pour off the clear portion and continue processing until blended. Add the poppy seeds. Process until mixed.

Note: The onion juice is best obtained by grating an onion on the fine side of a grater, or processing the onion in a food processor until puréed. This dressing is delicious on fruit salads of any kind, but has a particular affinity for grapefruit. Try drizzling on finely shredded red cabbage, thinly sliced avocado and sliced grapes.

Variation: Substitute 3 tablespoons minced onion for the onion juice. Use a red onion to yield a pink dressing which is great for a party.
MAKES ABOUT 3 CUPS

TOMATOES VINAIGRETTE

Ingredients
4 large tomatoes, sliced
6 tablespoons chopped fresh parsley
6 tablespoons olive oil
2 tablespoons vinegar
1 1/2 teaspoons minced fresh basil
1 teaspoon salt
1/8 teaspoon pepper
1 garlic clove, crushed
Chopped fresh parsley (optional)

METHOD OF PREPARATION
Arrange the tomatoes in a serving bowl. Sprinkle with 6 tablespoons parsley.

Combine the olive oil, vinegar, basil, salt, pepper and garlic in a jar with a lid, shaking to mix. Pour over the tomatoes.

Chill for 3 hours. Sprinkle with chopped fresh parsley.

Variation: May substitute 2 tablespoons dried parsley flakes for the 6 tablespoons chopped fresh parsley and 1/2 teaspoon dried whole basil for the minced fresh basil.

SERVES 8

MARINATED VEGETABLE SALAD

For the marinade
1 1/2 cups cider vinegar
1 cup vegetable oil
1/2 cup water
1/4 cup sugar
2 teaspoons salt
1 teaspoon oregano
1 teaspoon parsley flakes
1/4 teaspoon pepper

For the salad
2 pounds carrots, cut diagonally into thin slices
2 (14-ounce) cans artichoke hearts, drained, cut into halves
1 (15-ounce) can cocktail corn on the cob, drained
Florets of 1 small head cauliflower
Florets of 1 small bunch broccoli
8 ounces fresh mushrooms, cut into halves
8 ribs celery, cut into 1-inch slices
2 to 3 yellow squash, cut diagonally into slices

TO PREPARE THE MARINADE
Bring the cider vinegar, oil, water, sugar, salt, oregano, parsley flakes and pepper to a boil in a saucepan, stirring occasionally. Keep warm.

TO PREPARE THE SALAD
Combine the carrots, artichokes, corn on the cob, cauliflower, broccoli, mushrooms, celery and squash in a bowl and mix well. Pour the hot marinade over the vegetables, tossing lightly.

Marinate, covered, for 24 hours or longer, tossing occasionally.

Drain, discarding the marinade. Spoon into a large serving bowl.

SERVES 18 TO 20

GARDEN ANTIPASTO SALAD

Ingredients
1 (12-ounce) package garden-style pasta twirls
8 ounces salami, cubed
8 ounces provolone cheese, cubed
3/4 cup pitted black olives
3/4 cup green bell pepper strips
1/2 cup cherry tomato halves
1 (2-ounce) jar sliced pimento, drained
1 (8-ounce) bottle zesty Italian salad dressing

METHOD OF PREPARATION
Cook the pasta using package directions; drain.

Toss the pasta, salami, cheese, black olives, green pepper, cherry tomatoes and pimento in a large bowl and mix well.

Add the Italian salad dressing, tossing to coat.

Chill, covered, until serving time, stirring occasionally.

SERVES 10 TO 12

TABOULI

Ingredients
1 cup bulgur
1/2 cup extra-virgin olive oil
1/2 cup lemon juice
1/2 cup hot water
1 1/2 cups thinly sliced scallion bulbs and tops
2 medium tomatoes, coarsely chopped
1 cup minced fresh parsley
1/2 cup chopped fresh mint
Salt to taste
Pepper to taste

METHOD OF PREPARATION
Combine the bulgur, olive oil, lemon juice and hot water in a bowl and mix well.

Let stand at room temperature for 1 to 2 hours or until the liquid is absorbed. Stir in the scallions, tomatoes, parsley, mint, salt and pepper.

Chill, covered, until serving time.

Note: Chill, covered, for 8 to 10 hours to enhance the flavor.

Variation: Substitute dried mint for the chopped fresh mint.

SERVES 4 TO 6

SUNSHINE DRESSING

Ingredients
2/3 cup sugar
1/3 cup cider vinegar
1/2 teaspoon dry mustard
1/2 teaspoon onion juice
1/2 teaspoon salt
1 cup vegetable oil

METHOD OF PREPARATION
Process the sugar, cider vinegar, dry mustard, onion juice and salt in a blender until smooth.

Add the oil in a fine stream, processing constantly until blended.

Note: Toss with fresh spinach or an assortment of salad greens and sliced fresh fruit.

Variation: May substitute 2/3 cup packed brown sugar for the sugar.

MAKES ABOUT 1 1/2 CUPS

SOUPS & SANDWICHES

Soups & Sandwiches

Cowboy Beans, 75

Broccoli Cheese Soup, 75

Cheese Soup, 76

Big Boone's Chili, 76

White Bean Chili with Turkey and Cilantro Cream, 77

Chili con Queso Soup, 78

Ruby-Red Consommé, 78

Sherried Mushroom Soup, 79

Baked Potato Soup, 79

Butternut Squash Soup, 80

Taco Soup, 80

Tortilla Soup, 81

Texas Tortilla Soup, 81

Wild Rice and Ham Chowder, 82

Cobb Sandwiches, 82

Hot Croissant Sandwiches, 83

Stromboli, 83

Turkey Cranberry Croissants, 84

Sweet Hot Mustard, 84

COWBOY BEANS

Ingredients

1¹/2 pounds ground beef
2 (16-ounce) cans ranch-style beans
2 (16-ounce) cans pork and beans
2 onions, chopped
1 (7-ounce) can green chiles, drained, chopped
1 cup catsup
¹/2 cup packed brown sugar
¹/4 cup maple syrup
¹/4 cup mustard
Salt and pepper to taste

METHOD OF PREPARATION

Brown the ground beef in a skillet, stirring until crumbly; drain.

Combine the ground beef, ranch-style beans, pork and beans, onions, chiles, catsup, brown sugar, maple syrup, mustard, salt and pepper in a large heavy saucepan and mix well.

Simmer for 1¹/2 hours, stirring occasionally. Ladle into soup bowls.

Note: Serve with hot dogs or hamburgers, or with cornbread muffins as an entrée.

SERVES 6 TO 8

BROCCOLI CHEESE SOUP

Ingredients

1¹/2 pounds fresh broccoli
2 cups half-and-half
1 pound Velveeta cheese, cubed
³/4 teaspoon salt
¹/2 teaspoon pepper
¹/2 cup cornstarch
1 cup cold water

METHOD OF PREPARATION

Steam the broccoli in a steamer until tender or microwave in a microwave-safe dish on High for 8 minutes; drain.

Combine the half-and-half, cheese, salt and pepper in a double boiler.

Cook over boiling water until the cheese melts, stirring constantly. Stir in the broccoli. Add a mixture of the cornstarch and cold water and mix well.

Cook until the soup thickens, stirring frequently. Adjust the seasonings. Ladle into soup bowls.

SERVES 10

CHEESE SOUP

Ingredients

1/2 cup chopped green onions
1/2 cup chopped celery
1/2 cup grated carrot
3 tablespoons butter
2 (10-ounce) cans low-sodium chicken broth
2 (10-ounce) cans cream of potato soup
1 pound Velveeta cheese, cubed
3 ounces cream cheese, softened, cubed
Pepper to taste

METHOD OF PREPARATION

Sauté the green onions, celery and carrot in the butter in a saucepan. Stir in the broth; cover. Bring to a boil; reduce heat.

Cook until the vegetables are tender, stirring occasionally. Stir in the soup, Velveeta cheese and cream cheese.

Cook until the cheese melts, stirring constantly. Season with pepper. Ladle into soup bowls.

SERVES 4 TO 6

BIG BOONE'S CHILI

Ingredients

2 (16-ounce) cans tomatoes
4 cups water
5 pounds coarsely ground lean beef
2 large onions, chopped
5 tablespoons shortening
6 tablespoons chili powder
3 garlic cloves, minced
4 bay leaves
4 teaspoons cumin
2 teaspoons oregano
2 teaspoons (or more) salt
Cayenne or black pepper to taste
1 teaspoon coriander
3 to 5 tablespoons flour
Cold water or tomato juice

METHOD OF PREPARATION

Process the undrained tomatoes in a blender until puréed.

Combine the puréed tomatoes and 4 cups water in a 1 1/2- to 2-gallon stockpot and mix well.

Cook over medium heat, stirring occasionally.

Brown the ground beef with the onions in the shortening in a skillet, stirring until the ground beef is crumbly; drain. Add to the tomato mixture. Stir in the chili powder, garlic, bay leaves, cumin, oregano, salt and cayenne. Bring to a boil; reduce heat.

Simmer for 2 1/3 to 3 hours, stirring occasionally. Add additional water if needed for desired consistency.

Add the coriander 30 minutes before the end of the cooking process and mix well. Add a mixture of the flour and cold water just before the end of the cooking process. Cook until thickened, stirring constantly.

Discard the bay leaves. Ladle into chili bowls.

Note: Prepare the chili at least 1 day in advance to allow the flavors to intensify.

SERVES 12 TO 16

WHITE BEAN CHILI WITH TURKEY AND CILANTRO CREAM

For the cilantro cream
2/3 cup plain low-fat yogurt
3 tablespoons finely chopped fresh cilantro
3 tablespoons finely chopped fresh parsley

For the chili
1 pound dried white beans
1¹/2 pounds boneless skinless turkey breast, cut into halves
2 cups chopped onions
1 tablespoon vegetable oil
2 (4-ounce) cans diced green chiles
6 garlic cloves, minced
1¹/2 tablespoons oregano
1 tablespoon cumin
1 tablespoon chili powder
7 cups low-sodium chicken broth
18 ounces tomatillos, chopped
1 cup chopped fresh cilantro
1 cup chopped green onions
2 tablespoons fresh lime juice
Salt and pepper to taste
Sprigs of cilantro
¹/2 cup shredded Cheddar cheese (optional)

TO PREPARE THE CILANTRO CREAM

Combine the yogurt, cilantro and parsley in a bowl and mix well.

Chill, covered, in the refrigerator.

TO PREPARE THE CHILI

Sort and rinse the beans. Combine the beans with enough cold water to cover by 3 inches or more in a bowl. Let stand for 8 to 10 hours; drain.

Rinse the turkey and pat dry.

Sauté the onions in the oil in a heavy stockpot for 5 minutes. Stir in the chiles, garlic, oregano, cumin and chili powder.

Sauté for 5 minutes. Add the white beans, broth, tomatillos and 1 cup cilantro. Bring to a boil; reduce heat. Add the turkey.

Simmer for 20 minutes or until the turkey is cooked through, stirring occasionally. Transfer the turkey to a platter. Store, covered, in the refrigerator.

Simmer the chili for 2¹/2 hours or until the beans are tender, stirring occasionally.

Cut the turkey into ¹/2-inch pieces. Add the turkey, green onions and lime juice and mix well.

Simmer just until heated through, stirring occasionally. Season with salt and pepper.

Ladle the chili into bowls. Top with the cilantro cream and cilantro sprigs. Sprinkle with the cheese.

Note: The chili and cilantro cream may be prepared 1 day in advance and stored, covered, in the refrigerator. Reheat the chili over low heat just before serving and top with the cilantro cream.

SERVES 8

Chili con Queso Soup

Ingredients
1 large onion, finely chopped
6 tablespoons unsalted butter
2 (28-ounce) cans plum tomatoes, drained,
seeded, finely chopped
3 (4-ounce) cans mild green chiles, drained,
seeded, finely chopped
12 ounces cream cheese, cubed
2 (14-ounce) cans chicken broth
3 cups half-and-half
2 tablespoons plus 2 teaspoons fresh lemon juice, or to taste
Cayenne to taste
Salt to taste
Julienned corn tortilla strips
Finely chopped green onions
Shredded Monterey Jack cheese

Method of Preparation
Sauté the onion in the butter in a large saucepan over medium-low heat until tender. Stir in the tomatoes and chiles.

Cook over medium heat for 15 to 20 minutes or until the liquid is absorbed, stirring occasionally. Stir in the cream cheese.

Cook over low heat until the cream cheese melts, stirring constantly. Add the broth, half-and-half, lemon juice, cayenne and salt and mix well.

Cook over medium heat just until heated through, stirring constantly; do not boil.

Ladle into soup bowls. Serve with tortilla strips, green onions and Monterey Jack cheese.

SERVES 8 TO 10

Ruby-Red Consomme

Ingredients
4 cups tomato juice
2 cups chicken stock
1 rib celery, chopped
1 teaspoon chopped chives
1 teaspoon sugar
1/2 teaspoon Worcestershire sauce
1/2 teaspoon salt
1/2 teaspoon pepper
1 garlic clove, chopped
2 whole cloves
1 egg white, beaten
1 teaspoon lemon juice

Method of Preparation
Combine the tomato juice, chicken stock, celery, chives, sugar, Worcestershire sauce, salt, pepper, garlic and cloves in a saucepan and mix well.

Simmer for 45 minutes, stirring occasionally. Stir in the egg white and lemon juice; strain.

Ladle into soup bowls.

Note: Serve with toast points sprinkled with shredded cheese.

SERVES 6

SHERRIED MUSHROOM SOUP

Ingredients
2 tablespoons unsalted butter
1 tablespoon olive oil
3 large shallots, finely chopped
6 ounces mushrooms, sliced
6 ounces mushrooms, finely chopped
3 tablespoons cream sherry
2 cups low-sodium chicken broth
$1/4$ cup chopped fresh chives
Salt and pepper to taste

METHOD OF PREPARATION
Heat the butter and olive oil in a saucepan over medium heat until the foam subsides. Add the shallots and mushrooms and mix well.

Sauté over medium-high heat until the liquid from the mushrooms evaporates and the mushrooms begin to brown. Stir in the sherry.

Boil until the sherry evaporates. Stir in the broth.

Simmer for 15 minutes or until the mixture is reduced to about $2^1/2$ cups, stirring frequently. Stir in the chives. Season with salt and pepper.

Variation: Add 1 cup half-and-half or milk at the end of the cooking process and cook over low heat just until heated through; do not let boil. Ladle into soup bowls and top with fresh parsley. Substitute chopped scallion greens for the fresh chives.

SERVES 2

BAKED POTATO SOUP

Ingredients
4 large baking potatoes
$2/3$ cup butter or margarine
$2/3$ cup flour
6 cups milk
$3/4$ teaspoon salt
$1/2$ teaspoon pepper
$1^1/4$ cups shredded Cheddar cheese
4 green onions, chopped
12 slices crisp-fried bacon, crumbled
1 cup sour cream

METHOD OF PREPARATION
Prick the potatoes several times with a fork. Bake at 400 degrees for 1 hour or until tender. Let stand until cool.

Cut the potatoes lengthwise into halves. Scoop the pulp into a bowl, discarding the skins.

Heat the butter in a saucepan over low heat until melted. Add the flour, stirring until blended.

Cook for 1 minute, stirring constantly. Stir the milk in gradually.

Cook over medium heat until thickened, stirring constantly. Stir in the potato pulp, salt, pepper, 1 cup of the cheese, 2 tablespoons of the green onions and $1/2$ cup of the bacon.

Cook until heated through, stirring occasionally. Add the sour cream and mix well. May add additional milk if needed for desired consistency.

Ladle into soup bowls. Serve with the remaining cheese, green onions and bacon.

SERVES 6 TO 8

Butternut Squash Soup

Ingredients

2 large carrots, peeled, sliced
1 cup chopped onion
1 garlic clove, minced
2 tablespoons margarine
1 tablespoon minced gingerroot
2 teaspoons curry powder
1/4 teaspoon cinnamon
1/8 teaspoon nutmeg
2 medium butternut squash, peeled, cut into chunks
3 cups apple juice
40 crackers

Method of Preparation

Sauté the carrots, onion and garlic in the margarine in a saucepan over medium-high heat for 5 minutes or until the vegetables are tender. Stir in the gingerroot, curry powder, cinnamon and nutmeg.

Cook for 1 minute. Add the squash and apple juice and mix well. Bring to a boil; reduce heat.

Simmer, covered, for 15 minutes or until the squash is tender, stirring occasionally.

Process the squash mixture in batches in a blender or food processor until puréed. Return to the saucepan.

Cook just until heated through. Ladle into soup bowls. Serve with crackers.

Note: May serve chilled as well as hot.

Variation: For a thinner soup, add water until of the desired consistency.

Serves 8

Taco Soup

Ingredients

2 pounds ground beef
1 onion, chopped
2 (10-ounce) cans tomatoes with green chiles
1 (16-ounce) can pork and beans
1 (16-ounce) can pinto beans with jalapeños
1 (16-ounce) can ranch-style beans with jalapeños
1 (16-ounce) can whole kernel corn or hominy
1 envelope ranch salad dressing mix
1 envelope taco seasoning mix

Method of Preparation

Brown the ground beef with the onion in a saucepan, stirring until the ground beef is crumbly; drain. Stir in the undrained tomatoes, undrained beans, undrained corn, salad dressing mix and taco seasoning mix.

Simmer for 45 minutes, stirring occasionally. Ladle into soup bowls.

Note: May freeze the soup in portions for future use and heat as needed.

Variation: Serve with 1 or more of the following toppings: shredded Cheddar cheese, chopped fresh tomatoes, chopped avocado, sour cream and/or tortilla chips.

Serves 8 to 10

Tortilla Soup

Ingredients

1 dried ancho chile pepper
1/4 cup olive oil
4 corn tortillas, cut into 1-inch pieces
1 large onion, coarsely chopped
1 medium green bell pepper, chopped
3 garlic cloves, minced
4 cups chicken broth
1/2 teaspoon cumin
1/2 teaspoon freshly ground black pepper
2 tomatoes, chopped
2 tablespoons chopped fresh cilantro
1 tablespoon chopped fresh parsley

Method of Preparation

Remove the stem and seeds from the chile pepper.

Sauté the chile pepper in the olive oil in a heavy saucepan until tender. Remove the chile pepper to a dish, reserving the pan drippings. Chop the chile pepper.

Fry the tortilla pieces in the reserved pan drippings until brown. Drain the chips, reserving the pan drippings.

Sauté the onion, green pepper and garlic in the reserved pan drippings until tender. Add the broth, cumin and black pepper and mix well. Bring to a boil; reduce heat.

Simmer, covered, for 20 minutes, stirring occasionally. Stir in the chile pepper and tomatoes.

Simmer for 10 minutes, stirring occasionally. Stir in the cilantro and parsley just before serving.

Reserve 1/4 of the tortilla chips. Place the remaining tortilla chips in the bottom of 6 soup bowls. Ladle the soup over the chips. Top with the reserved chips.

Serves 6

Texas Tortilla Soup

Ingredients

1 pound boneless chicken thighs and breasts
1/4 cup vegetable oil
2 tablespoons margarine
1 large onion, chopped
2 large carrots, thinly sliced
6 ribs celery, thinly sliced
1 jalapeño, finely minced
2 large garlic cloves, minced (optional)
1/2 cup flour
1 teaspoon cumin
1 teaspoon chili powder
1 teaspoon salt
1 teaspoon lemon pepper
4 (15-ounce) cans low-sodium chicken broth
1 (15-ounce) can tomatoes
1 to 3 teaspoons hot pepper sauce
Unsalted tortilla chips
1 cup sour cream
1 to 2 avocados, chopped
1 cup shredded Cheddar cheese

Method of Preparation

Rinse the chicken and pat dry; chop.

Heat the oil and margarine in a heavy saucepan until the margarine melts. Add the chicken, onion, carrots, celery, jalapeño and garlic and mix well.

Sauté for 5 minutes. Stir in a mixture of the flour, cumin, chili powder, salt and lemon pepper. Add the broth, tomatoes and hot pepper sauce and mix well.

Simmer for 1 hour, stirring occasionally.

Arrange some tortilla chips in soup bowls. Ladle the soup over the chips. Top with the sour cream, chopped avocados and cheese.

Note: It takes a little more time, but try making your own tortilla chips. Cut 8 corn tortillas into strips and fry in hot oil until light brown. Drain on paper towels.

Serves 6 to 8

Wild Rice and Ham Chowder

Ingredients

1½ cups water
¾ cup wild rice
½ cup chopped onion
3 garlic cloves, minced
¼ cup margarine
½ cup flour
4 cups water
4 chicken bouillon cubes
1½ cups chopped potatoes
½ cup chopped carrot
½ teaspoon thyme
½ teaspoon nutmeg
⅛ teaspoon pepper
1 bay leaf
1 (17-ounce) can corn
1 pound chopped cooked ham
1 cup half-and-half
1 tablespoon chopped fresh parsley

Method of Preparation

Combine 1½ cups water and rice in a saucepan. Bring to a boil; reduce heat.

Simmer for 35 to 40 minutes or until tender; do not drain.

Sauté the onion and garlic in the margarine in a saucepan. Stir in the flour.

Cook for 1 minute. Stir in 4 cups water and the bouillon cubes. Add the potatoes, carrot, thyme, nutmeg, pepper and bay leaf and mix well.

Simmer, covered, for 15 to 20 minutes, stirring occasionally. Add the corn and mix well.

Simmer for 15 minutes longer, stirring occasionally. Stir in the ham, half-and-half, rice and parsley.

Cook just until heated through, stirring occasionally. Discard the bay leaf. Ladle into soup bowls.

Serves 6

Cobb Sandwiches

Ingredients

4 boneless skinless chicken breast halves
Salt and pepper to taste
¼ cup olive oil
¼ cup balsamic vinegar
1 tablespoon Dijon mustard
1 avocado
Lemon juice to taste
⅓ cup mayonnaise
8 slices challah or other egg bread, toasted
4 lettuce leaves
1 tomato, thinly sliced
8 ounces bleu cheese, thinly sliced
8 slices crisp-fried bacon

Method of Preparation

Rinse the chicken and pat dry. Season both sides with salt and pepper. Place in a dish. Pour a mixture of the olive oil, balsamic vinegar and Dijon mustard over the chicken, turning to coat.

Marinate in the refrigerator for 30 minutes or longer, turning occasionally. Drain, discarding the marinade.

Grill the chicken over hot coals for 7 minutes per side or until cooked through. Let stand until cool. Cut diagonally into slices.

Slice the avocado and sprinkle with lemon juice.

Spread the mayonnaise on the bread slices. Layer 4 slices of the bread with the lettuce, tomato, avocado, bleu cheese, bacon and chicken; top with the remaining bread slices.

Serves 4

HOT CROISSANT SANDWICHES

Ingredients

2 tablespoons margarine, softened
2 tablespoons finely chopped onion
2 tablespoons Dijon mustard
2 teaspoons poppy seeds
4 croissants, split
Thinly sliced Swiss cheese
Thinly sliced cooked turkey
Thinly sliced cooked ham

METHOD OF PREPARATION

Combine the margarine, onion, Dijon mustard and poppy seeds in a bowl and mix well.

Spread the cut sides of the croissants with the margarine mixture. Layer the cheese, turkey and ham over the bottom halves of the croissants; top with remaining croissant halves. Wrap each sandwich individually in heavy-duty foil.

Freeze until firm. Place the frozen sandwiches on a baking sheet.

Bake at 350 degrees for 30 minutes. Bake for 20 minutes if sandwiches are not frozen.

Note: Great to have on hand for a simple and quick luncheon entrée. Serve with a fresh fruit salad.

SERVES 4

STROMBOLI

Ingredients

1 (16-ounce) loaf frozen bread dough, thawed
4 ounces thinly sliced ham
4 ounces thinly sliced salami
1/2 teaspoon whole basil
1/2 teaspoon whole oregano
3 ounces provolone cheese, sliced
1 cup shredded mozzarella cheese
2 tablespoons melted butter or margarine
1 teaspoon cornmeal

METHOD OF PREPARATION

Pat the bread dough into a 10x15-inch rectangle on a lightly greased baking sheet. Arrange the ham slices lengthwise down the center; top with the salami. Sprinkle with 1/4 teaspoon of the basil and 1/4 teaspoon of the oregano. Arrange the provolone cheese over the herbs; sprinkle with the mozzarella cheese, remaining basil and remaining oregano.

Moisten the edges of the dough with water. Bring the long edges of the rectangle to the center; press edges to seal. Seal the ends.

Brush the dough with 1 tablespoon of the butter; sprinkle with the cornmeal. Invert on the baking sheet. Brush with the remaining butter.

Bake at 375 degrees for 20 to 22 minutes or until light brown. Cut into 4 portions.

SERVES 4

Turkey Cranberry Croissants

Ingredients
8 ounces cream cheese, softened
1/4 cup orange marmalade
1/2 cup chopped pecans
6 croissants or rolls, split
1 pound thinly sliced cooked turkey
3/4 cup whole cranberry sauce
6 lettuce leaves

Method of Preparation
Combine the cream cheese, marmalade and pecans in a bowl and mix well.

Spread the cut sides of the croissants with the cream cheese mixture. Layer the turkey on the bottom halves.

Spread 2 tablespoons of the cranberry sauce on each layered half; top with the lettuce and the remaining croissant halves.

Serves 6

Sweet Hot Mustard

Ingredients
3 ounces dry mustard
1 cup white vinegar
2 eggs, beaten
3/4 cup sugar

Method of Preparation
Combine the dry mustard and vinegar in a bowl and mix well. Let stand at room temperature for 2 to 10 hours.

Combine the mustard mixture with a mixture of the eggs and sugar in a saucepan and mix well.

Cook over low heat until thickened, stirring constantly. Spoon into hot sterilized jars; seal with 2-piece lids.

Store in the refrigerator.

Note: Makes great Christmas gifts!

Makes About 2 Cups

BREADS

BREADS

*Bread Machine Recipes

BASIC BISCUIT MIX

Ingredients
12 cups flour
1/4 cup plus 2 tablespoons baking powder
2 tablespoons salt
2 cups shortening

METHOD OF PREPARATION
Sift the flour, baking powder and salt into a bowl and mix well. Cut in the shortening until crumbly. Spoon into a covered container.

Store in the refrigerator or a cool place. This mix may be used in any of the following recipes.
MAKES 14 CUPS

FOR BISCUITS
Combine 2 cups Basic Biscuit Mix and 1/2 cup milk. Roll as desired. Bake on an ungreased baking sheet at 450 degrees for 12 to 15 minutes. Makes 10 to 12 Biscuits.

FOR MUFFINS
Combine 2 cups Basic Biscuit Mix and 2 tablespoons sugar. Add a mixture of 1 beaten egg and 3/4 cup milk, stirring just until moistened. Fill muffin cups sprayed with nonstick cooking spray 2/3 full. Bake for 12 to 15 minutes. Makes 10 to 12 Muffins.

FOR PANCAKES
Mix 2 cups Basic Biscuit Mix, 1 1/4 cups milk and 2 beaten eggs until smooth. Bake on a lightly greased griddle using manufacturer's directions. Makes 6 to 8 Pancakes.

FOR NUT BREAD
Combine 3 cups Basic Biscuit Mix, 3/4 cup sugar, 1 cup milk, 1 cup chopped nuts and 1 beaten egg. Spoon into a greased 5x9-inch loaf pan. Bake at 350 degrees for 1 hour. Makes 1 Loaf.

SOURDOUGH BISCUITS

Ingredients
1/2 cup sugar
2 envelopes dry yeast
2 cups lukewarm water
6 cups flour
4 teaspoons baking powder
1 1/2 teaspoons salt
1/4 teaspoon baking soda
1 cup buttermilk
2/3 cup vegetable oil

METHOD OF PREPARATION
Dissolve the sugar and yeast in the lukewarm water in a large bowl and mix well.

Add the flour, baking powder, salt, baking soda, buttermilk and oil, stirring until a soft dough forms.

Roll the dough on a lightly floured surface; cut with a biscuit cutter. Place the biscuits on a greased baking sheet.

Bake at 425 degrees until light brown.

Note: Prepare the dough up to 1 week in advance and store, covered, in the refrigerator. Bake as needed.

MAKES 3 DOZEN BISCUITS

VELVET CREAM BISCUITS

Ingredients
4 cups flour
2 tablespoons baking powder
2 tablespoons sugar
1 teaspoon salt
2 1/2 cups whipping cream
1/4 cup melted butter

METHOD OF PREPARATION

Combine the flour, baking powder, sugar and salt in a bowl and mix well. Add the whipping cream, stirring just until moistened.

Knead the dough on a lightly floured surface 10 to 12 times. Roll 1/2 inch thick; cut with a 2-inch biscuit cutter.

Place the biscuits on a greased baking sheet. Brush with the butter.

Bake at 425 degrees for 12 to 14 minutes or until light brown.

Note: To make ahead, bake the biscuits for 7 to 8 minutes and freeze. To serve, thaw completely and bake at 425 degrees for 5 to 6 minutes.

MAKES ABOUT 30 BISCUITS

YEAST BISCUITS

Ingredients
3 envelopes dry yeast
1/4 cup lukewarm water
2 cups buttermilk
1/2 cup sugar
1/2 cup shortening
1 teaspoon salt
1 teaspoon baking powder
1 teaspoon baking soda
5 cups flour
1/4 cup melted butter

METHOD OF PREPARATION

Dissolve the yeast in the lukewarm water and mix well.

Combine the buttermilk, sugar, shortening, salt, baking powder and baking soda in a bowl and mix well. Add 2 cups of the flour and mix well. Stir in the yeast mixture. Add the remaining 3 cups flour and mix well.

Knead the dough on a lightly floured surface until smooth. Roll 1/4 to 1/2 inch thick; cut with a biscuit cutter. Brush each biscuit with the melted butter; fold in half. Place on a baking sheet.

Freeze until firm. Place the biscuits in an airtight freezer container.

Take the desired amount of biscuits out of the freezer when needed. Place on a baking sheet. Let rise for 2 hours.

Bake at 375 degrees until light brown.

MAKES 30 TO 36 BISCUITS

BLACK-EYED PEA CORN BREAD

Ingredients

1 pound pork sausage, crumbled
1 onion, chopped
1 cup cornmeal
1/2 cup flour
1 teaspoon salt
1/2 teaspoon baking soda
1 cup buttermilk
1/2 cup vegetable oil
2 eggs
1 (15-ounce) can black-eyed peas
8 ounces Cheddar cheese, shredded
3/4 cup cream-style corn
Chopped green bell pepper to taste

METHOD OF PREPARATION

Brown the sausage with the onion in a skillet, stirring until the sausage is crumbly; drain.

Combine the cornmeal, flour, salt and baking soda in a bowl and mix well. Stir in a mixture of the buttermilk, oil and eggs. Add the sausage mixture, black-eyed peas, cheese, corn and green pepper and mix well. Spoon into a greased 9x13-inch baking pan.

Bake at 350 degrees for 50 to 55 minutes or until light brown.

Note: Eliminate the salt and baking soda if using cornmeal mix to prepare the corn bread.

SERVES 8 TO 10

BEER BREAD WITH DILL

Ingredients

3 cups self-rising flour
1 (12-ounce) can beer, at room temperature
1/3 cup sugar
1 tablespoon chopped fresh dill-weed
Butter to taste, softened

METHOD OF PREPARATION

Combine the flour, beer, sugar and dillweed in a bowl and mix well. Spoon into a 5x9-inch loaf pan sprayed with nonstick cooking spray.

Bake at 350 degrees for 45 minutes. Remove from the oven. Spread the top with butter. Slice when cool.

Note: Wrap the loaf in foil and freeze for future use. To serve, thaw the bread and reheat, wrapped in foil, in a 325-degree oven for 20 minutes. Left-over bread is delicious toasted for breakfast.

Variation: Substitute the dillweed with any fresh herb of your choice. Oregano is a good choice when serving the bread with Italian food.

MAKES 1 LOAF

CHEESE BREAD

Ingredients
3/4 cup chopped onion
2 tablespoons margarine
1 1/2 cups baking mix
1/4 teaspoon salt
1/2 cup milk
1/2 cup low-fat cottage cheese
1 egg
2 tablespoons melted margarine
1/4 cup grated Parmesan cheese
1 tablespoon sesame seeds

METHOD OF PREPARATION

Sauté the onion in 2 tablespoons margarine in a small skillet.

Combine the baking mix and salt in a bowl and mix well. Stir in the milk, cottage cheese and egg. Add the onion mixture and mix well.

Spoon the batter into an 8x8-inch baking pan. Drizzle with the melted margarine; sprinkle with the Parmesan cheese and sesame seeds.

Bake at 425 degrees for 20 minutes. Reduce the oven temperature to 350 degrees.

Bake for 5 minutes longer.

SERVES 4 TO 6

CHEESE FRENCH BREAD

Ingredients
1/2 cup butter, softened
1/4 cup mayonnaise
2 cups shredded mozzarella cheese
1/2 cup finely chopped black olives
1 teaspoon onion powder
1/2 teaspoon garlic powder
1 (16-ounce) loaf French bread, cut lengthwise into halves

METHOD OF PREPARATION

Combine the butter and mayonnaise in a bowl and mix well. Stir in the cheese, olives, onion powder and garlic powder. Spread over the cut sides of the French bread. Place on a baking sheet.

Bake at 350 degrees for 10 minutes or until the cheese melts.

Variation: Spread a mixture of 2 cups mayonnaise, 2 cups shredded Monterey Jack cheese and a 7-ounce can of green chiles between the slices and over the top of a 16-ounce loaf of sliced French bread. Bake, wrapped in foil, at 350 degrees for 20 minutes.

SERVES 12

ZUCCHINI BREAD

Ingredients
3 eggs, beaten
3 cups grated zucchini
2 cups sugar
1 cup vegetable oil
1 tablespoon vanilla extract
3 cups sifted flour
1 tablespoon cinnamon
2 teaspoons baking powder
1 teaspoon salt
3/4 teaspoon baking soda
1/2 cup chopped nuts

METHOD OF PREPARATION

Combine the eggs, zucchini, sugar, oil and vanilla in a bowl and mix well. Stir in a sifted mixture of the flour, cinnamon, baking powder, salt and baking soda. Add the nuts and mix well.

Spoon into 2 greased and floured 5x9-inch loaf pans.

Bake at 325 degrees for 1 hour or until the loaves test done.

Note: May bake the bread in 4 miniature loaf pans.

MAKES 2 LOAVES

COUNTRY CLUB MUFFINS

Ingredients
2 cups packed brown sugar
2 cups chopped walnuts
4 eggs
1/2 teaspoon salt
1 1/4 cups flour
2 teaspoons vanilla extract
1/4 cup melted butter

METHOD OF PREPARATION

Mix the brown sugar, walnuts, eggs, salt, flour, vanilla and butter in the order listed in a bowl.

Fill greased and floured muffin cups 3/4 full.

Bake at 300 degrees for 20 to 30 minutes or until the muffins test done.

Note: The unique, nutty flavor of these muffins make them a favorite.

MAKES 2 DOZEN MUFFINS

LEMON POPPY SEED MUFFINS

Ingredients
2 cups flour
2 teaspoons baking powder
1 teaspoon salt
1¼ cups sugar
1 cup butter or margarine, softened
4 egg yolks, beaten
½ cup fresh or frozen lemon juice
4 egg whites, stiffly beaten
2 teaspoons grated lemon zest
3 tablespoons poppy seeds, lightly toasted

METHOD OF PREPARATION
Sift the flour, baking powder and salt together.

Cream the sugar and butter in a mixer bowl until smooth. Add the egg yolks.

Beat until light and fluffy. Add the lemon juice alternately with the flour mixture, mixing just until moistened; do not overmix.

Fold in the egg whites, lemon zest and poppy seeds. Fill buttered muffin cups ¾ full.

Bake at 375 degrees for 20 minutes.

MAKES 1 DOZEN MUFFINS

ORANGE CRUNCH MUFFINS

For the topping
½ cup packed brown sugar
¼ cup flour
¼ teaspoon cinnamon
2 tablespoons butter, softened
½ cup chopped nuts

For the muffins
1½ cups sifted flour
¼ cup sugar
¼ cup packed brown sugar
2 teaspoons baking powder
½ teaspoon salt
½ teaspoon cinnamon
½ cup vegetable oil
½ cup milk
1 egg, lightly beaten
1 teaspoon grated orange peel

For the icing
¾ cup sifted confectioners' sugar
1 tablespoon fresh orange juice
½ teaspoon vanilla extract

TO PREPARE THE TOPPING
Combine the brown sugar, flour, cinnamon and butter in a bowl and mix well. Stir in the nuts.

TO PREPARE THE MUFFINS
Combine the flour, sugar, brown sugar, baking powder, salt and cinnamon in a bowl and mix well. Add the oil, milk, egg and orange peel, stirring just until moistened. Spoon into greased muffin cups. Top with the topping.

Bake at 400 degrees for 20 minutes or until the muffins test done. Let stand until cool.

TO PREPARE THE ICING
Combine the confectioners' sugar, orange juice and vanilla in a bowl and mix well. Spread over the top of the muffins.

MAKES 1 DOZEN MUFFINS

ORANGE PECAN MUFFINS

Ingredients
1/2 cup butter or margarine, softened
1 cup sugar
2 eggs
1 cup flour
1 teaspoon baking soda
1/2 teaspoon salt
1 cup buttermilk
1 cup flour
1 cup finely chopped pecans
Grated peel of 1 orange

METHOD OF PREPARATION
Spray miniature muffins cups with nonstick cooking spray.

Cream the butter and sugar in a mixer bowl until light and fluffy, scraping the bowl occasionally. Add the eggs, beating until blended. Add a mixture of 1 cup flour, baking soda and salt alternately with the buttermilk, mixing just until moistened.

Stir in a mixture of 1 cup flour, pecans and orange peel. Fill the prepared muffins cups 1/2 full.

Bake at 350 degrees for 15 to 20 minutes or until light brown.

MAKES 5 DOZEN MUFFINS

POPPY SEED GEMS

Ingredients
1 cup sugar
1/2 cup butter, softened
2 eggs
1 cup plain yogurt
1 tablespoon vanilla extract
2 cups flour
4 teaspoons poppy seeds
1/2 teaspoon salt
1/4 teaspoon baking soda

METHOD OF PREPARATION
Cream the sugar and butter in a mixer bowl until light and fluffy. Add the eggs 1 at a time, beating well after each addition. Beat in the yogurt and vanilla until blended.

Add a mixture of the flour, poppy seeds, salt and baking soda, stirring just until moistened. Spoon into miniature muffin cups sprayed with nonstick cooking spray.

Bake at 400 degrees for 7 to 10 minutes; do not overbake. The muffins will not appear to be done or brown at end of baking process.

Let stand until cool.

Note: Delicious served at a brunch or tea with raspberry jam.

MAKES 2 DOZEN MINIATURE MUFFINS

PUMPKIN MUFFINS

Ingredients
2 cups flour
2 cups sugar
1 tablespoon cinnamon
1 teaspoon baking soda
1 teaspoon salt
1 small can pumpkin
1¼ cups vegetable oil
4 eggs
Cinnamon and sugar to taste

METHOD OF PREPARATION

Combine the flour, 2 cups sugar, 1 tablespoon cinnamon, baking soda and salt in a mixer bowl and mix well. Add the pumpkin, oil and eggs.

Beat for 1 minute. Spoon into muffin cups sprayed with nonstick cooking spray. Sprinkle with cinnamon and sugar to taste.

Bake at 325 degrees for 15 to 20 minutes or until the muffins test done.

Note: May bake in a bundt pan in a 325-degree oven for 1 hour.

MAKES 1 DOZEN MUFFINS

SAUSAGE MUFFINS

Ingredients
8 ounces pork sausage
2 cups flour
2 tablespoons sugar
1 tablespoon baking powder
¼ teaspoon salt
1 cup milk
1 egg, lightly beaten
¼ cup melted butter or margarine
½ cup shredded Cheddar cheese

METHOD OF PREPARATION

Line muffin cups with paper liners; spray with nonstick cooking spray.

Brown the sausage in a skillet, stirring until crumbly; drain.

Combine the flour, sugar, baking powder and salt in a bowl and mix well. Make a well in the center of the dry ingredients.

Combine the milk, egg and butter in a bowl and mix well. Pour into the well, stirring just until moistened. Stir in the sausage and cheese. Fill the prepared muffin cups ⅔ full.

Bake at 375 degrees for 20 minutes or until golden brown. Remove the muffins from the pan immediately.

Note: Do not overbake.

MAKES 1 DOZEN MUFFINS

ALMOND PASTE TWIRL

For the filling
1/3 cup sugar
2 tablespoons butter, softened
1/4 cup ground almonds
1/4 teaspoon almond extract

For the bread
3 to 31/4 cups flour
1 envelope dry yeast
1 cup milk
6 tablespoons butter
1/3 cup sugar
1/2 teaspoon salt
1 egg

For the icing
11/2 cups confectioners' sugar, sifted
2 tablespoons melted butter
1 to 2 tablespoons hot water
1/2 teaspoon vanilla extract
1/8 teaspoon almond extract

TO PREPARE THE FILLING
Combine the sugar, butter, almonds and flavoring in a bowl and mix well.

TO PREPARE THE BREAD
Mix 2 cups of the flour and the yeast in a mixer bowl.

Combine the milk, butter, sugar and salt in a saucepan. Heat just until the butter melts. Stir into the flour mixture. Add the egg.

Beat at low speed for 30 seconds, scraping the bowl constantly. Beat at high speed for 3 minutes.

Stir in enough of the remaining flour to make a soft dough. Knead on a lightly floured surface for 3 to 5 minutes or until smooth.

Shape into a ball and place in a greased bowl, turning to coat the surface.

Let rise, covered, for 1 hour or until doubled in bulk. Punch the dough down.

Let rest for 10 minutes. Roll into a 12x18-inch rectangle on a lightly floured surface.

Spread the filling over the rectangle. Roll as for a jelly roll; pinch to seal the seam.

Arrange seam side down or form into a ring on a greased baking sheet. Cut with kitchen shears every 1/2 inch to within 1/2 inch of bottom. Pull slices alternately left and right.

Let rise for 45 minutes or until doubled in bulk. Bake at 375 degrees for 20 to 25 minutes.

TO PREPARE THE ICING
Beat the confectioners' sugar, butter, hot water and flavorings in a mixer bowl until of drizzling consistency. Drizzle over the bread.

SERVES 12 TO 16

CARDAMOM BREAD

Ingredients
2 envelopes dry yeast
1 tablespoon sugar
1/2 cup lukewarm water
2 cups milk
1 cup sugar
1/2 cup butter or margarine
2 teaspoons salt
9 cups bread flour
3 eggs
2 teaspoons cardamom
1 egg, lightly beaten

METHOD OF PREPARATION

Dissolve the yeast and 1 tablespoon sugar in the lukewarm water and mix well.

Combine the milk, 1 cup sugar, butter and salt in a microwave-safe dish. Microwave until the butter melts and mix well.

Combine 6 cups of the bread flour, 3 eggs and the milk mixture in a bowl. Stir the cardamom into the yeast mixture. Add the yeast mixture to the flour mixture and mix well.

Pour the flour mixture over the remaining 3 cups bread flour on a bread board. Knead until well mixed. Shape into a ball. Place in a greased glass bowl, turning to coat the surface.

Let rise until doubled in bulk. Punch the dough down.

Let rise again until doubled in bulk. Punch the dough down. Divide the dough into 3 equal portions. Divide each portion into 3 portions and shape into balls. Roll each ball into a rope. Braid 3 ropes to form a loaf; seal the ends. Place on a nonstick baking sheet. Repeat the process with the remaining 2 portions of dough.

Let rise for 30 minutes. Brush with the lightly beaten egg.

Bake at 350 degrees until golden brown.

Note: This bread freezes well for holiday giving.

MAKES 3 LOAVES

CROISSANTS

Ingredients
2 envelopes dry yeast
1 cup lukewarm water
5 cups flour
3/4 cup evaporated milk
1/3 cup sugar
1/4 cup melted butter
1 egg
1 1/2 teaspoons salt
1 cup butter, chilled
1 egg, beaten
1 teaspoon water

METHOD OF PREPARATION

Sprinkle the yeast over the lukewarm water in a mixer bowl. Let stand until softened. Stir in 1 cup of the flour, evaporated milk, sugar, melted butter, 1 egg and salt.

Beat until smooth, scraping the bowl occasionally.

Cut the chilled butter into the remaining 4 cups flour in a bowl. Add the yeast mixture, gently mixing with a spatula just until moistened. Cover with plastic wrap sprayed with nonstick cooking spray.

Chill for 4 hours to 4 days. Shape into a ball.

Knead on a lightly floured surface 6 times. Divide the dough into 4 equal portions.

Roll 1 portion at a time into a circle, leaving remaining portions of dough wrapped in plastic wrap in the refrigerator. Cut into wedges. Roll the wedges up from the wide end. Place point side down on an ungreased baking sheet; may be frozen at this time. Repeat the process with the remaining dough portions.

Let rise, loosely covered, in a warm place. Brush with a mixture of 1 egg and 1 teaspoon water.

Bake at 375 degrees for 10 to 13 minutes or until golden brown.

MAKES 30 CROISSANTS

Honey Whole Wheat Bread

Ingredients
1 cup milk
3/4 cup shortening
1/2 cup honey
2 teaspoons salt
2 envelopes dry yeast
3/4 cup lukewarm (105- to 115-degree) water
3 eggs, lightly beaten
4 1/2 cups all-purpose flour
1 1/2 cups whole wheat flour
1 teaspoon butter, softened

Method of Preparation

Heat the milk in a saucepan until bubbles form around the edge. Remove from heat. Add the shortening, honey and salt, stirring until the shortening melts. Cool to 105 to 115 degrees. Check the temperature with a thermometer. Dissolve the yeast in the lukewarm water in a mixer bowl. Stir in the milk mixture. Add the eggs.

Combine the all-purpose flour and whole wheat flour in a bowl and mix well. Add 2/3 of the flour mixture to the yeast mixture.

Beat at low speed until blended, scraping the bowl occasionally. Beat at medium speed for 2 minutes or until smooth. Add the remaining flour mixture, beating with a wooden spoon until blended. Mix by hand 20 to 30 times to develop gluten. Cover with waxed paper and a kitchen towel.

Let rise in a warm place for 1 hour or until doubled in bulk. Punch the dough down. Beat with a spoon for 30 seconds or until smooth. Spoon into a lightly greased 3-quart baking dish or heatproof bowl, spreading evenly.

Let rise, covered, for 40 minutes or until doubled in bulk; the dough should rise slightly above the edges of the dish. Cut a 4-inch cross 1/2 inch deep in the top of the dough with a sharp knife.

Bake at 375 degrees for 45 to 50 minutes or until brown; bread should sound hollow when tapped.

Remove to a wire rack to cool. Spread the butter over the top. Serve warm.

Serves 16

Herbed Rolls

Ingredients
2 cups milk
1/2 cup shortening
1/2 cup sugar
1 cake yeast
4 1/2 to 7 cups flour
1 tablespoon salt
1 teaspoon baking soda
1 teaspoon baking powder
1 1/2 tablespoons sesame seeds
1 tablespoon minced parsley
1 tablespoon chopped chives
1/2 teaspoon dillweed
Melted butter

Method of Preparation

Bring the milk, shortening and sugar to a boil in a saucepan. Cool the mixture to 105 to 115 degrees.

Combine the milk mixture and yeast cake in a bowl. Let stand for 10 minutes and mix well. Stir in 3 to 4 cups of the flour or just enough to make a soft dough.

Let rise for 2 hours. Stir in the salt, baking soda and baking powder. Add the sesame seeds and herbs and mix well. Add 1 1/2 to 3 cups of the remaining flour to make a stiff dough.

Chill, covered, in the refrigerator.

Roll into a 1/4-inch-thick rectangle on a lightly floured surface 1 hour before baking. Cut into 1/2x4-inch strips with a pizza cutter; roll strips. Arrange close together in a greased baking pan. Brush with melted butter.

Let rise for 45 minutes. Bake at 350 degrees for 15 minutes or until brown.

Variation: Add 1 or any combination of the herbs to the dough.

Makes 6 Dozen Rolls

ICEBOX DINNER ROLLS

Ingredients
1 envelope dry yeast
1/4 cup lukewarm water
1 cup milk, scalded, cooled
3 eggs
4 cups flour
1/2 cup sugar
1 teaspoon salt
1 cup shortening
Melted butter

METHOD OF PREPARATION
Dissolve the yeast in the lukewarm water in a bowl and mix well.

Beat the milk and eggs in a mixer bowl until blended. Stir in the yeast mixture.

Sift the flour, sugar and salt into a bowl and mix well. Cut in the shortening until crumbly. Add the milk mixture and mix well.

Chill, covered, for 2 to 8 hours. Divide the dough into 2 equal portions.

Roll the dough into a 1/4-inch-thick circle on a lightly floured surface. Cut into wedges. Roll wedges up from wide end; dip in melted butter. Place on a baking sheet.

Let rise in a warm place.

Bake at 400 degrees until brown.

MAKES 3 DOZEN ROLLS

ORANGE ROLLS

Ingredients
12 brown and serve rolls
2 tablespoons melted butter
1 cup sugar
Juice of 1 medium orange
2 tablespoons finely grated orange peel

METHOD OF PREPARATION
Brush the top and sides of the rolls with the melted butter.

Combine the sugar, orange juice and orange peel in a bowl and mix well. Coat the top and sides of the rolls with the mixture; do not coat the bottoms. Place on a baking sheet.

Bake using package directions. Serve immediately.

Note: Let stand until cool and slightly firm and store in the refrigerator for later use.

MAKES 1 DOZEN ROLLS

Basic Pizza Dough

Ingredients
1 tablespoon cornmeal
2/3 cup [1 cup]* water
4 teaspoons [2 tablespoons] olive oil or vegetable oil
1/2 teaspoon [3/4 teaspoon] salt
2 cups [3 cups] bread flour
1 1/2 teaspoons [2 teaspoons] bread machine yeast

Method of Preparation
Grease a 12-inch pizza pan for a thick crust, a 14-inch pizza pan for a thin crust or a 9x13-inch baking pan for a thick crust and sprinkle with the cornmeal.

Add the water, olive oil, salt, bread flour and yeast to the bread machine pan in the order recommended by the manufacturer.

Set the machine on the dough mode or on the manual cycle.

Remove the dough from the bread machine and place on a lightly floured surface. Knead in additional flour if needed to make an easily handled dough. Roll to fit the pan; place on the pan or pat over the bottom and side of the pan.

Top with 1/2 to 3/4 cup sauce, 8 to 12 ounces cooked meat or 4 to 5 ounces pepperoni, 1/2 to 1 cup chopped onion or green bell pepper or any vegetable and 1 to 1 1/2 cups shredded cheese. Bake at 425 degrees for 15 to 25 minutes or until the edges are brown and the cheese is bubbly.

Note: For the 1 1/2-pound recipe, bake in two 12-inch pizza pans for a thin crust, a 14-inch pizza pan for a thick crust or a 10x15-inch baking sheet for a thin crust.

Variation: For whole wheat pizza dough, substitute a mixture of 1 cup [1 1/2 cups] whole wheat flour and 1 cup [1 1/2 cups] bread flour for the bread flour.

For basil-Parmesan pizza dough, add 3 table-spoons [1/4 cup] grated Parmesan cheese and 3/4 teaspoon [1 teaspoon] basil with the flour.

For taco pizza dough, add 2 tablespoons [3 table-spoons] cornmeal and 1 tablespoon [4 teaspoons] taco seasoning mix with the flour and omit the salt.

*Use measurements in brackets to make a 1 1/2-pound recipe.

Makes 1 Recipe

Double Cheese Wheat Bread

Ingredients
1/2 cup [2/3 cup]* cup milk
1/3 cup [1/2 cup] water
3/4 teaspoon [1 teaspoon] salt
1 1/2 cups [2 cups] bread flour
1/2 cup [1 cup] whole wheat flour
1/4 cup [1/2 cup] shredded Cheddar cheese
3 tablespoons [1/4 cup] grated Parmesan cheese
1 tablespoon sugar
1 1/2 teaspoons [2 teaspoons] bread machine yeast

Method of Preparation
Add the milk, water, salt, bread flour, whole wheat flour, Cheddar cheese, Parmesan cheese, sugar and yeast to the bread machine pan in the order recommended by the manufacturer, adding the cheeses with the flours.

Set your machine on the basic white bread cycle with light color setting.

Note: Store the bread, wrapped in foil or plastic wrap, in the refrigerator for up to 3 days. Let the bread stand at room temperature for 1 hour before serving or heat, wrapped in foil, in a 350-degree oven for 20 to 30 minutes.

*Use measurements in brackets to make a 1 1/2-pound loaf.

Makes 1 One-Pound Loaf

CLASSIC FRENCH BREAD

Ingredients
3/4 cup [1 1/4 cups]* water
1/2 teaspoon [3/4 teaspoon] salt
2 1/4 cups [3 1/2 cups] bread flour
1 1/2 teaspoons [2 teaspoons] bread machine yeast
Cornmeal
Vegetable oil to taste
1 egg white
1 tablespoon water

METHOD OF PREPARATION

Add 3/4 cup water, salt, bread flour and yeast to the bread machine pan in the order recommended by the manufacturer. Set the machine on the dough mode or on the manual setting.

Remove the dough from the bread machine and place on a lightly floured surface. Knead in additional flour if needed to make an easily handled dough.

Roll into a 10x15-inch rectangle. [Divide the dough into 2 portions and roll each portion into an 8x10-inch rectangle for a 1 1/2-pound recipe.] Roll tightly beginning at long end. Pinch the seam and ends to seal; taper the ends by gently rolling back and forth. Place seam side down on a greased baking sheet sprinkled with cornmeal. Brush lightly with oil.

Let rise, covered, in a warm place for 10 to 15 minutes or until almost doubled in bulk. Cut 3 or 4 diagonal slashes 1/4 inch deep in the top.

Whisk the egg white and 1 tablespoon water lightly in a bowl. Brush some of the egg white mixture over the top of the loaf.

Bake at 375 degrees for 20 minutes. Brush with the remaining egg white mixture. Bake for 5 to 10 minutes longer or until the loaf sounds hollow when tapped. Remove to a wire rack to cool.

Note: For even browning when baking 2 loaves, switch positions of baking sheets halfway through the baking process.

*Use measurements in brackets to make a 1 1/2-pound recipe.

MAKES 1 ONE-POUND LOAF [2 LOAVES]

DRIED TOMATO AND ROSEMARY BREAD

Ingredients
2/3 cup [1 cup]* water
2 tablespoons [3 tablespoons] minced unsalted sun-dried tomatoes
1 tablespoon olive oil or vegetable oil
3/4 teaspoon [1 teaspoon] salt
2 cups [3 cups] bread flour
3 tablespoons [1/4 cup] nonfat dry milk
2 teaspoons [1 tablespoon] sugar
1/2 teaspoon [1 teaspoon] rosemary
1/2 teaspoon [3/4 teaspoon] paprika
1 1/2 teaspoons [2 teaspoons] bread machine yeast

METHOD OF PREPARATION

Add the water, sun-dried tomatoes, olive oil, salt, bread flour, nonfat dry milk, sugar, rosemary, paprika and yeast to the bread machine pan in the order recommended by the manufacturer, adding the sun-dried tomatoes with the water.

Set the machine on the basic white bread cycle with medium to normal color setting.

Note: Do not use oil-pack sun-dried tomatoes in this recipe.

*Use measurements in brackets to make a 1 1/2-pound loaf.

MAKES 1 ONE-POUND LOAF

GREEK-STYLE BREAD

Ingredients

2 ounces [3 ounces]* feta cheese
2/3 cup [1 cup] milk
1 tablespoon olive oil or vegetable oil
3/4 teaspoon [1 teaspoon] salt
2 cups [3 cups] bread flour
3 tablespoons [1/4 cup] sliced black olives
2 teaspoons [1 tablespoon] sugar
1 1/2 teaspoons [2 teaspoons] bread machine yeast

METHOD OF PREPARATION

Drain the feta cheese and pat dry; crumble.

Add the feta cheese, milk, olive oil, salt, bread flour, black olives, sugar and yeast to the bread machine pan in the order recommended by the manufacturer, adding the cheese and black olives with the flour.

Set the machine on the basic white bread cycle with medium /normal color setting.

Store, wrapped in foil or plastic wrap, in the refrigerator. Let stand at room temperature before serving.

*Use measurements in brackets to make a 1 1/2-pound loaf.

MAKES 1 ONE-POUND LOAF

PIMENTO OLIVE LOAF

Ingredients

1/2 cup [3/4 cup]* water
1 (2-ounce) jar sliced pimento
1 tablespoons [2 tablespoons] drained sliced black olives
1 tablespoon butter or margarine
3/4 teaspoon [1 teaspoon] salt
2 cups [3 cups] bread flour
2 tablespoons [3 tablespoons] nonfat dry milk
2 teaspoons [1 tablespoon] sugar
1 1/2 teaspoons [2 teaspoons] bread machine yeast

METHOD OF PREPARATION

Add the water, undrained pimento, black olives, butter, salt, bread flour, nonfat dry milk, sugar and yeast to the bread machine pan in the order recommended by the manufacturer, adding the pimento and olives with the water.

Set the machine on the basic white bread cycle with medium to normal color setting. The time-bake feature may be used.

*Use measurements in brackets to make a 1 1/2-pound loaf.

MAKES 1 ONE-POUND LOAF

OLD-FASHIONED CINNAMON ROLLS

For the filling

1/3 cup [1/2 cup]* coarsely chopped almonds, toasted
3 tablespoons [1/4 cup] sugar
1 teaspoon [1 1/4 teaspoons] cinnamon

For the dough

1/3 cup [3/4 cup] milk
2 tablespoons [3 tablespoons] water
1 egg
3 tablespoons [1/4 cup] butter or margarine, chopped
1/2 teaspoon [3/4 teaspoon] salt
2 1/4 cups [3 1/3 cups] bread flour
2 tablespoons [3 tablespoons] sugar
1 1/2 teaspoons [2 teaspoons] bread machine yeast
1 tablespoon [2 tablespoons] butter or margarine, softened

TO PREPARE THE FILLING

Combine the almonds, sugar and cinnamon in a bowl and mix well.

TO PREPARE THE DOUGH

Add the milk, water, egg, 3 tablespoons butter, salt, bread flour, sugar and yeast to the bread machine pan in the order recommended by the manufacturer.

Set the machine on the dough mode or on the manual cycle.

Remove the dough from the machine and place on a lightly floured surface. Knead in additional flour if needed to make an easily handled dough. If dough is too elastic, cover and let rest for 10 minutes before shaping.

FOR 1-POUND RECIPE

Roll the dough into an 8x12-inch rectangle. Spread with 1 tablespoon butter; sprinkle with the filling. Roll tightly beginning at long end; pinch the seam to seal. Cut into 9 equal slices. Place the slices cut side up in a greased 8x8-inch baking pan. Let rise, covered, in a warm place for 20 to 30 minutes or until almost doubled in bulk. Bake at 350 degrees for 25 to 30 minutes or until brown. Cool slightly. Remove to a platter. Drizzle with your favorite glaze. Serve warm.

FOR 1 1/2-POUND RECIPE

Divide the dough into 2 equal portions. Roll each portion into an 8x9-inch rectangle. Spread each rectangle with half the butter; sprinkle each rectangle with half the filling. Roll as for a jelly roll; pinch the seam to seal. Cut each roll into 6 slices. Place all the rolls in a greased 9x9-inch baking pan. Bake using directions for 1-pound recipe.

*Use measurements in brackets to make a 1 1/2-pound recipe.

SERVES 9 [12]

PULL-APART MONKEY ROLLS

Ingredients
1/2 cup milk
2 tablespoons water
1 egg
1 tablespoon butter or margarine
1/2 teaspoon salt
2 1/4 cups bread flour
4 teaspoons sugar
1 1/2 teaspoons bread machine yeast
2 tablespoons melted butter or margarine
1/3 cup sugar
1/2 teaspoon cinnamon

METHOD OF PREPARATION

Add the milk, water, egg, 1 tablespoon butter, salt, bread flour, 4 teaspoons sugar and yeast to the bread machine pan in the order recommended by the manufacturer.

Set the machine on the dough mode or on the manual cycle.

Remove the dough from the bread machine and place on a lightly floured surface. Knead in additional flour if needed to make an easily handled dough. Divide the dough into 20 equal portions. Shape each portion into a ball.

Dip each dough ball in 2 tablespoons melted butter and roll in a mixture of 1/3 cup sugar and cinnamon. Arrange half the dough in the bottom of a greased 6 1/2- to 8-cup ovenproof ring mold or fluted tube pan with nonremovable bottom. Make a second layer, positioning the dough balls for the second layer between the dough balls in the first layer. Drizzle with the remaining butter; sprinkle with the remaining sugar mixture.

Let rise, covered, in a warm place for 30 to 45 minutes or until almost doubled in bulk.

Bake at 375 degrees for 25 to 30 minutes or until brown. Cool in the pan for 1 minute. Invert onto a serving platter. Serve warm.

SERVES 20

SOUR CREAM AND CHIVE POTATO BREAD

Ingredients
1/2 cup [3/4 cup]* water
1/3 cup [1/2 cup] chopped peeled potato
1/4 cup [1/3 cup] sour cream
Milk
1 tablespoon butter or margarine
3/4 teaspoon [1 teaspoon] salt
2 1/4 cups [3 1/2 cups] bread flour
1 tablespoon [4 teaspoons] minced chives
2 teaspoons [1 tablespoon] sugar
1 1/4 teaspoons [1 1/2 teaspoons] bread machine yeast

METHOD OF PREPARATION

Combine the water and potato in a saucepan. Bring to a boil; reduce heat.

Cook, covered, for 8 to 9 minutes or until tender; do not drain. Let stand until cool. Mash the potato. Add the sour cream and enough milk to measure 1 cup [1 1/3 cups].

Add the potato mixture, butter, salt, bread flour, chives, sugar and yeast to the bread machine pan in the order recommended by the manufacturer, treating the potato mixture as the liquid.

Set the machine on the basic white bread cycle with medium to normal color setting.

Variation: Substitute low-fat yogurt for the sour cream.

*Use measurements in brackets to make a 1 1/2-pound loaf.

MAKES 1 ONE-POUND LOAF

Sour Cream Poppy Seed Bread

Ingredients

1/3 cup [1/2 cup]* sour cream
3 tablespoons [1/2 cup] water
1 egg
1 tablespoon [2 tablespoons] butter or margarine, chopped
3/4 teaspoon [1 teaspoon] salt
2 cups [3 cups] bread flour
1 tablespoon [4 teaspoons] sugar
1 teaspoon [1 1/2 teaspoons] poppy seeds
1 1/2 teaspoons [2 teaspoons] bread machine yeast

Method of Preparation

Add the sour cream, water, egg, butter, salt, bread flour, sugar, poppy seeds and yeast to the bread machine pan in the order recommended by the manufacturer, adding the sour cream with the water.

Set the machine on the basic white bread cycle with medium to normal color setting.

Variation: Use low-fat plain yogurt instead of the sour cream.

*Use measurements in brackets to make a 1 1/2-pound loaf.

Makes 1 One-Pound Loaf

Swiss Fennel Bread

Ingredients

1/2 cup [3/4 cup]* shredded Swiss cheese
2 tablespoons [3 tablespoons] bread flour
1/2 cup [2/3 cup] milk
1/4 cup [1/3 cup] water
1 tablespoon butter or margarine
3/4 teaspoon [1 teaspoon] salt
1 1/4 cups [1 2/3 cups] bread flour
2/3 cup [1 cup] whole wheat flour
2 teaspoons [1 tablespoon] sugar
3/4 teaspoon [1 teaspoon] fennel seeds
1 1/2 teaspoons [2 teaspoons] bread machine yeast

Method of Preparation

Combine the Swiss cheese and 2 tablespoons bread flour in a bowl and mix well.

Add the cheese mixture, milk, water, butter, salt, 1 1/4 cups bread flour, wheat flour, sugar, fennel seeds and yeast to the bread machine pan in the order recommended by the manufacturer.

Set the machine on the basic white bread cycle with medium to normal color setting.

Note: Store, wrapped, in the refrigerator. Let stand at room temperature before serving.

*Use measurements in brackets to make a 1 1/2-pound loaf.

Makes 1 One-Pound Loaf

Breakfast
& Brunch

Breakfast & Brunch

Roulade of Cheese Souffle

For the filling
2 (10-ounce) packages frozen chopped spinach,
cooked, drained
1/4 cup finely chopped onion
2 tablespoons butter
1 cup sour cream
1/4 cup shredded sharp Cheddar cheese
1 teaspoon nutmeg
1/4 teaspoon salt

For the soufflé
1/3 cup butter
6 tablespoons flour
1/2 teaspoon salt
1/8 teaspoon cayenne
1 1/4 cups milk
1/2 cup grated Parmesan cheese
1/2 cup coarsely shredded sharp Cheddar cheese
7 egg yolks, beaten
7 egg whites, at room temperature
1/4 teaspoon salt
1/4 teaspoon cream of tartar
Grated Parmesan cheese to taste
Cheddar cheese slices (optional)
Tomato slices
Sprigs of parsley

To Prepare the Filling

Push the spinach through a sieve to remove excess moisture.

Sauté the onion in the butter in the skillet until brown. Stir in the spinach, sour cream, cheese, nutmeg and salt. Remove from heat.

To Prepare the Souffle

Heat the butter in a saucepan until melted. Remove from heat. Whisk in the flour, 1/2 teaspoon salt and cayenne until blended. Add the milk gradually and mix well. Return to heat. Bring to a boil, stirring constantly; reduce heat.

Simmer until thickened, stirring constantly. Add 1/2 cup Parmesan cheese and shredded Cheddar cheese and mix well.

Simmer until blended, stirring constantly. Stir a small amount of the hot mixture into the egg yolks; stir the egg yolks into the hot mixture. Remove from heat.

Beat the egg whites, 1/4 teaspoon salt and cream of tartar in a mixer bowl until stiff peaks form. Fold 1/3 of the beaten egg whites into the cheese mixture. Fold in the remaining egg whites. Spoon into a 10x15-inch baking pan sprayed with nonstick cooking spray.

Bake at 350 degrees for 18 minutes or until puffed, golden brown and firm to the touch.

Loosen the edges of the soufflé. Invert onto waxed paper lightly sprinkled with Parmesan cheese. Spread with the filling. Roll as for a jelly roll. Place seam side down on a greased baking sheet. Arrange cheese slices over the top.

Broil 4 inches from the heat source until the cheese melts.

Transfer to a serving platter with a large spatula. Top with tomato slices and parsley sprigs.

Note: Soufflé may be prepared in advance, wrapped in foil, and stored in the refrigerator or freezer. Reheat wrapped in foil; do not broil the cheese slices until just before serving.

Variation: Try this seafood filling for a change. Combine 2 cups drained crab meat, 1/2 cup mayonnaise, 1/2 cup sour cream and 1/8 teaspoon lemon juice and spread over the soufflé.

Serves 8

BREAKFAST SOUFFLE

Ingredients

1 pound hot or regular sausage
8 to 12 ounces bacon, crisp-fried, drained
12 slices bread, cubed
2 cups shredded sharp Cheddar cheese
8 eggs
4 cups milk
1 teaspoon salt
1 teaspoon dry mustard
Dash of Worcestershire sauce

METHOD OF PREPARATION

Brown the sausage in a skillet, stirring until crumbly; drain. Combine the sausage and bacon in a bowl and mix well.

Sprinkle 1/2 of the bread in a greased 3-quart baking dish. Top with 1 cup of the cheese. Layer the bacon mixture, remaining bread and remaining cheese in the order listed over the prepared layers.

Beat the eggs, milk, salt, dry mustard and Worcestershire sauce in a mixer bowl until blended. Pour over the prepared layers. Chill, covered, for 8 to 10 hours.

Bake at 325 degrees for 45 to 60 minutes or until brown.

Note: May freeze for future use. Thaw in the refrigerator before baking.

SERVES 10 TO 12

BRUNCH ENCHILADAS

Ingredients

1 pound sausage
2 cups shredded Cheddar cheese
1/2 cup chopped green onions
1/2 cup chopped green bell pepper
8 to 10 (7-inch) flour tortillas
4 eggs
2 cups light cream or half-and-half
1 tablespoon flour
1/4 teaspoon salt
1/4 teaspoon garlic powder
Tabasco sauce to taste
2 cups shredded Cheddar cheese

METHOD OF PREPARATION

Brown the sausage in a skillet, stirring until crumbly; drain.

Combine the sausage, 2 cups cheese, green onions and green pepper in a bowl and mix well. Spoon approximately 1/2 cup of the sausage mixture in the center of each tortilla; roll. Place seam side down in a greased 9x13-inch baking dish.

Beat the eggs in a mixer bowl until blended. Add the light cream, flour, salt, garlic powder and Tabasco sauce, beating until smooth. Pour over the tortillas. Chill, covered, for 8 to 10 hours.

Bake at 350 degrees for 40 to 45 minutes; cover with foil during the last part of the baking process. Remove the foil and sprinkle with 2 cups cheese.

Bake for 5 to 10 minutes longer or until bubbly. Let stand for 10 minutes before serving.

SERVES 8 TO 10

Brunch Pizza

Ingredients

1 pound pork sausage
1 (8-count) can crescent rolls
1 cup frozen hash brown potatoes, thawed
1 cup shredded sharp Cheddar cheese
5 eggs, beaten
1/4 cup milk
1/2 teaspoon salt
1/8 teaspoon pepper
2 tablespoons grated Parmesan cheese
Whole pimentos (optional)
Sprigs of oregano

Method of Preparation

Brown the sausage in a skillet, stirring until crumbly; drain.

Separate the crescent roll dough into 8 triangles. Arrange the triangles with points toward the center in a greased 12-inch pizza pan, pressing the bottom and side to cover the pan; seal the perforations.

Spoon the sausage over the prepared layer; sprinkle with the hash brown potatoes and Cheddar cheese. Pour a mixture of the eggs, milk, salt and pepper over the top.

Bake at 375 degrees for 25 minutes. Sprinkle with the Parmesan cheese.

Bake for 5 minutes longer. Top with pimentos and oregano.

Note: Crescent roll dough can be separated into 2 rectangles and pressed into a 10x15-inch pan.

Serves 6 to 8

Chile Verde Casserole

Ingredients

6 (6- to 7-inch) corn tortillas
1/4 cup vegetable oil
4 (4-ounce) cans whole green chiles, split, seeded
1 pound Monterey Jack cheese, shredded
1 pound Cheddar cheese, shredded
2 cups milk
6 eggs, beaten
1/4 cup flour
1 teaspoon salt
Sour cream (optional)
Picante sauce (optional)

Method of Preparation

Grease a 3-quart baking dish; spray with nonstick cooking spray. Soften the tortillas in hot oil in a skillet; drain.

Line the bottom of the prepared dish with the tortillas. May cut additional softened corn tortillas into quarters and line the sides of the dish. Arrange the chiles over the tortillas. Sprinkle the Monterey Jack cheese and Cheddar cheese over the chiles.

Beat the milk, eggs, flour and salt in a mixer bowl until blended. Pour over the prepared layers.

Bake at 300 degrees for 30 minutes. Increase the oven temperature to 325 degrees.

Bake for 15 minutes longer. Serve with sour cream and picante sauce.

Serves 18

EGG AND SAUSAGE SQUARES

Ingredients
1 pound sausage
4 ounces mushrooms, sliced
$^1/_2$ cup chopped onion
2 tomatoes, chopped
8 ounces mozzarella cheese, shredded
1$^1/_4$ cups buttermilk baking mix
1 cup milk
12 eggs
1$^1/_2$ teaspoons seasoned salt
$^1/_2$ teaspoon pepper
$^1/_2$ teaspoon Italian seasoning

METHOD OF PREPARATION
Brown the sausage in a skillet, stirring until crumbly; drain.

Layer the sausage, mushrooms, onion, tomatoes and cheese in a greased 9x13-inch baking dish.

Beat the baking mix, milk, eggs, seasoned salt, pepper and Italian seasoning in a mixer bowl until blended. Pour over the prepared layers.

Bake at 350 degrees for 30 minutes or until brown. Cut into squares.

Note: Cut into smaller portions and serve as an appetizer.

SERVES 12

GREEN CHILE STRATA

Ingredients
4 flour tortillas
2 (4-ounce) cans chopped green chiles
4 ounces Canadian bacon or ham, cut into slivers
2 cups shredded Monterey Jack cheese
3 eggs, beaten
1 cup milk
1 teaspoon salt

METHOD OF PREPARATION
Grease a 9x13-inch baking pan.

Cut the tortillas to fit the bottom of the pan without overlapping. Line the bottom with the tortillas. Layer the chiles, Canadian bacon and cheese $^1/_2$ at a time in the prepared pan.

Beat the eggs, milk and salt in a mixer bowl until blended. Pour over the prepared layers. Chill, covered, for 30 minutes to 8 hours.

Bake at 350 degrees for 45 to 60 minutes or until the strata is slightly puffed and bubbly.

Cool for 5 minutes. Cut into squares.

SERVES 6

Herbed Breakfast Casseroles

For the crust
3 1/2 cups flour
1 cup finely ground almonds
1/2 cup confectioners' sugar
Pinch of salt
3/4 cup butter, softened
1 egg
1 egg yolk

For the filling
1/2 cup chopped onion
1 tablespoon butter
1/3 cup finely chopped smoked ham
6 to 8 slices crisp-fried bacon, crumbled
3 cups cream
8 eggs, beaten
1/4 teaspoon salt
1/2 teaspoon freshly ground pepper
1/4 teaspoon nutmeg
3 tablespoons finely chopped fresh basil
1 tablespoon finely chopped fresh thyme
3 ounces cream cheese, cubed
1/2 cup shredded Cheddar cheese
1/2 cup shredded Monterey Jack cheese
1 bunch scallions, chopped
1/3 cup sliced almonds

To Prepare the Crust

Combine the flour, almonds, confectioners' sugar and salt in a bowl and mix well. Cut the butter into the flour mixture until crumbly. Stir in a mixture of the egg and egg yolk.

Shape into 2 round patties and place on a platter. Chill for 30 minutes.

Crumble the mixture into two 9-inch tart pans or a 9x13-inch baking dish. Press over the side and bottom of each tart pan.

Bake at 350 degrees until light brown.

To Prepare the Filling

Sauté the onion in the butter in a skillet until tender.

Sprinkle equal portions of the onion, ham and bacon in each tart pan.

Whisk the cream and eggs in a bowl. Add the salt, pepper, nutmeg, basil and thyme and mix well. Pour 1/2 of the egg mixture into each tart pan. Top with the cream cheese, Cheddar cheese and Monterey Jack cheese. Sprinkle with the scallions and almonds.

Bake at 350 degrees for 30 to 40 minutes. Cool slightly before serving.

Note: May cool thoroughly, wrap and freeze for future use.

Serves 16

Quiche Lorraine

For the pastry
1¹/₂ cups flour
¹/₄ teaspoon salt
¹/₂ cup shortening
4 to 5 tablespoons cold water

For the quiche
9 slices crisp-fried bacon, crumbled
1 cup chopped ham
1 cup whipping cream
3 eggs
2 cups shredded Swiss cheese
1 teaspoon flour
Butter to taste

To Prepare the Pastry

Combine the flour and salt in a bowl and mix well. Cut in the shortening until crumbly. Add the water 1 tablespoon at a time, mixing with a fork until the mixture forms a ball.

Roll into a circle 2 inches larger than a pie plate on a lightly floured surface. Fit into the pie plate; crimp or flute the edge. Prick the bottom and sides with a fork.

Bake at 350 degrees for 10 minutes or until golden brown.

To Prepare the Quiche

Chill 2 mixer bowls in the freezer.

Sprinkle the bacon and ham over the bottom of the baked layer.

Beat the whipping cream in a chilled mixer bowl. Beat the eggs in the remaining chilled mixer bowl until thick. Add the eggs to the whipped cream, beating until blended. Stir in the cheese and flour. Pour over the prepared layers. Dot with butter.

Bake at 350 degrees for 40 minutes.

Serves 8

Company Quiche Lorraine

Ingredients
1¹/₂ all-ready pie pastries
16 slices crisp-fried bacon, crumbled
¹/₂ cup chopped onion
2 cups shredded Swiss cheese
1 (6-ounce) can mushrooms, drained, chopped
6 eggs, lightly beaten
2¹/₂ cups whipping cream
1 teaspoon salt
¹/₂ teaspoon pepper

Method of Preparation

Roll the pie pastries on a lightly floured surface. Pat into a 9x13-inch baking pan, sealing the edges. Sprinkle the bacon, onion, cheese and mushrooms over the prepared layer.

Whisk the eggs, whipping cream, salt and pepper in a bowl. Pour over the prepared layers.

Bake at 425 degrees for 15 minutes. Reduce the oven temperature to 300 degrees.

Bake for 30 to 35 minutes longer or until set.

Note: This is a great company dish because it makes a large casserole instead of the traditional pie.

Serves 10 to 12

Tomato Quiche

Ingredients

1 unbaked (10-inch) deep-dish pie shell
8 ounces Swiss cheese, shredded
3 large tomatoes, peeled, chopped
1 small onion, chopped
3 tablespoons butter
1 teaspoon salt
1/4 teaspoon thyme
3 eggs, beaten
1 cup half-and-half

Method of Preparation

Bake the pie shell at 400 degrees for 10 minutes. Sprinkle with the cheese.

Combine the tomatoes, onion, butter, salt and thyme in a saucepan.

Cook over medium heat until the mixture is reduced by 1/2, stirring frequently. Spoon over the cheese.

Beat the eggs and half-and-half in a mixer bowl until blended. Pour over the prepared layers.

Bake at 425 degrees for 10 minutes. Reduce the oven temperature to 350 degrees.

Bake for 35 minutes longer or until set. Let stand for 10 to 15 minutes before serving.

Note: May substitute 1 can of stewed tomatoes for the fresh tomatoes.

Serves 6 to 8

Cinnamon Cake

Ingredients

Cinnamon and sugar to taste
1 cup margarine, softened
4 eggs
2 cups flour
2 cups sugar
2 teaspoons baking powder
2 teaspoons baking soda
2 teaspoons vanilla extract
2 cups sour cream

Method of Preparation

Grease a bundt pan and sprinkle some cinnamon and sugar in the bottom.

Combine the margarine, eggs, flour, sugar, baking powder, baking soda, vanilla and sour cream in a bowl and mix well.

Layer 1/2 of the batter, cinnamon and sugar and remaining batter in the prepared pan. Sprinkle with cinnamon and sugar.

Bake at 375 degrees for 45 to 60 minutes or until the cake tests done.

Variation: Use fat-free sour cream.

Serves 16

Sour Cream Coffee Cake

For the topping
1/4 cup packed brown sugar
1 teaspoon cinnamon
1 cup chopped nuts

For the coffee cake
2 cups sugar
1 cup butter, softened
2 cups flour
2 eggs
1 cup sour cream
1 teaspoon baking powder
1 teaspoon vanilla extract
1/4 teaspoon salt

To Prepare the Topping
Combine the brown sugar, cinnamon and nuts in a bowl and mix well.

To Prepare the Coffee Cake
Beat the sugar and butter in a mixer bowl until creamy. Add the flour, eggs, sour cream, baking powder, vanilla and salt and mix well.

Layer the batter and topping 1/2 at a time in a greased tube pan.

Bake at 350 degrees for 45 to 60 minutes or until the coffee cake tests done.

Note: This coffee cake will fall when removed from the oven, but serve it without any apologies.

Variation: Bake in 2 loaf pans for approximately 1 hour or until the loaves test done.

Serves 16

French Breakfast Puffs

Ingredients
1 1/2 cups flour
1 1/2 teaspoons baking powder
1/2 teaspoon salt
1/4 teaspoon nutmeg
1/2 cup sugar
1/3 cup shortening
1 egg
1/2 cup milk
6 tablespoons melted butter
1/2 cup sugar
1 teaspoon cinnamon

Method of Preparation
Combine the flour, baking powder, salt and nutmeg in a bowl and mix well.

Beat 1/2 cup sugar, shortening and egg in a mixer bowl until creamy. Add the flour mixture alternately with the milk, beating well after each addition. Fill greased muffin cups 2/3 full.

Bake at 350 degrees for 20 to 25 minutes or until golden brown.

Remove the muffins from the oven; dip in the melted butter. Coat with a mixture of 1/2 cup sugar and cinnamon. Serve warm.

Serves 12

QUICHE MUFFINS

Ingredients
1 cup milk
2/3 cup melted butter
4 eggs
3 cups baking mix
2 cups shredded zucchini
2 1/4 cups chopped ham
3/4 cup shredded Cheddar cheese
3/4 cup shredded Swiss cheese
3/4 cup shredded provolone cheese
1/4 cup chopped green onions with tops

METHOD OF PREPARATION
Combine the milk, butter, eggs and baking mix in a bowl, stirring just until moistened. Add the zucchini, ham, Cheddar cheese, Swiss cheese, provolone cheese and green onions and mix well.

Spoon the batter into 8 jumbo muffin cups.

Bake at 350 degrees for 25 to 30 minutes or until the muffins test done. Cool in the pan until firm.

Note: May bake in 28 regular muffin cups or 96 miniature muffin cups. May prepare the batter in advance and store in an airtight container in the refrigerator.

SERVES 8

DUTCH PANCAKES

Ingredients
1/2 cup butter
1 cup flour
1 cup milk
6 eggs
Pinch of salt
Whipped cream to taste
Honey to taste

METHOD OF PREPARATION
Heat the butter in a 9x13-inch baking pan in the oven until melted.

Combine the flour, milk, eggs and salt in a bowl and mix well. Pour over the melted butter.

Bake at 425 degrees for 20 minutes.

Serve hot with a beaten mixture of whipped cream and honey.

Variation: Serve with a mixture of confectioners' sugar and lemon juice.

SERVES 8 TO 10

PUMPKIN PANCAKES

Ingredients
2 cups baking mix
2 tablespoons brown sugar
2 teaspoons cinnamon
1 cup evaporated milk
1/2 cup canned pumpkin
2 tablespoons vegetable oil
2 eggs
1 teaspoon vanilla extract

METHOD OF PREPARATION

Combine the baking mix, brown sugar, cinnamon, evaporated milk, pumpkin, oil, eggs and vanilla in the order listed in a bowl and mix well. Spoon the batter onto a hot griddle.

Bake using manufacturer's directions. Serve with syrup and whipped cream.

Note: For variety, serve with honey butter. Combine butter, honey and confectioners' sugar and mix until of a spreading consistency.

SERVES 6

BAVARIAN APPLE TORTE

For the crust
1/2 cup butter, softened
1/3 cup sugar
1 cup flour
1/4 teaspoon vanilla extract

For the filling
8 ounces cream cheese, softened
1/4 cup sugar
1 egg
1/2 teaspoon vanilla extract

For the topping
4 cups sliced peeled apples
1/2 cup sugar
1/2 teaspoon vanilla extract
1/2 cup chopped pecans

TO PREPARE THE CRUST

Cream the butter and sugar in a mixer bowl. Stir in the flour and vanilla. Pat over the bottom and 2 inches up the side of a greased 9-inch springform pan.

TO PREPARE THE FILLING

Beat the cream cheese, sugar, egg and vanilla in a mixer bowl until blended. Spread over the prepared layer.

TO PREPARE THE TOPPING

Combine the apples, sugar and vanilla in a bowl and mix gently. Spoon evenly over the filling. Sprinkle with the pecans.

Bake at 450 degrees for 10 minutes. Reduce the oven temperature to 400 degrees.

Bake for 25 minutes longer. Let stand until cool. Remove the side of the springform pan and place the torte on a serving platter; slice.

SERVES 12

BREAKFAST TRIFLE

Ingredients
Granola
Sliced fresh fruit
Vanilla yogurt

METHOD OF PREPARATION

Layer the granola, fruit and yogurt alternately in a trifle dish, glass bowl or dessert goblets.

Sprinkle with additional granola or top with fresh fruit.

Note: If using frozen fruit, partially thaw and serve immediately.

Variation: Substitute crumbled sweet muffins, cake or bread for the granola and any flavored yogurt for the vanilla yogurt.

BERRY JAM

Ingredients
1 (20-ounce) can crushed pineapple
3 1/2 cups sugar
1 package Sure-Jel
1 (10-ounce) package frozen raspberries
Paraffin, melted

METHOD OF PREPARATION

Combine the pineapple, sugar, Sure-Jel and raspberries in a heavy saucepan. Bring to a rolling boil, stirring constantly.

Boil for 5 minutes, stirring frequently; skim. Cool slightly.

Spoon the jam into parfait glasses. Top with the paraffin to seal.

Note: Decorate with cotton and striped straws to give the appearance of a soda.

MAKES 4 EIGHT-OUNCE JARS

Pear Jelly

Ingredients
4 cups (1/8x1-inch) pear chunks
1 cup sugar

Method of Preparation

Combine the pears and sugar in a saucepan.

Cook over low heat for 1 1/2 hours or until the pears are tender but not mushy, stirring occasionally. Spoon into hot sterilized jars; seal with 2-piece lids.

Store in the refrigerator.

Note: If the pears are extremely juicy and the jelly is not of the desired consistency at the end of the cooking process, remove the pears to a bowl. Cook the liquid until thickened or of the desired consistency and stir in the pears. Sterilize jars by boiling in water for 10 minutes.

Makes 4 Pint Jars

Tropical Fruit Salsa

Ingredients
1 cup chopped mango
1 cup chopped fresh pineapple
1 cup chopped red bell pepper
2/3 cup chopped kiwifruit
1/2 cup finely chopped red onion
1/4 cup finely chopped fresh cilantro
1 to 2 teaspoons fresh lime juice
1/2 to 1 teaspoon minced jalapeño
Salt and white pepper to taste

Method of Preparation

Combine the mango, pineapple, red pepper, kiwifruit, red onion, cilantro, lime juice and jalapeño in a bowl and mix well. Season with salt and white pepper.

Spoon into a serving bowl.

Note: May be prepared up to 3 hours in advance.

Variation: Substitute canned pineapple for the fresh pineapple.

Makes 4 Cups

ENTREES

ENTREES

BRISKET

Ingredients
Celery salt to taste
Garlic salt to taste
Lemon pepper to taste
Onion salt to taste
1 (7- to 9-pound) brisket
6 tablespoons liquid smoke
1/2 cup Worcestershire sauce
Salt and pepper to taste
1 (8-ounce) bottle barbecue sauce

METHOD OF PREPARATION

Sprinkle celery salt, garlic salt, lemon pepper and onion salt evenly over the brisket. Place in the center of a sheet of heavy-duty foil. Sprinkle with the liquid smoke.

Fold the sides of the foil to the center to seal. Marinate in the refrigerator for 8 to 10 hours.

Remove the brisket from the refrigerator 6 1/2 hours before serving. Pour the Worcestershire sauce over the brisket. Season with salt and pepper; seal. Place in a baking pan.

Bake at 300 degrees for 5 hours. Uncover the brisket and pour the barbecue sauce over the brisket.

Bake, uncovered, for 1 hour longer. Let stand for 20 minutes before slicing. Serve with additional barbecue sauce.

SERVES 12 TO 16

SIRLOIN ROAST WITH ANCHO CHILE SAUCE

For the ancho chile sauce
3 ancho chiles
1 onion, chopped
2 shallots, chopped
3 garlic cloves, chopped
2 tablespoons vegetable oil
2 cups chicken stock
3 tomatoes, chopped
2 jalapeños, seeded, chopped
2 tablespoons sugar
Salt to taste
1 cup chopped fresh cilantro

For the roast
1 (5-pound) beef sirloin roast, trimmed
2 tablespoons garlic powder
2 teaspoons salt
Sprigs of fresh cilantro

TO PREPARE THE ANCHO CHILE SAUCE

Remove the stems and seeds from the chiles. Toast the chiles in a hot skillet for a few seconds.

Soak the chiles in warm water to cover in a bowl for 1 hour or until rehydrated.

Process the chiles and some of the liquid in a blender until puréed.

Sauté the onion, shallots and garlic in the oil in a saucepan for a few seconds. Add the stock, tomatoes, jalapeños and chile purée. Bring to a boil; reduce heat. Simmer for a few minutes, stirring occasionally. Stir in the sugar and salt. Process in a blender until puréed. Add the cilantro.

Process until puréed. Season with salt.

TO PREPARE THE ROAST

Rub the roast with a mixture of the garlic powder and salt. Place in a roasting pan.

Bake at 350 degrees for 1 1/2 hours or to 140 degrees on a meat thermometer for rare, 160 degrees for medium or 170 degrees for well done.

Let stand for 20 minutes before carving. Top each serving with some of the ancho chile sauce and fresh cilantro sprigs.

SERVES 12 TO 15

GRILLED STUFFED BEEF TENDERLOIN WITH BORDELAISE SAUCE

For the stuffing

12 ounces fresh mushrooms, finely chopped
6 ounces ham, chopped
1/2 cup minced green onions
1/4 teaspoon salt
1/4 teaspoon pepper
1/2 cup butter
3 cups white bread cubes
2 tablespoons water

For the bordelaise sauce

4 shallots, minced
2 tablespoons butter
1 1/2 cups red wine
1/2 teaspoon thyme
1/2 teaspoon marjoram
1 1/2 cups beef bouillon
2 tablespoons chopped fresh parsley
1/2 teaspoon lemon juice
1 tablespoon butter
2 tablespoons flour
2 to 3 teaspoons water
Salt and pepper to taste

For the tenderloins

2 (1 1/2-pound) beef tenderloins
1 1/2 pounds bacon

TO PREPARE THE STUFFING

Sauté the mushrooms, ham, green onions, salt and pepper in the butter in a skillet until tender. Remove from heat. Add the bread cubes and water, tossing to mix. Prepare 1 1/2 hours before serving or early in the day and store in the refrigerator.

TO PREPARE THE BORDELAISE SAUCE

Sauté the shallots in 2 tablespoons butter until tender; do not brown. Add the wine, thyme and marjoram and mix well.

Simmer until reduced by 1/2, stirring frequently. Stir in the bouillon.

Simmer for 5 to 10 minutes or until of the desired consistency, stirring occasionally. Add the parsley and lemon juice and mix well.

Simmer for 5 minutes, stirring occasionally. Add 1 tablespoon butter, stirring until melted. Stir in a mixture of the flour and water gradually.

Simmer until thickened, stirring constantly. Season with salt and pepper.

TO PREPARE THE TENDERLOINS

Cut a pocket 1 1/2 inches deep down the length of each tenderloin. Spoon 1/2 of the stuffing into each pocket, packing firmly. Wrap 1 slice of bacon at a time around each tenderloin, overlapping each slice. Secure the bacon with skewers.

Grill over hot coals for 15 minutes per side for rare to medium or until done to taste. Let stand for 10 minutes before slicing.

Arrange the slices on a heated platter. Serve with the bordelaise sauce.

SERVES 8 TO 12

DIJON BEEF TENDER

Ingredients

1 (1¹/₂-pound) beef tenderloin
Olive oil
Dijon mustard
Garlic salt to taste
Lemon pepper to taste

METHOD OF PREPARATION

Preheat the oven to 500 degrees, letting the oven heat for 30 minutes.

Coat the tenderloin with olive oil and Dijon mustard. Season generously with garlic salt and lemon pepper on all sides. Place on a baking sheet.

Bake at 500 degrees for 20 minutes. Turn off the oven.

Let stand with the oven door closed for 1 hour or until the oven is cool. Remove the beef and slice. Serve at room temperature.

SERVES 6

TENDERLOIN OF BEEF WITH WINE GRAVY

Ingredients

¹/₂ teaspoon salt
¹/₂ teaspoon pepper
1 (3¹/₂-pound) beef tenderloin
2 garlic cloves, crushed
4 ounces fresh mushrooms, sliced
¹/₄ cup butter
1 cup red wine
¹/₂ teaspoon garlic salt

METHOD OF PREPARATION

Rub the salt and pepper over the tenderloin. Rub with the garlic. Place the tenderloin on a rack in a shallow baking pan.

Bake at 375 degrees for 30 minutes for rare, 45 minutes for medium or 1 hour for well done. Transfer to a heated platter, reserving the pan drippings.

Sauté the mushrooms in the butter in a skillet. Stir in the red wine and garlic salt.

Simmer for 5 minutes, stirring occasionally. Add the reserved pan drippings and mix well.

Simmer just until heated through. Pour over the tenderloin or serve separately.

SERVES 6

LONDON BROIL WITH TARRAGON BUTTER

For the tarragon butter
2 medium shallots
2¹/₂ tablespoons chopped fresh parsley
4 teaspoons tarragon vinegar
1¹/₂ teaspoons chopped fresh tarragon
¹/₂ teaspoon freshly ground pepper
¹/₂ cup butter, chilled, chopped

For the London broil
1 (1¹/₂-pound) flank steak
1 cup vegetable oil
1 cup vinegar
1 garlic clove, minced
Salt and pepper to taste
Fresh tarragon

TO PREPARE THE TARRAGON BUTTER

Mince the shallots in a food processor fitted with a steel blade. Add the parsley, tarragon vinegar, tarragon and pepper.

Process briefly. Add the butter.

Process until mixed. Shape into a ball on waxed paper or parchment paper. Chill or freeze, covered, until firm.

TO PREPARE THE LONDON BROIL

Score the flank steak. Place in a shallow dish. Pour a mixture of the oil, vinegar and garlic over the steak, turning to coat.

Marinate in the refrigerator for 2 to 3 hours, turning occasionally.

Place the steak on a rack in a broiler pan.

Broil 3 inches from the heat source for 5 minutes. Season with salt and pepper; turn.

Broil for 5 minutes longer for medium-rare or until done to taste. Season with salt and pepper; sprinkle with tarragon.

Let stand for 15 minutes before slicing. Top each serving with the tarragon butter.

Variation: Substitute ¹/₂ teaspoon dried tarragon for the fresh tarragon when preparing the Tarragon Butter.

SERVES 6

SIRLOIN STEAK WITH TARRAGON AND MUSHROOM SAUCE

Ingredients
4 (10-ounce) sirloin steaks
Salt and pepper to taste
¹/₂ cup olive oil
1¹/₂ cups sliced mushrooms
2 shallots, chopped
4 garlic cloves, chopped
¹/₂ cup white wine
2 tomatoes, peeled, seeded, chopped
¹/₂ cup chicken stock or veal stock
¹/₃ cup chopped fresh tarragon

METHOD OF PREPARATION

Season the steaks with salt and pepper. Sauté the steaks in the hot olive oil in a skillet for 1 minute per side or until done to taste. Remove the steaks to a heated serving platter, reserving the pan drippings.

Add the mushrooms, shallots and garlic to the reserved pan drippings. Sauté for a few seconds. Deglaze with the white wine.

Cook until the liquid is slightly reduced, stirring constantly. Stir in the tomatoes, stock and tarragon.

Cook until of the desired consistency, stirring constantly. Season with salt and pepper. Pour the sauce over the steaks. Serve immediately.

SERVES 4

BEEF AND CHEESE ENCHILADAS

Ingredients
2 pounds ground chuck
1 1/2 pounds ground round
3/4 to 1 cup grated onion
2 tablespoons chili powder
1 tablespoon cumin
1 1/2 teaspoons flour
2 garlic cloves, minced
Salt and pepper to taste
2 (15-ounce) cans tomato sauce
1 1/2 tomato sauce cans water
1/2 cup vegetable oil
24 corn tortillas
3 (10-ounce) cans enchilada sauce
2 1/2 pounds American cheese, shredded
Chopped onion (optional)

METHOD OF PREPARATION
Brown the ground chuck and ground round in a skillet, stirring until crumbly; drain. Stir in 3/4 to 1 cup onion, chili powder, cumin, flour, garlic, salt and pepper. Add the tomato sauce and water and mix well.

Simmer for 30 minutes, stirring occasionally; skim off the fat.

Heat the oil in a skillet over medium heat until hot. Dip each tortilla in the oil to soften. Dip each tortilla in the enchilada sauce.

Spoon 2 tablespoons of the ground beef mixture, 2 tablespoons of the cheese and some of the chopped onion on each tortilla; roll to enclose the filling. Arrange in two 9x13-inch baking dishes.

Stir the remaining enchilada sauce into the remaining ground beef mixture, adding additional water if needed for the desired consistency. Pour over the enchiladas. Sprinkle with the remaining cheese.

Bake at 350 degrees for 20 to 30 minutes or until brown and bubbly.

SERVES 16 TO 18

SPINACH ENCHILADA CASSEROLE

Ingredients
12 corn tortillas
1 1/2 pounds lean ground beef
1 small onion, chopped
1 garlic clove, minced
1 (10-ounce) package frozen chopped spinach, thawed
1 to 1 1/2 cups picante sauce
1 (8-ounce) can tomato sauce
2 medium tomatoes, seeded, chopped
1 large red bell pepper, chopped
1 tablespoon lime juice
1 teaspoon salt
1 cup sour cream
3/4 cup shredded Monterey Jack cheese
3/4 cup shredded Cheddar cheese or Monterey Jack cheese
Shredded lettuce (optional)
1/2 cup sliced black olives (optional)

METHOD OF PREPARATION
Arrange 6 tortillas over the bottom and up the sides of a greased 9x13-inch baking dish, overlapping as necessary.

Brown the ground beef with the onion and garlic in a skillet, stirring until the ground beef is crumbly; drain.

Squeeze the moisture from the spinach. Stir the spinach, picante sauce, tomato sauce, tomatoes, red pepper, lime juice and salt into the ground beef mixture.

Simmer for 15 minutes, stirring occasionally. Spread 1/2 of the ground beef mixture in the prepared baking dish. Top with the remaining tortillas, overlapping as necessary. Spread with the sour cream and remaining ground beef mixture.

Bake at 350 degrees for 30 minutes or until bubbly. Sprinkle with the Monterey Jack cheese and Cheddar cheese.

Let stand for 10 minutes. Cut into squares. Top each serving with lettuce and black olives.

Note: May prepare and store in refrigerator for up to 6 hours in advance. Let stand at room temperature for 30 minutes before baking.

SERVES 8

MEXICAN LASAGNA

Ingredients
18 corn tortillas
2 pounds ground beef
1¹/₂ cups water
2 envelopes taco seasoning mix
4 garlic cloves, crushed
¹/₂ teaspoon cayenne
2 cups sour cream
1 tablespoon chili powder
1 (24-ounce) jar salsa
1 cup sliced green onions
3 cups shredded Monterey Jack cheese
3 cups shredded Cheddar cheese

METHOD OF PREPARATION
Arrange 6 of the tortillas over the bottom and up the sides of a 9x13-inch baking dish, overlapping as necessary.

Brown the ground beef in a skillet, stirring until crumbly; drain. Stir in the water, taco seasoning, garlic and cayenne.

Simmer for 10 minutes, stirring occasionally.

Combine the sour cream and chili powder in a bowl and mix well.

Layer 1 cup salsa, ¹/₂ of the ground beef mixture, ¹/₂ cup of the green onions, 1 cup of the sour cream mixture, 1 cup of the Monterey Jack cheese and 1 cup of the Cheddar cheese in the prepared baking dish. Arrange 6 more of the tortillas over the prepared layers. Repeat the layers. Top with the remaining tortillas and remaining salsa.

Bake at 375 degrees for 40 minutes. Sprinkle with the remaining Monterey Jack cheese and remaining Cheddar cheese.

Bake for 5 minutes longer or until the cheese melts.

SERVES 8 TO 10

MEXICAN PILE-ON

Ingredients
1 cup rice
1 (8-ounce) package tortilla chips, crushed
4 cups chili, heated
1¹/₂ cups shredded Cheddar cheese
1 medium onion, chopped
¹/₂ head lettuce, chopped
1 large tomato, chopped
1 cup sour cream
1 avocado, chopped
1 (2-ounce) can sliced black olives, drained
Picante sauce

METHOD OF PREPARATION
Cook the rice using package directions.

Layer the chips, rice, chili, cheese, onion, lettuce, tomato, sour cream, avocado, black olives and picante sauce in the order listed on 6 dinner plates, allowing ²/₃ cup chips and ²/₃ cup chili per serving.

SERVES 6

LAMB SHISH KABOBS WITH WHITE RICE

For the marinade and lamb
Juice of 2 lemons
1/2 cup pineapple juice
1/4 cup vegetable oil
2 tablespoons chopped fresh parsley
2 tablespoons grated onion
1 tablespoon chili powder
2 teaspoons salt
1 teaspoon ginger
1 teaspoon curry powder
1 garlic clove, crushed
3 pounds leg of lamb, cut into 1 1/2-inch cubes

For the shish kabobs
3 to 4 red or green bell peppers, parboiled, cut into chunks
1 pineapple, cut into chunks
20 large mushrooms
15 cherry tomatoes
12 pearl onions, parboiled
Hot cooked white rice

TO PREPARE THE MARINADE
Combine the lemon juice, pineapple juice, oil, parsley, onion, chili powder, salt, ginger, curry powder and garlic in a bowl and mix well.

Combine the marinade and lamb in a glass bowl, turning to coat.

Marinate in the refrigerator for 5 to 7 hours, turning occasionally.

Drain, reserving the marinade.

TO PREPARE THE SHISH KABOBS
Thread the lamb on skewers. Skewer the red or green peppers, pineapple, mushrooms, cherry tomatoes and pearl onions on separate skewers.

Grill the lamb and vegetable kabobs over hot coals until done to taste, basting with the reserved marinade frequently.

Serve the lamb and vegetable kabobs over hot cooked rice.

SERVES 8 TO 10

SPICY CRUSTED HAM

Ingredients
1 (5- to 6-pound) boneless smoked ham, cooked
1/3 cup packed light brown sugar
3 tablespoons fine dry bread crumbs
1/4 teaspoon dry mustard
1/4 teaspoon allspice
1/4 teaspoon freshly ground pepper
1/3 cup dark corn syrup
8 to 10 whole cloves

METHOD OF PREPARATION
Place the ham fat side up on a rack in a shallow roasting pan. Score the ham at 1-inch intervals with a sharp knife. Score the ham in the opposite direction, creating a diamond pattern. Insert a meat thermometer in the center of the thickest portion of the ham. Cover with foil.

Bake at 325 degrees for 2 hours or to 140 degrees on the meat thermometer.

Combine the brown sugar, bread crumbs, dry mustard, allspice and pepper in a bowl and mix well. Bring the corn syrup to a boil in a saucepan. Set aside.

Stud the ham with the whole cloves 30 minutes before the end of the cooking process. Brush the top and side of the ham with the corn syrup; sprinkle with 1/3 of the bread crumb mixture.

Bake for 10 minutes. Drizzle with 1/2 of the remaining corn syrup and sprinkle with 1/2 of the remaining bread crumb mixture.

Bake for 10 minutes. Drizzle with the remaining corn syrup and sprinkle with the remaining bread crumb mixture.

Bake for 10 minutes.

SERVES 10 TO 12

STUFFED PORK ROAST

For the stuffing
4 ounces pork sausage
1 3/4 cups herb-seasoned stuffing
1 cup chopped peeled tart apple
1/2 cup hot water
1/2 cup chopped celery
1/3 cup raisins
1 tablespoon chopped onion
1/2 teaspoon salt
1/2 teaspoon sage
1/8 teaspoon pepper

For the roast
1 (5-pound) rolled boneless pork loin roast
1/2 teaspoon salt
1/2 teaspoon pepper
1/2 teaspoon coriander
1 (10-ounce) jar cherry preserves
2 tablespoons orange marmalade

TO PREPARE THE STUFFING

Cook the sausage until slightly pink. Drain and pat dry with paper towels.

Combine the sausage, stuffing, apple, hot water, celery, raisins, onion, salt, sage and pepper in a bowl and mix well. May blend in a food processor for a finer texture.

TO PREPARE THE ROAST

Separate the roast into 2 portions; trim the excess fat. Slice each portion lengthwise, cutting to but not through the outer edge to form a large rectangle. Open the slices like a book. Pound 1/2 inch thick between sheets of waxed paper.

Sprinkle the cut sides equally with the salt, pepper and coriander. Spoon the stuffing down the center of 1 portion. Top with the remaining portion. Secure with kitchen twine at 2- to 3-inch intervals.

Place the roast on a greased rack in a shallow roasting pan. Insert a meat thermometer into the thickest portion of the pork, making sure it does not touch fat or the stuffing.

Bake at 325 degrees for 1 1/2 hours or to 145 degrees on the meat thermometer. Brush with a mixture of the cherry preserves and orange marmalade.

Bake for 1 hour longer or to 160 degrees on the meat thermometer, basting frequently with the cherry preserves mixture.

Remove the kitchen twine from the roast. Arrange on a serving platter. Garnish with celery leaves.

Note: The cooking time for a pork roast will vary according to poundage. A good guide to follow is 30 to 35 minutes per pound.

SERVES 10 TO 12

APRICOT PECAN STUFFED PORK TENDERLOINS

For the stuffing

1½ cups dried apricots
½ cup pecan pieces
1 garlic clove
½ teaspoon salt
¼ teaspoon pepper
1 tablespoon thyme
2 tablespoons vegetable oil
1 tablespoon molasses

For the tenderloins

2 (½-pound) pork tenderloins
Vegetable oil to taste
1 tablespoon thyme
1 cup chicken broth

TO PREPARE THE STUFFING

Combine the apricots, pecans, garlic, salt and pepper in a food processor container fitted with a steel blade.

Process until coarsely chopped. Add the thyme, oil and molasses.

Process until finely chopped but not smooth.

TO PREPARE THE TENDERLOINS

Cut a pocket down the length of each tenderloin to within ½ inch of the edge. Unfold the tenderloins. Pound ½ inch thick between sheets of waxed paper.

Spread the cut side of the tenderloins with equal portions of the stuffing; secure each tenderloin with kitchen twine. Place seam side down in a shallow baking pan. Brush lightly with oil; sprinkle with the thyme.

Pour the broth over the tenderloins.

Bake at 350 degrees for 45 to 60 minutes or until meat thermometer inserted in thickest portion registers 160 degrees.

SERVES 4 TO 6

GRILLED PORK TENDERLOINS

Ingredients

3 (1½-pound) pork tenderloins
½ cup teriyaki sauce
½ cup soy sauce
3 tablespoons brown sugar
2 green onions, chopped
1 garlic clove, crushed
1 tablespoon sesame seeds
½ teaspoon ginger
½ teaspoon pepper
1 tablespoon vegetable oil

METHOD OF PREPARATION

Place the tenderloins in a shallow dish.

Combine the teriyaki sauce, soy sauce, brown sugar, green onions, garlic, sesame seeds, ginger, pepper and oil in a bowl and mix well. Pour over the tenderloins, turning to coat.

Marinate, covered, in the refrigerator for 2 to 4 hours, turning occasionally.

Grill with cover down over medium-hot coals for 20 minutes or until meat thermometer inserted in thickest portion registers 160 degrees, turning once.

SERVES 12 TO 16

PORK CHOPS WITH GLAZED PEACHES

For the peaches
4 medium peaches, cut into halves
2 tablespoons brown sugar
1 tablespoon water

For the pork chops
1/3 cup Dijon mustard
1/4 cup packed brown sugar
1 tablespoon steak sauce
4 pork loin chops, 3/4 inch thick
Sprigs of parsley

TO PREPARE THE PEACHES

Grill the peach halves over hot coals for 5 to 8 minutes or until hot and light brown, turning and basting with a mixture of the brown sugar and water occasionally.

Prepare approximately 10 minutes before serving.

TO PREPARE THE PORK CHOPS

Combine the Dijon mustard, brown sugar and steak sauce in a bowl and mix well. Add the pork chops, turning to coat. Let stand for 20 minutes. Drain, reserving the mustard sauce.

Grill over medium-hot coals for 10 to 12 minutes or until light brown and cooked through, turning and basting with the remaining mustard sauce occasionally.

Arrange the pork chops on 4 dinner plates. Top with parsley sprigs. Serve with the glazed peaches.

SERVES 4

CHICKEN WITH SEASONED POTATOES

Ingredients
1 (3-pound) chicken, cut up
1/3 cup flour
1 teaspoon salt
1 teaspoon paprika
Dash of pepper
1/2 cup butter
2 cups (1/2-inch-thick) unpeeled slices new potatoes
Salt and pepper to taste
3/4 cup sliced green onions
2 chicken bouillon cubes
1 cup hot water
1 cup sour cream
Sprigs of parsley

METHOD OF PREPARATION

Rinse the chicken and pat dry.

Combine the flour, salt, paprika and pepper in a food storage bag and shake to mix. Add the chicken pieces in batches, shaking to coat.

Brown the chicken in the butter in a skillet. Push the chicken to the center of the skillet. Arrange the potatoes around the chicken. Season the potatoes with salt and pepper. Sprinkle the green onions over the top.

Dissolve the bouillon cubes in the hot water and pour over the chicken, potatoes and green onions.

Simmer, covered, for 35 minutes or until the chicken is tender. Transfer the chicken and potatoes to a serving platter, reserving the pan drippings.

Stir the sour cream into the pan drippings. Cook until heated through, stirring constantly. Drizzle over the chicken and vegetables. Top with parsley sprigs.

Note: This dish works best if prepared in an electric skillet.

SERVES 4

CHICKEN BREASTS WITH ALMONDS

Ingredients

2 pounds boneless chicken breasts
1/4 cup flour
1/4 teaspoon salt
1/8 teaspoon ground pepper
1/2 cup sliced almonds
1/4 cup margarine
1/2 teaspoon rosemary
1/2 cup dry white wine

METHOD OF PREPARATION

Rinse the chicken and pat dry. Coat with a mixture of the flour, salt and pepper.

Sauté the almonds in the margarine in a skillet until brown. Remove the almonds with a slotted spoon to a bowl, reserving the pan drippings. Stir the rosemary into the pan drippings.

Brown the chicken on both sides in the reserved pan drippings over medium heat. Stir in the white wine.

Cook, covered, over low heat for 5 to 10 minutes or until the chicken is cooked through. Remove the chicken with a slotted spoon to a heated serving platter, reserving the pan drippings.

Bring the reserved pan drippings to a boil. Stir in the almonds. Spoon over the chicken.

SERVES 6 TO 8

BARBEQUED CHICKEN WITH HONEY MUSTARD GLAZE

Ingredients

6 chicken breast halves
1 (8-ounce) can tomato sauce
1/2 cup olive oil or corn oil
1/2 cup orange juice
1/4 cup vinegar
1 1/2 teaspoons oregano
1 teaspoon salt
6 peppercorns or 1/2 teaspoon pepper
1 garlic clove, minced
1/4 cup honey
1/2 teaspoon dry mustard

METHOD OF PREPARATION

Rinse the chicken and pat dry. Arrange in a shallow dish.

Combine the tomato sauce, olive oil, orange juice, vinegar, oregano, salt, peppercorns and garlic in a jar with a tightfitting lid, shaking to mix. Pour over the chicken, turning to coat.

Marinate, covered, in the refrigerator for 2 to 10 hours, turning occasionally. Drain, reserving the marinade. Bring the reserved marinade to a boil in a saucepan.

Grill the chicken over medium-hot coals for 45 to 50 minutes or until cooked through, turning and basting with the reserved marinade frequently.

Brush with a mixture of the honey and dry mustard just before the end of the cooking process.

Note: Reduce the cooking time if boneless chicken breasts are used.

SERVES 6

BASIL GRILLED CHICKEN

For the basil cheese butter
1/2 cup butter or margarine, softened
2 tablespoons minced fresh basil
1 tablespoon grated Parmesan cheese
1/4 teaspoon garlic powder
1/8 teaspoon salt
1/8 teaspoon pepper

For the chicken
4 skinless chicken breast halves
3/4 teaspoon coarsely ground pepper
1/3 cup melted butter or margarine
1/4 cup chopped fresh basil
Sprigs of basil (optional)

TO PREPARE THE BASIL CHEESE BUTTER
Combine butter, basil, cheese, garlic powder, salt and pepper in a mixer bowl. Beat at low speed until mixed, scraping the bowl occasionally. Set aside.

TO PREPARE THE CHICKEN
Rinse the chicken and pat dry. Press pepper into the meaty sides of the chicken. Brush lightly with a mixture of melted butter and basil, reserving the remaining mixture.

Grill the chicken over medium-hot coals for 8 to 10 minutes per side or until cooked through, turning and basting with the reserved butter mixture frequently.

Arrange the chicken on a serving platter. Top with basil sprigs. Serve with the basil cheese butter.

SERVES 4

CHICKEN FAJITAS

Ingredients
2 1/2 to 3 pounds boneless skinless chicken breasts
Juice and grated peel of 4 limes
2 quarts water
1/2 cup red wine (optional)
1 large tomato, chopped
1/4 large onion, chopped
2 jalapeños, chopped
1/2 bunch cilantro, chopped
1 tablespoon meat tenderizer
1 teaspoon Worcestershire sauce
1 teaspoon garlic powder
1 teaspoon salt
1 teaspoon pepper
10 to 12 flour tortillas, heated

METHOD OF PREPARATION
Rinse the chicken and pat dry. Arrange in a glass dish or bowl. Drizzle with the lime juice and sprinkle with the lime peel.

Combine the water, red wine, tomato, onion, jalapeños, cilantro, meat tenderizer, Worcestershire sauce, garlic powder, salt and pepper in a bowl and mix well. Pour over the chicken, turning to coat.

Marinate, covered, in the refrigerator for 10 to 12 hours, turning occasionally. Drain, discarding the marinade.

Grill over hot coals until cooked through.

Serve with the flour tortillas, grilled red and green bell peppers and grilled onions.

Variation: Substitute lean flank steak or skirt steak for the chicken.

SERVES 10 TO 12

CHICKEN MARINARA

Ingredients
6 boneless skinless chicken breast halves
2 eggs, beaten
3/4 cup Italian-style bread crumbs
Salt and pepper to taste
Italian seasoning to taste
1/4 cup margarine
1 (32-ounce) jar spaghetti sauce
3 ounces mozzarella cheese, cut into 6 slices
6 ounces Swiss cheese, cut into 6 slices
1/4 cup milk
1 tablespoon grated Parmesan cheese
Hot cooked spaghetti

METHOD OF PREPARATION
Rinse the chicken and pat dry. Pound 1/4 inch thick between 2 sheets of plastic wrap with a meat mallet. Dip the chicken in the eggs; coat with the bread crumbs. Sprinkle with salt, pepper and Italian seasoning.

Sauté the chicken in the margarine in a skillet for 2 minutes per side or until light brown.

Pour 1/2 of the spaghetti sauce into a 9x13-inch baking dish. Arrange the chicken over the sauce.

Bake at 350 degrees for 25 minutes. Arrange 1 slice of the mozzarella cheese and 1 slice of the Swiss cheese on each chicken breast. Top with a mixture of the remaining spaghetti sauce and milk; sprinkle with the Parmesan cheese.

Bake for 5 minutes longer. Serve with hot cooked spaghetti.

Note: Prepared spaghetti sauce makes this quick and easy. Impress your company—they will think you have been cooking all day.

SERVES 6

CHICKEN SANTA CRUZ

Ingredients
12 chicken tenders
3 tablespoons lemon juice
3 to 4 large red or green bell peppers
2 tablespoons olive oil
2 garlic cloves, minced
2 large onions, sliced, cut into halves
2 teaspoons cumin seeds
1 teaspoon oregano
1 teaspoon red pepper flakes
1/2 teaspoon salt, or to taste
Freshly ground black pepper
3 tablespoons finely chopped fresh parley or cilantro

METHOD OF PREPARATION
Rinse the chicken and pat dry. Combine with the lemon juice in a bowl and mix well.

Cut the red peppers into halves. Cut the halves into 1-inch strips. Cut each strip horizontally into thirds.

Heat the olive oil in a skillet until hot. Add the red peppers, garlic, onions, cumin seeds, oregano and red pepper flakes, stirring until coated.

Cook, covered, over medium heat for 10 minutes, stirring occasionally. Add the chicken tenders and mix well.

Cook, covered, for 10 minutes longer or until the chicken is cooked through, stirring occasionally. Season with the salt and black pepper; sprinkle with the parsley.

Note: Serve with a rice or corn casserole and a green salad with fresh orange sections.

SERVES 4 TO 6

CHICKEN SUPREME

Ingredients

6 boneless chicken breast halves
1 cup sour cream
2 tablespoons lemon juice
1 teaspoon celery salt
1 teaspoon paprika
1/4 teaspoon garlic powder
1/4 teaspoon pepper
1 cup bread crumbs
1/2 cup melted butter

METHOD OF PREPARATION

Rinse the chicken and pat dry. Coat with a mixture of the sour cream, lemon juice, celery salt, paprika, garlic powder and pepper. Arrange in a shallow dish.

Marinate in the refrigerator for 8 to 10 hours; do not cover.

Coat the chicken in the bread crumbs. Arrange in a shallow dish. Drizzle with 1/2 of the butter.

Bake at 350 degrees for 40 minutes. Drizzle with the remaining butter.

Bake for 15 minutes longer or until the chicken is cooked through.

SERVES 6

THREE-CITRUS GRILLED CHICKEN

Ingredients

4 boneless chicken breast halves
1/4 red onion, thinly sliced
1/3 cup fresh orange juice
1/4 cup olive oil
1/4 cup frozen lemon juice concentrate, thawed
1/4 cup fresh lemon juice
1/4 cup honey
3 tablespoons fresh lime juice
3 tablespoons chopped fresh mint
1 tablespoon grated orange peel
2 teaspoons grated lemon peel
1 1/4 teaspoons grated lime peel
1/4 teaspoon cumin
1/4 teaspoon cinnamon
1/8 teaspoon ground pepper
1/8 teaspoon salt

METHOD OF PREPARATION

Rinse the chicken and pat dry.

Combine the red onion, orange juice, olive oil, lemon juice concentrate, lemon juice, honey, lime juice, mint, orange peel, lemon peel, lime peel, cumin, cinnamon, pepper and salt in a bowl and mix well. Add the chicken, tossing to coat.

Marinate, covered, in the refrigerator for 2 to 10 hours, tossing occasionally. Drain, reserving the marinade. Bring the marinade to a boil in a saucepan. Remove from heat.

Grill the chicken over medium-hot coals for 18 minutes or until cooked through, turning and basting with the reserved marinade frequently. Transfer to a heated serving platter.

Bring the remaining marinade to a boil in a saucepan. Serve with the chicken.

SERVES 4

CHICKEN IN PASTRY

Ingredients
6 boneless skinless chicken breast halves
1 medium onion, chopped
2 tablespoons melted butter or margarine
4 mushrooms, sliced
2 large carrots, cut into 1-inch strips
1 rib celery, chopped
1 cup chicken broth
1/3 cup dry white wine
1 tablespoon Worcestershire sauce
1/4 teaspoon parsley flakes
1/4 teaspoon chopped chives
1/4 teaspoon dry mustard
1/8 teaspoon garlic powder
1/8 teaspoon chervil
1/8 teaspoon white pepper
1/8 teaspoon freshly ground black pepper
1 bay leaf
2 tablespoons water
1 tablespoon plus 1 teaspoon cornstarch
1 (10-ounce) can cream of mushroom soup
1/2 cup sour cream
1/2 cup shredded Swiss cheese
1/2 cup shredded mild or sharp Cheddar cheese
2 tablespoons grated Parmesan cheese
1 recipe (2-crust) pie pastry

METHOD OF PREPARATION

Rinse the chicken and pat dry. Cut into 1-inch pieces.

Sauté the chicken and onion in the butter in a large skillet for 5 minutes. Add the mushrooms, carrots, celery, broth, white wine, Worcestershire sauce, parsley flakes, chives, dry mustard, garlic powder, chervil, white pepper, black pepper and bay leaf and mix well.

Simmer, covered, for 10 minutes, stirring occasionally. Discard the bay leaf. Stir in a mixture of the water and cornstarch.

Bring to a boil over medium heat, stirring constantly. Remove from heat. Stir in the soup, sour cream, Swiss cheese, Cheddar cheese and Parmesan cheese.

Roll 1/2 of the pastry 1/8 inch thick on a lightly floured surface. Fit into a 21/2-quart pie plate. Spoon the chicken mixture over the prepared layer.

Roll the remaining pastry 1/8 inch thick on a lightly floured surface. Cut 1/2 of the pastry into 1/2-inch strips with a fluted pastry wheel.

Moisten the edge of the pastry in the pie plate. Arrange the pastry strips in a lattice design over the chicken mixture. Trim the edge and seal.

Make leaf cutouts with the remaining pastry. Arrange around the inner edge of the pie plate.

Bake at 400 degrees for 30 to 40 minutes or until light brown.

SERVES 6

CHICKEN ENCHILADAS WITH TOMATILLO SAUCE

For the tomatillo sauce
1 1/2 pounds fresh tomatillos
1 cup water
Salt to taste
1/3 cup chopped onion
2 garlic cloves
2 to 3 jalapeños, coarsely chopped
1/4 cup chopped fresh coriander or cilantro
2 corn tortillas
3 tablespoons vegetable oil
1/2 teaspoon sugar

For the enchiladas
2 cups sour cream
1/4 cup finely chopped onion
1/4 cup minced fresh coriander or cilantro
1 teaspoon minced garlic
Salt to taste
2 cups chopped cooked white-meat chicken
3/4 cup butter
18 corn tortillas
2 cups shredded white Cheddar cheese

To Prepare the Tomatillo Sauce

Remove the skins of the tomatillos. Combine the tomatillos, water and salt in a saucepan. Bring to a rolling boil.

Boil, covered, for 5 minutes. Combine the tomatillos, 1/2 cup cooking liquid, onion, garlic, jalapeños and coriander in a blender container or food processor container.

Process for 1 minute or until puréed. Reserve 1 cup of the sauce to serve with the enchiladas.

Sauté the tortillas in the hot oil in a skillet until crisp. Drain, reserving the pan drippings. Add the tortillas to the remaining tomatillo sauce.

Process until blended.

Combine the reserved pan drippings and tomatillo sauce in a large skillet. Stir in the sugar.

Cook over medium heat for 10 minutes, stirring occasionally.

To Prepare the Enchiladas

Combine the sour cream, onion, coriander and garlic and mix well. Season with salt.

Sauté the chicken lightly in 1/4 cup of the butter in a skillet. Remove from heat.

Heat the remaining butter in a skillet until melted. Sauté the tortillas a few at a time in the butter for 5 to 6 seconds per side or until soft but not crisp, turning once. Pat dry with paper towels.

Fill each tortilla with a small amount of the sour cream mixture, some of the chicken, some of the tomatillo sauce and some of the cheese; roll to enclose the filling. Secure with wooden picks.

Arrange the enchiladas side by side in a 9x13-inch baking pan. Spread with the remaining sour cream mixture, remaining tomatillo sauce and remaining cheese.

Bake at 350 degrees for 15 to 20 minutes or until hot. Serve with the reserved tomatillo sauce.

Note: May substitute two 15-ounce cans tomatillos for the fresh tomatillos. Canned tomatillos do not require cooking.

SERVES 6

CHICKEN OLE

For the sauce

2 (10-ounce) cans cream of chicken soup
1 (12-ounce) can evaporated milk
1 pound Velveeta cheese, cubed
1 (4-ounce) can green chiles
1 (2-ounce) jar pimento

For the filling

2 cups chopped onions
3 tablespoons butter or margarine
8 ounces mushrooms, sliced
4 cups chopped cooked chicken
2 cups sour cream
1 (10-ounce) can cream of chicken soup
1 (4-ounce) can chopped green chiles
$^1/_2$ cup sliced almonds, toasted
$^1/_2$ teaspoon oregano
$^1/_4$ teaspoon salt
$^1/_8$ teaspoon pepper
20 flour tortillas
2 cups shredded Cheddar cheese

TO PREPARE THE SAUCE

Combine the soup, evaporated milk and cheese in a saucepan.

Cook over low heat until blended. Stir in the chiles and pimento.

TO PREPARE THE FILLING

Sauté the onions in 1 tablespoon of the butter in a skillet until tender. Remove the onions with a slotted spoon to a bowl. Add the remaining 2 tablespoons butter to the skillet.

Sauté the mushrooms in the butter until tender. Stir in the onions, chicken, sour cream, soup, chiles, almonds, oregano, salt and pepper.

Spread some of the sauce in the bottom of two 9x13-inch baking dishes sprayed with nonstick cooking spray.

Fill each tortilla with $^1/_3$ cup of the chicken mixture; roll to enclose the filling. Arrange side by side in the prepared baking dishes. Spread liberally with the desired amount of sauce, pressing between the tortillas and around the edges. Freeze any remaining sauce for future use.

Bake at 350 degrees for 35 minutes. Sprinkle with the cheese.

Bake just until the cheese melts.

SERVES 10

ALMOND CHICKEN

Ingredients
2 cups chopped cooked chicken
3/4 cup mayonnaise
3/4 cup chopped celery
1/4 cup slivered almonds
2 tablespoons lemon juice
1 1/2 teaspoons finely grated onion
Salt to taste
1/2 cup shredded cheese
1 cup crushed potato chips

METHOD OF PREPARATION

Combine the chicken, mayonnaise, celery, almonds, lemon juice, onion and salt in a bowl and mix well. Spoon into a baking dish.

Sprinkle with the shredded cheese; top with the potato chips.

Bake at 400 degrees for 15 minutes or until brown and bubbly.

SERVES 4 TO 6

CHICKEN SOPA

Ingredients
12 corn tortillas
Vegetable oil
1 large onion, chopped
Garlic salt to taste
1 to 2 tablespoons butter
1 (10-ounce) can cream of mushroom soup
1 (10-ounce) can cream of chicken soup
2 (10-ounce) cans tomatoes with green chiles
1 cup evaporated milk
1 (3-pound) chicken, cooked, chopped
8 ounces Monterey Jack cheese, shredded
8 ounces longhorn cheese, shredded
2 cups sour cream

METHOD OF PREPARATION

Soften the tortillas in hot oil in a skillet. Drain and cut into halves. Line a greased 3-quart baking dish with the tortillas.

Sauté the onion and garlic salt in the butter in a skillet until the onion is tender.

Combine the onion, soups, tomatoes and evaporated milk in a saucepan and mix well.

Cook just until heated through, stirring frequently.

Layer the soup mixture, chicken, Monterey Jack cheese and longhorn cheese 1/2 at a time in the prepared baking dish. Spread with the sour cream.

Bake, covered, at 325 degrees for 1 to 1 1/2 hours or until bubbly.

Note: May store in the refrigerator or freeze for future use before baking. Thaw in the refrigerator before baking.

SERVES 6 TO 8

CHICKEN TETRAZZINI

Ingredients
1 cup thinly sliced celery
1 cup chopped green bell pepper
1/2 cup chopped onion
1 (4-ounce) can sliced mushrooms
1/2 cup butter or margarine
1/4 cup flour
1 cup milk
2 cups chopped cooked chicken
8 ounces sharp Cheddar cheese, shredded
1/4 cup dry sherry
2 tablespoons Worcestershire sauce
2 teaspoons salt
1/4 teaspoon pepper
1/4 cup chopped pimento
1 garlic clove, crushed
1 (8-ounce) package spaghetti, cooked, drained
3/4 cup grated Parmesan cheese

METHOD OF PREPARATION

Sauté the celery, green pepper, onion and mushrooms in the butter in a large saucepan until tender. Stir in the flour. Add the milk gradually, stirring constantly.

Cook until thickened, stirring constantly. Add the chicken, Cheddar cheese, sherry, Worcestershire sauce, salt, pepper, pimento and garlic and mix well.

Cook until the cheese melts, stirring constantly. Add the spaghetti and mix well. Spoon into a baking dish. Sprinkle with the Parmesan cheese.

Bake at 350 degrees for 15 to 20 minutes or until brown and bubbly.

Note: May be prepared 1 day in advance, stored in the refrigerator and baked just before serving or may be frozen for future use.

SERVES 8 TO 10

GRILLED QUAIL WITH CURRANT SAUCE

Ingredients
14 quail
1 (14-ounce) can chicken stock
2 teaspoons cornstarch
1/2 cup sherry
1/2 cup red wine
1/3 cup currants
4 to 6 tablespoons unsalted butter, chopped
1/4 cup olive oil
3 shallots, minced
5 to 6 sprigs of thyme or 1 teaspoon dried thyme
Hot cooked rice or noodles
4 to 5 large sprigs of thyme

METHOD OF PREPARATION

Rinse the quail and pat dry.

Grill the quail over hot coals for 15 minutes or until cooked through. Let stand until cool.

Debone the quail, reserving 1 cup of the bones.

Combine the stock and cornstarch in a saucepan, stirring until the cornstarch dissolves. Add the sherry, red wine, currants, butter, olive oil, shallots, 5 to 6 sprigs of thyme and reserved bones and mix well.

Cook over medium heat until of the desired consistency; strain.

Spoon the hot cooked rice or noodles onto a serving platter. Top with the quail; drizzle with the currant sauce. Arrange 4 to 5 sprigs of thyme around the quail.

Variation: Substitute 1/3 cup golden raisins for the currants.

SERVES 5 TO 6

QUAIL STUFFED WITH JALAPENOS

Ingredients
8 quail
4 jalapeños, cut lengthwise into halves, seeded
1 onion, thinly sliced (optional)
1 (8-ounce) can water chestnuts, drained (optional)
Pepper to taste
8 slices bacon
Salt to taste

METHOD OF PREPARATION
Rinse the quail and pat dry.

Make slits on both sides of the breast of the quail. Stuff each slit with a jalapeño half or stuff 1 side with a jalapeño and the other side with an onion slice or water chestnut. Sprinkle with pepper. Wrap each bird with a slice of bacon; secure with a wooden pick.

Grill over hot coals for 20 to 30 minutes or until cooked through, turning frequently. Season with salt.

Note: May substitute 8 doves for the quail.

Variation: Marinate dove or quail in Italian salad dressing for several hours to enhance flavor.

SERVES 4

CRUSTACEAN CASSEROLE

Ingredients
2 pounds crab meat
8 slices sourdough bread, torn
1 pound Swiss cheese, cubed
1/2 cup sliced almonds
4 cups milk
3 eggs, beaten
1 teaspoon dry mustard
1/2 whole nutmeg, finely grated
1/3 cup dry sherry

METHOD OF PREPARATION
Layer the crab meat, bread, cheese and almonds in a 9x13-inch baking dish.

Combine the milk, eggs, dry mustard and nutmeg in a bowl and mix well. Pour over the prepared layers.

Chill, covered, for 4 to 10 hours. Pour the sherry over the top just before baking.

Bake at 350 degrees for 45 minutes or until set.

Note: Imitation crab meat made from whitefish may be substituted for the crab meat.

SERVES 8

ORANGE ROUGHY PARMESAN

Ingredients
1/2 cup freshly grated Parmesan cheese
1/4 cup butter, softened
3 tablespoons mayonnaise
3 tablespoons chopped green onions
1/4 teaspoon salt
Freshly ground pepper to taste
Dash of Tabasco sauce
2 pounds orange roughy fillets
2 tablespoons fresh lemon juice

METHOD OF PREPARATION
Combine the cheese, butter, mayonnaise, green onions, salt, pepper and Tabasco sauce in a bowl and mix well.

Arrange the fillets in a buttered baking dish. Drizzle with the lemon juice. Let stand for 10 minutes.

Broil the fillets 3 to 4 inches from the heat source for 5 minutes. Spread with the cheese mixture.

Broil for 2 to 3 minutes longer or until the fish flakes easily.

Variation: Substitute your favorite skinless white fish for the orange roughy.

SERVES 4

BARBEQUE SHRIMP

Ingredients
1 1/2 to 2 pounds shrimp
1 cup melted butter
2 to 3 garlic cloves, crushed
2 tablespoons paprika
1 teaspoon salt
Pepper to taste

METHOD OF PREPARATION
Peel and devein the shrimp, leaving the tails intact. Arrange in a shallow baking dish.

Combine the butter, garlic, paprika and salt in a bowl and mix well. Pour over the shrimp, turning to coat. Sprinkle heavily with pepper; shrimp should appear black.

Marinate, covered with plastic wrap, in the refrigerator for 2 hours or longer. Remove the cover.

Bake at 450 degrees for 10 minutes. Turn the shrimp.

Bake for 10 minutes longer. Drain the butter mixture into a saucepan and keep warm.

Broil the shrimp for 5 minutes.

Arrange the shrimp in individual serving bowls. Drizzle with the warm butter mixture.

Note: Serve with crusty French bread.

SERVES 3 TO 4

CAJUN SHRIMP CREOLE

Ingredients
2 tablespoons bacon drippings
2 tablespoons flour
2 onions, chopped
1 large green bell pepper, chopped
2 garlic cloves, crushed or minced
2 teaspoons chopped fresh parsley
1 (16-ounce) can stewed tomatoes
$1/2$ teaspoon salt
$1/3$ teaspoon thyme
$1/8$ to $1/2$ teaspoon red pepper flakes
2 bay leaves
$1 1/2$ cups frozen cocktail shrimp, thawed, drained
2 teaspoons Worcestershire sauce
Hot cooked white rice

METHOD OF PREPARATION

Combine the bacon drippings and flour in a saucepan and mix well.

Cook until of the consistency of a dark brown roux, stirring constantly. Add the onions, green pepper, garlic and parsley.

Sauté until the onions are brown. Stir in the tomatoes, salt, thyme, red pepper flakes and bay leaves. Add the shrimp and mix well.

Cook over low heat for 30 to 90 minutes, stirring occasionally. Discard the bay leaves and stir in the Worcestershire sauce just before serving.

Ladle over hot cooked rice in individual serving bowls.

Note: The flavor of the Creole is enhanced by the longer cooking time.

SERVES 4 TO 6

PASTA WITH ASPARAGUS

Ingredients
5 garlic cloves, minced
1 teaspoon red pepper flakes
2 to 3 dashes of hot pepper sauce
$1/4$ cup olive oil
1 tablespoon butter or margarine
1 pound fresh asparagus, cut into $1 1/2$-inch pieces
$1/4$ teaspoon pepper
Salt to taste
$1/4$ cup grated Parmesan cheese
8 ounces mostaccioli or rigatoni, cooked, drained

METHOD OF PREPARATION

Cook the garlic, red pepper flakes and hot pepper sauce in the olive oil and butter in a skillet for 2 to 3 minutes, stirring constantly. Add the asparagus, pepper and salt and mix well.

Sauté for 8 to 10 minutes or until the asparagus is tender-crisp. Stir in the cheese.

Spoon the asparagus mixture over the hot pasta in a bowl, tossing to coat.

Serve immediately.

SERVES 4 TO 6

PASTA PRIMAVERA

Ingredients

1 pound fresh asparagus, trimmed
2 cups fresh broccoli florets
1 medium onion, chopped
1 large garlic clove, chopped
1 tablespoon olive oil
1 large carrot, cut into diagonal slices
1 medium red bell pepper, coarsely chopped
1 medium yellow bell pepper, coarsely chopped
1 cup whipping cream
1/2 cup chicken broth
3 green onions, chopped
2 tablespoons chopped fresh basil, or
2 teaspoons dried basil
1/2 teaspoon salt
8 ounces linguine, broken, cooked, drained
8 ounces fresh mushrooms, sliced
1 cup freshly grated Parmesan cheese
1/4 teaspoon freshly ground pepper

METHOD OF PREPARATION

Cut the asparagus diagonally into 1 1/2-inch pieces. Combine the asparagus and broccoli in a steamer.

Steam, covered, over boiling water for 6 to 8 minutes or until the vegetables are tender-crisp. Remove from heat.

Sauté the onion and garlic in the olive oil in a skillet until tender. Add the carrot and bell peppers and mix well.

Sauté until the carrot and bell peppers are tender-crisp; drain.

Combine the whipping cream, broth, green onions, basil and salt in a saucepan and mix well.

Cook over medium-high heat for 5 minutes, stirring occasionally.

Combine the hot linguine, asparagus mixture, carrot mixture, whipping cream mixture and mushrooms in a bowl, tossing gently to mix. Sprinkle with the cheese and pepper and toss gently. Serve immediately.

SERVES 8

TORTILLA BLACK BEAN CASSEROLE

Ingredients

2 cups chopped onions
1 1/2 cups chopped green bell peppers
1 (15-ounce) can chopped tomatoes
3/4 cup picante sauce
2 garlic cloves, minced
2 teaspoons cumin
2 (15-ounce) cans black beans, drained
12 (6-inch) corn tortillas
2 cups shredded low-fat Monterey Jack cheese
2 medium tomatoes, sliced (optional)
2 cups shredded lettuce (optional)
Sliced green onions (optional)
Sliced black olives (optional)
1/2 cup low-fat sour cream or plain yogurt (optional)

METHOD OF PREPARATION

Bring the onions, green peppers, undrained tomatoes, picante sauce, garlic and cumin to a boil in a saucepan; reduce heat.

Simmer for 10 minutes, stirring occasionally. Stir in the black beans.

Spread 1/3 of the black bean mixture in a 9x13-inch baking dish. Arrange 1/2 of the tortillas over the black bean mixture, overlapping as necessary. Sprinkle 1/2 of the cheese over the tortillas. Layer half the remaining black bean mixture, the remaining tortillas and the remaining black bean mixture over the layers.

Bake, covered, at 350 degrees for 30 to 35 minutes or until bubbly. Sprinkle with the remaining cheese.

Let stand for 10 minutes. Top with the tomatoes, lettuce, green onions and black olives. Cut into squares. Serve with the sour cream or yogurt.

Note: Cut into smaller portions and serve as a side dish.

Variation: Substitute red kidney beans for the black beans.

SERVES 6 TO 8

BARBEQUE SAUCE

Ingredients
2 cups catsup
1/2 cup light corn syrup
1/4 cup packed brown sugar
1/4 cup Worcestershire sauce
2 tablespoons liquid smoke
1 teaspoon lemon juice
Dash of hot pepper sauce (optional)

METHOD OF PREPARATION
Combine the catsup, corn syrup, brown sugar, Worcestershire sauce, liquid smoke, lemon juice and hot pepper sauce in a bowl and mix well.

Spoon into a covered container.

Store in the refrigerator. Use as desired.

MAKES 2 1/2 TO 3 CUPS

BLACKENED SEASONING

Ingredients
5 teaspoons salt
2 teaspoons paprika
2 teaspoons garlic powder
2 teaspoons cayenne
2 teaspoons onion powder
1 1/2 teaspoons black pepper
1 1/2 teaspoons white pepper
1 teaspoon whole oregano
1 teaspoon thyme

METHOD OF PREPARATION
Combine the salt, paprika, garlic powder, cayenne, onion powder, black pepper, white pepper, oregano and thyme in a bowl and mix well.

Store in an airtight container.

Note: Coat meat, fish or poultry with melted butter and then in the blackened seasoning mixture; meat should be at least 3/4 inch thick. Heat a skillet over high heat for 2 minutes or until white ash forms. Place the meat, fish or poultry in the skillet and drizzle with 1 teaspoon melted butter. Cook for 10 minutes or until charred; turn. Drizzle with 1 teaspoon melted butter. Cook approximately 10 minutes longer.

Try redfish, black grouper, skinless chicken and ribeyes with this seasoning mixture.

MAKES 6 TABLESPOONS

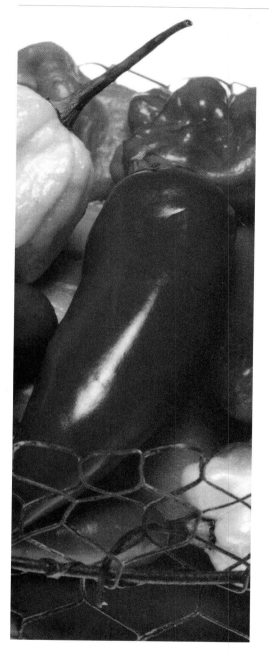

$\mathcal{S}$IDE $\mathcal{D}$ISHES

Asparagus Bundles with Hazelnut Dressing, 147

Asparagus Casserole, 147

Asparagus Parmesan, 148

Best Baked Beans, 148

Cuban Black Beans, 149

Tasty Black Beans, 149

Cheese and Sour Cream Green Beans, 150

Green Beans with Almonds, 150

Green Beans with Wine Sauce, 151

Southern Broccoli, 151

Brussels Sprouts with Scallions, 152

Orange-Glazed Brussels Sprouts, 152

Glazed Carrots with Bacon and Onion, 153

Cauliflower and Wild Rice, 153

Tangy Mustard Cauliflower with Vegetable Medley, 154

Corn and Rice, 154

Grilled Corn on the Cob, 155

Shoe Peg Corn with Chiles, 155

Baked Mushrooms, 156

Herbed Baked Potatoes, 156

New Potato Casserole, 157

Savory Spinach, 157

Spinach Cheese Casserole, 158

Bacon Cheese Squash, 158

Squash and Hominy Casserole, 158

Zucchini Parmigiana, 159

Garden Vegetable Casserole, 159

Mixed Vegetable Casserole, 160

Grits Soufflé, 160

Pecan Rice, 160

Rice Green Chile Casserole, 161

Tex-Mex Rice, 161

Wild Rice and Oyster Casserole, 162

Rum-Baked Pears, 162

ASPARAGUS BUNDLES WITH HAZELNUT DRESSING

For the hazelnut dressing
3/4 cup vegetable oil
1/2 cup finely chopped hazelnuts, toasted
2 tablespoons raspberry vinegar
Salt and freshly ground pepper to taste

For the asparagus
2 pounds thin asparagus
4 green onions with tops
Salt to taste

TO PREPARE THE HAZELNUT DRESSING

Heat the oil in a saucepan or microwave in a microwave-safe dish until hot. Pour over the hazelnuts in a glass bowl or jar.

Let stand, covered, at room temperature for 24 to 36 hours. Strain, pressing lightly. Store the oil and nuts separately in the refrigerator for up to 2 weeks if desired.

Whisk the hazlenut oil and raspberry vinegar together in a bowl. Season with salt and pepper. Store, covered, in the refrigerator until serving time or for up to several days.

TO PREPARE THE ASPARAGUS

Trim the asparagus, leaving spears approximately 5 inches long. Separate into bundles of 6 to 8 spears each; tips should point in the same direction.

Cut off the green onion tops where the white ends and cut the green tops lengthwise into halves, reserving the white portion for another use. Place the tops in a microwave-safe dish. Add water to cover by 1/4 inch.

Microwave, covered, on High for 1 to 2 minutes or until wilted. Cool slightly. Tie the asparagus bundles with the strips of green onion.

Bring 1 inch salted water to a boil in a skillet. Add the asparagus bundles.

Simmer for 4 minutes or until tender-crisp. Plunge the bundles into cold water to stop the cooking process. Drain and pat dry.

Drizzle the hazelnut vinaigrette over the asparagus bundles on individual serving plates; sprinkle with the hazelnuts.

Note: The asparagus may be prepared 1 day in advance. Arrange on a double thickness of paper towels in a shallow dish and cover with plastic wrap. Store in the refrigerator.

SERVES 8

ASPARAGUS CASSEROLE

Ingredients
2 (16-ounce) cans asparagus, drained
3 hard-cooked eggs, sliced
2 tablespoons butter
2 tablespoons flour
1 1/2 cups milk
1 1/4 cups shredded Cheddar cheese
3/4 cup crushed butter crackers
2 tablespoons butter

METHOD OF PREPARATION

Place the asparagus on paper towels and pat dry. Arrange in a baking dish. Top with the eggs.

Heat 2 tablespoons butter in a saucepan until melted. Stir in the flour until blended. Add the milk gradually, stirring constantly.

Cook until thickened, stirring constantly. Stir in the cheese.

Cook just until the cheese melts, stirring constantly. Pour over the prepared layers. Top with a mixture of the crackers and 2 tablespoons butter.

Bake at 350 degrees for 20 to 25 minutes or until brown and bubbly.

SERVES 4 TO 6

SIDE DISHES

ASPARAGUS PARMESAN

Ingredients

1 pound asparagus, trimmed
1/2 teaspoon sugar
1/8 teaspoon salt
1/4 cup butter
1 tablespoon (heaping) grated Parmesan cheese

METHOD OF PREPARATION

Cut the asparagus spears into 1-inch pieces.
Sprinkle the asparagus with the sugar and salt.
Steam or boil in a 3-quart saucepan for 15 minutes or until tender-crisp; drain.

Heat the butter in a skillet until melted. Add the asparagus; sprinkle with the cheese.

Sauté lightly. Arrange on a serving platter. Serve immediately.

SERVES 3 TO 4

BEST BAKED BEANS

Ingredients

4 slices bacon
2 onions, chopped
1 cup chopped green bell pepper
1 cup chopped fresh parsley
1 cup chopped celery
2 garlic cloves, crushed
2 large cans pork and beans
1 (16-ounce) can tomatoes with green chiles
1 (2-ounce) jar chopped pimento
1 tablespoon prepared mustard
1 teaspoon chili powder
Salt and pepper to taste

METHOD OF PREPARATION

Fry the bacon in a skillet until crisp. Drain, reserving the drippings. Crumble the bacon.

Sauté the onions, green pepper, parsley, celery and garlic in the reserved pan drippings in the skillet until tender. Add the pork and beans, tomatoes, pimento, prepared mustard, chili powder, salt, pepper and crumbled bacon and mix well. Spoon into a baking dish or slow cooker.

Bake at 300 degrees for 1 1/2 hours.

SERVES 8 TO 10

CUBAN BLACK BEANS

Ingredients

1 pound dried black beans
1 large onion, chopped
5 garlic cloves, minced
1/4 cup olive oil
6 cups water
1 (6-ounce) can tomato paste
1 tablespoon vinegar
2 teaspoons salt
1 teaspoon pepper
1/2 teaspoon sugar
Hot cooked rice
Chopped tomatoes
Chopped green onions
Shredded Cheddar cheese

METHOD OF PREPARATION

Sort and rinse the black beans. Combine with enough water to cover in a bowl. Let stand for 8 hours; drain.

Sauté the onion and garlic in the olive oil in a skillet until tender.

Bring the beans, onion mixture, 6 cups water, tomato paste, vinegar, salt, pepper and sugar to a boil in a stockpot; reduce heat.

Simmer until the beans are tender, stirring occasionally.

Serve over hot cooked rice. Top each serving with tomatoes, green onions and cheese.

Variation: Add a can of tomatoes with green chiles to spice up the beans.

SERVES 8 TO 10

TASTY BLACK BEANS

Ingredients

1 pound dried black beans
4 cups water
1 to 2 (14-ounce) cans beef, chicken or vegetable broth
1 cup red wine
1/4 cup finely chopped fresh cilantro
4 garlic cloves, minced
1 tablespoon Tony Chachere's seasoning
1 tablespoon cumin
Juice of 1/2 lemon
1 tablespoon vinegar

METHOD OF PREPARATION

Sort and rinse the black beans. Combine with enough water to cover in a bowl. Let stand for 8 to 10 hours; drain.

Combine the black beans, 4 cups water, broth, red wine, cilantro, garlic, Tony Chachere's seasoning and cumin in a slow cooker.

Cook on High for 5 to 6 hours. Stir in the lemon juice and vinegar.

Cook on Low for 2 hours or until the beans are tender.

Note: A great alternative to pinto beans.

Variation: Prepare black bean burritos with any combination of the following ingredients: black beans, brown rice, shredded Monterey Jack cheese, salsa, plain yogurt, chopped avocado and/or chopped tomato.

SERVES 6

CHEESE AND SOUR CREAM GREEN BEANS

Ingredients
1/2 cup chopped onion
1 tablespoon parsley
2 tablespoons butter or margarine
2 tablespoons flour
1 teaspoon salt
1/2 teaspoon pepper
1/2 teaspoon grated lemon peel
5 cups drained canned green beans
1 cup sour cream
1/2 cup shredded American cheese
1/2 cup bread crumbs
2 tablespoons melted butter or margarine

METHOD OF PREPARATION
Sauté the onion and parsley in 2 tablespoons butter in a saucepan until tender; do not brown. Reduce the heat to medium-low.

Stir in the flour, salt, pepper and lemon peel. Add the green beans and sour cream and mix well.

Cook just until heated through. Spoon into a 6x10-inch baking dish. Sprinkle with the cheese. Top with a mixture of the bread crumbs and 2 tablespoons melted butter.

Broil until brown and bubbly.

Note: May be prepared in advance and stored, covered, in the refrigerator. Reheat in a 350-degree oven for 30 minutes. Broil for several minutes until brown.

Variation: Substitute crushed butter crackers for the bread crumbs.

SERVES 6 TO 8

GREEN BEANS WITH ALMONDS

Ingredients
2 tablespoons sliced almonds
2 teaspoons butter or margarine
1 1/4 pounds green beans, trimmed
2 tablespoons butter or margarine
1/2 cup chicken broth
1/4 teaspoon salt
1/4 teaspoon pepper
1 tablespoon water
1 teaspoon cornstarch
1 1/2 teaspoons lemon juice

METHOD OF PREPARATION
Sauté the almonds in 2 teaspoons butter in a skillet until light brown.

Cut the green beans into French-style strips. Cook the beans in 2 tablespoons butter in a skillet over high heat for 5 minutes, stirring frequently. Stir in the broth, salt and pepper. Bring to a boil; reduce heat.

Simmer, covered, for 8 to 10 minutes, stirring occasionally.

Stir in a mixture of the water and cornstarch. Cook for 1 minute, stirring constantly. Add the lemon juice and mix well.

Spoon into a serving bowl; sprinkle with the almonds.

SERVES 5

Green Beans with Wine Sauce

Ingredients
1/2 cup water
1 pound fresh green beans, trimmed
1 onion, coarsely chopped
4 garlic cloves, minced
2 tablespoons olive oil
4 large tomatoes, peeled, seeded, coarsely chopped
1/2 cup dry white wine
1 (2-ounce) can sliced black olives, drained
1 tablespoon lemon juice
1/4 teaspoon coarsely ground pepper

Method of Preparation
Bring the water to a boil in a saucepan over high heat. Add the beans. Reduce the heat to medium.

Cook, covered, for 10 minutes or until the beans are tender; drain. Keep the beans warm.

Sauté the onion and garlic in the olive oil in a skillet over high heat for 5 minutes or until tender-crisp. Stir in the tomatoes and white wine. Bring to a boil; reduce heat.

Simmer for 20 minutes, stirring occasionally. Stir in the black olives. Pour over the green beans in a serving bowl. Drizzle with the lemon juice; sprinkle with the pepper.

Serves 6

Southern Broccoli

Ingredients
2 (10-ounce) packages frozen chopped broccoli
1 (8-ounce) can water chestnuts, drained
1/2 cup chopped pecans
1 1/2 envelopes onion soup mix
1/2 cup melted butter

Method of Preparation
Steam the broccoli in a steamer for 5 minutes; drain the broccoli.

Combine the broccoli, water chestnuts, pecans, soup mix and butter in a bowl and mix well. Spoon into a buttered baking dish.

Bake at 350 degrees for 30 minutes or until brown and bubbly.

Note: Showy, yet easy to prepare, and perfect for the novice cook.

Serves 8

BRUSSELS SPROUTS WITH SCALLIONS

Ingredients
26 brussels sprouts, trimmed
3 tablespoons unsalted butter
4 scallions, thinly sliced diagonally
1 teaspoon fresh lime juice, or to taste
Salt and white pepper to taste

METHOD OF PREPARATION

Cut the brussels sprouts into halves; slice lengthwise into quarters.

Heat the butter in a skillet over medium-high heat until the foam subsides. Sauté the brussels sprouts and scallions in the butter for 10 minutes or until tender and light brown.

Combine the brussels sprouts mixture, lime juice, salt and white pepper in a bowl and mix well.

Variation: Add 2 teaspoons poppy seeds with the lime juice.

SERVES 4

ORANGE-GLAZED BRUSSELS SPROUTS

Ingredients
1 pound fresh brussels sprouts, trimmed
2 tablespoons unsalted butter
1 teaspoon sugar
1/4 teaspoon salt
1/4 cup orange marmalade

METHOD OF PREPARATION

Combine the brussels sprouts with enough water to cover in a saucepan.

Simmer for 10 to 12 minutes or until tender; drain. Remove to a bowl.

Heat the butter in the same saucepan until melted. Stir in the sugar, salt and marmalade.

Cook until hot, stirring constantly. Add the brussels sprouts, stirring gently to coat. Spoon into a serving bowl.

SERVES 3 TO 4

Glazed Carrots with Bacon and Onion

Ingredients
1 pound carrots, peeled, diagonally sliced
3 slices bacon
1 small onion, chopped
3 tablespoons brown sugar
1/8 teaspoon pepper

Method of Preparation
Bring the carrots and enough water to cover to a boil in a saucepan.

Cook for 15 minutes or until tender-crisp; drain.

Fry the bacon in a skillet until crisp. Drain, reserving 1 tablespoon of the pan drippings. Crumble the bacon.

Sauté the onion in the reserved pan drippings until tender. Stir in the brown sugar, pepper and carrots.

Cook until heated through, stirring frequently. Spoon into a serving bowl. Sprinkle with the bacon.

Serves 4

Cauliflower and Wild Rice

Ingredients
2 3/4 cups water
1 cup wild rice, rinsed
1 tablespoon margarine
1 teaspoon salt
Florets of 1 head cauliflower
1 teaspoon salt
3 tablespoons butter
3 tablespoons flour
1/4 to 1/2 cup milk
1 cup shredded Cheddar cheese
1/3 cup shredded Swiss cheese
Bread crumbs or cracker crumbs

Method of Preparation
Bring the water, wild rice, margarine and 1 teaspoon salt to a boil in a saucepan.

Boil until tender; drain. Spread in a large greased baking dish.

Combine the cauliflower and 1 teaspoon salt with a small amount of water in a saucepan. Bring to a boil.

Boil until tender-crisp; drain. Arrange over the rice.

Heat the butter in a saucepan over medium heat until melted. Stir in the flour until blended. Add the milk gradually, stirring constantly.

Cook until of a cream sauce consistency, stirring constantly. Pour over the prepared layers. Sprinkle with the Cheddar cheese and Swiss cheese. Top with bread crumbs.

Bake at 350 degrees for 30 minutes or until brown and bubbly.

Serves 4

TANGY MUSTARD CAULIFLOWER WITH VEGETABLE MEDLEY

Ingredients
1 medium head cauliflower
3 stalks fresh broccoli
1 zucchini, sliced
1 yellow squash, sliced
12 fresh mushrooms
1/2 cup mayonnaise
1 teaspoon onion flakes
1 teaspoon prepared mustard
1/2 cup shredded Cheddar cheese
Garlic powder to taste
Lemon pepper to taste

METHOD OF PREPARATION

Place the cauliflower in the center of a microwave-safe platter; cover with plastic wrap.

Microwave on High for 5 minutes. Arrange the broccoli, zucchini, yellow squash and mushrooms around the cauliflower; cover.

Microwave on High for 5 to 6 minutes.

Combine the mayonnaise, onion flakes and prepared mustard in a bowl and mix well. Pour over the cauliflower.

Sprinkle some of the cheese over the cauliflower; sprinkle the remaining cheese lightly over the remaining vegetables. Sprinkle all the vegetables with garlic powder and lemon pepper.

Let stand for 5 minutes before serving.

SERVES 8 TO 10

CORN AND RICE

Ingredients
1 onion, chopped
1 green bell pepper, chopped
1/2 cup butter
2 eggs, beaten
2 (16-ounce) cans cream-style corn
1 cup uncooked instant rice
Salt and pepper to taste
Shredded Cheddar cheese

METHOD OF PREPARATION

Sauté the onion and green pepper in the butter in a skillet. Combine the onion mixture, eggs, corn, rice, salt and pepper in a bowl and mix well.

Spoon into a baking dish.

Bake at 350 degrees for 30 minutes. Sprinkle with Cheddar cheese.

Bake for 5 minutes longer or until the cheese melts.

SERVES 8 TO 10

GRILLED CORN ON THE COB

Ingredients
¹/2 cup butter or margarine, softened
2 tablespoons minced fresh chives
1 tablespoon lemon juice
4 ears of corn, shucked

METHOD OF PREPARATION

Combine the butter, chives and lemon juice in a bowl and mix well.

Place each ear of corn on a sheet of heavy-duty foil. Spread each ear of corn with the butter mixture; wrap securely.

Grill over hot coals for 15 to 20 minutes or until tender, turning at 5-minute intervals.

Variation: Add basil, thyme or rosemary to the butter mixture for a stronger herb flavor.

SERVES 4

SHOE PEG CORN WITH CHILES

Ingredients
8 ounces cream cheese, softened
¹/2 cup melted butter
3 (16-ounce) cans Shoe Peg or white corn, drained
1 (4-ounce) can chopped green chiles

METHOD OF PREPARATION

Combine the cream cheese and butter in a bowl and mix well.

Stir in the corn and undrained chiles. Spoon into a baking dish.

Bake, covered, at 325 degrees for 30 minutes.

SERVES 10 TO 12

SIDE DISHES

BAKED MUSHROOMS

Ingredients
1 pound fresh mushrooms
2 tablespoons flour
1 tablespoon parsley flakes
1 tablespoon dried minced onion
1 teaspoon Dijon mustard
1 teaspoon salt
1 teaspoon pepper
1/2 teaspoon nutmeg
1/2 teaspoon curry powder
Dash of garlic powder
1 cup cream

METHOD OF PREPARATION
Arrange the mushrooms in a baking dish.

Combine the flour, parsley flakes, minced onion, Dijon mustard, salt, pepper, nutmeg, curry powder and garlic powder in a bowl and mix well. Stir in the cream.

Pour over the mushrooms in the prepared dish. Bake at 350 degrees for 1 hour.

SERVES 4

HERBED BAKED POTATOES

Ingredients
4 medium potatoes
1 teaspoon salt
2 to 3 tablespoons melted butter
1/4 cup chopped fresh parsley, chives, thyme or sage
1/4 cup shredded Cheddar cheese
1 1/2 tablespoons grated Parmesan cheese

METHOD OF PREPARATION
Peel the potatoes if desired. Cut each potato vertically into thin slices, cutting to but not through the bottom of the potato.

Place in a baking dish; fan slightly. Sprinkle with the salt; drizzle with the butter. Sprinkle with the herbs.

Bake at 425 degrees for 50 minutes. Sprinkle with the Cheddar cheese and Parmesan cheese.

Bake for 10 to 15 minutes longer or until the potatoes are tender and light brown.

Note: Lay a wooden spoon adjacent to the potato. Slice the potato, letting the knife blade hit the spoon handle to avoid cutting all the way through the potato.

Variation: Substitute 2 to 3 teaspoons dried herbs for the fresh herbs.

SERVES 4

New Potato Casserole

Ingredients

6 to 8 unpeeled medium to large new potatoes
6 slices bacon
1 onion, chopped
1 small jar pimento-stuffed green olives, drained, sliced
1 cup sour cream
1/2 cup mayonnaise
Butter
12 ounces Monterey Jack cheese, shredded

Method of Preparation

Combine the new potatoes with enough water to cover in a saucepan. Cook until tender; drain. Chop the potatoes.

Fry the bacon in a skillet until crisp. Drain, reserving the pan drippings. Crumble the bacon.

Sauté the onion in the reserved pan drippings in the skillet until tender.

Combine the olives, sour cream and mayonnaise in a bowl and mix well. Add the potatoes, onion and bacon and mix gently. Spoon into a buttered 9x13-inch baking dish. Dot with butter; sprinkle with the cheese.

Bake at 350 degrees for 35 to 40 minutes or until golden brown.

Serves 10 to 12

Savory Spinach

Ingredients

2 (10-ounce) packages frozen chopped spinach, thawed
3 1/2 cups herb-seasoned stuffing
1/2 large onion, chopped
3/4 cup melted margarine or butter
1/2 cup grated Parmesan cheese
3 to 4 eggs, beaten
1/2 to 1 teaspoon pepper
1/2 teaspoon garlic salt
1/2 teaspoon thyme

Method of Preparation

Combine the spinach, dry stuffing, onion, margarine, cheese, eggs, pepper, garlic salt and thyme in a bowl and mix well. Spoon into a baking dish.

Bake at 325 degrees for 15 minutes.

Variation: Top broiled tomatoes with the spinach mixture or stuff into mushroom caps. For an elegant dish, partially bake the spinach mixture and spoon into phyllo pastry and enclose. Bake for an additional 10 minutes.

Serves 6

SPINACH CHEESE CASSEROLE

Ingredients
3 to 4 (10-ounce) packages frozen chopped spinach,
thawed, drained
3 cups small curd cottage cheese
6 eggs, beaten
8 ounces American cheese, cubed
6 tablespoons butter or margarine, chopped
1 to 2 tablespoons flour (optional)

METHOD OF PREPARATION
Squeeze the moisture from the spinach.

Combine the cottage cheese and eggs in a bowl
and mix well. Stir in the cheese and butter. Add the
spinach and mix well.

Add the flour if the mixture is too moist and mix
well. Spoon into a greased 9x13-inch baking dish

Bake at 325 degrees for 1 hour or until set.

Note: Bake the casserole at 350 degrees if using a
metal baking pan.

SERVES 15

BACON CHEESE SQUASH

Ingredients
4 slices bacon
4 large yellow squash, sliced
2 green onions, sliced
1/2 cup sour cream
1 egg, beaten
1/2 cup shredded Swiss cheese
3/4 cup shredded Cheddar cheese

METHOD OF PREPARATION
Fry the bacon in a skillet until crisp. Drain,
reserving the pan drippings. Crumble the bacon.

Sauté the squash and green onions in the
reserved pan drippings in the skillet for 8 to 10
minutes. Stir in a mixture of the sour cream and
egg. Add 1/2 of the bacon and mix well.

Spoon half the squash mixture into a greased
2-quart baking dish; sprinkle with the Swiss cheese.
Top with the remaining squash mixture. Sprinkle
with the Cheddar cheese and remaining bacon.

Bake at 350 degrees for 20 minutes or until
bubbly.

SERVES 6

SQUASH AND HOMINY CASSEROLE

Ingredients
2 pounds yellow squash, sliced
1 large onion, sliced
Salt to taste
4 (16-ounce) cans yellow hominy
1 pound Monterey Jack cheese, shredded
1 1/2 cups sour cream
1 cup (or less) melted butter
2 to 3 jalapeños, seeded, chopped

METHOD OF PREPARATION
Combine the squash, onion and salt with enough
water to cover in a saucepan.

Cook until the vegetables are tender; drain.

Bring the hominy to a boil in a saucepan; drain.

Combine the squash mixture, hominy, cheese,
sour cream, butter and jalapeños in a bowl and
mix well. Season with salt. Spoon into a 9x13-inch
baking dish.

Bake at 350 degrees for 20 minutes or until
bubbly.

SERVES 10 TO 12

Zucchini Parmigiana

Ingredients
4 cups sliced zucchini
1 cup chopped onion
1 garlic clove, crushed
2 tablespoons vegetable oil
2 tablespoons butter
2 cups tomato purée
1/2 teaspoon basil
1/2 teaspoon salt
Dash of pepper
1 pound mozzarella cheese, sliced
2 tablespoons grated Parmesan cheese

Method of Preparation
Steam the zucchini in a large saucepan until tender; drain.

Sauté the onion and garlic in the oil and butter in a skillet for 5 minutes or until tender. Stir in the tomato purée, basil, salt and pepper. Bring to a boil; reduce heat.

Simmer for 10 minutes, stirring occasionally. Spoon half the mixture into a lightly greased 1 1/2-quart baking dish. Arrange the zucchini and mozzarella cheese over the prepared layer, overlapping the slices as necessary. Spread with the remaining tomato purée mixture. Sprinkle with the Parmesan cheese.

Bake at 400 degrees for 25 minutes.
Serves 8

Garden Vegetable Casserole

Ingredients
1 cup chopped potato
1 cup chopped zucchini
1 cup chopped carrot
1/2 cup chopped onion
1 cup water
1/4 cup flour
2 cups milk
1/4 cup butter or margarine
1 teaspoon salt
1/4 teaspoon celery seeds
1/4 teaspoon ground pepper
4 hard-cooked eggs, thinly sliced (optional)
1/2 cup shredded Cheddar cheese
1/4 cup melted butter or margarine
1/4 cup plain bread crumbs.

Method of Preparation
Combine the potato, zucchini, carrot, onion and water in a skillet.

Cook over medium-high heat until tender; drain.

Return the vegetable mixture to the skillet. Sprinkle with the flour and mix well. Stir in the milk, 1/4 cup butter, salt, celery seeds and pepper.

Cook over medium heat for 10 to 15 minutes or until thickened, stirring frequently. Spoon half the mixture into a greased 9-inch round baking dish; top with the eggs. Spoon the remaining vegetable mixture over the eggs; sprinkle with the cheese. Top with a mixture of 1/4 cup melted butter and bread crumbs.

Bake at 400 degrees for 15 to 20 minutes or until brown and bubbly.

Note: May be prepared 1 day in advance, stored in the refrigerator, and baked the day of serving. Bake for 25 to 30 minutes or until bubbly.
Serves 8 to 10

MIXED VEGETABLE CASSEROLE

Ingredients
1 (16- to 20-ounce) package frozen broccoli
1 (16- to 20-ounce) package frozen cauliflower
1 (16- to 20-ounce) package frozen carrots
1 1/2 pounds Velveeta cheese, shredded
2 sleeves butter crackers, crumbled
1 cup melted butter or margarine

METHOD OF PREPARATION
Microwave the broccoli, cauliflower and carrots in separate microwave-safe dishes using package directions until tender-crisp; drain.

Layer the broccoli, 1/3 of the cheese, cauliflower, 1/3 of the cheese, carrots and remaining cheese in a 9x13-inch baking dish sprayed with nonstick cooking spray. Sprinkle with the cracker crumbs; drizzle with the butter.

Bake at 350 degrees for 20 to 30 minutes or until brown and bubbly.

SERVES 10 TO 12

GRITS SOUFFLE

Ingredients
1 1/2 cups grits
6 cups boiling water
8 ounces cheese, shredded or cubed
1/2 cup butter
2 teaspoons seasoned salt
1 teaspoon onion salt
1 teaspoon garlic salt
3/4 teaspoon Worcestershire sauce
3 eggs, lightly beaten
Paprika to taste

METHOD OF PREPARATION
Cook the grits in the boiling water in a saucepan for 5 minutes. Stir in the cheese, butter, seasoned salt, onion salt, garlic salt and Worcestershire sauce. Stir 3 to 4 tablespoons of the hot mixture into the eggs; stir the eggs into the hot mixture. Spoon into a buttered 2-quart soufflé dish; sprinkle heavily with paprika.

Chill, covered, for 8 to 10 hours.

Bake at 350 degrees for 1 1/2 hours or until set and light brown.

SERVES 16

PECAN RICE

Ingredients
6 tablespoons butter
1 cup chopped pecans
1 small onion, chopped
1 cup white rice
1 cup wild rice
2 cups chicken stock
2 cups water
1/2 teaspoon thyme
1/2 teaspoon pepper
3 tablespoons chopped fresh parsley

METHOD OF PREPARATION
Heat 3 tablespoons of the butter in a skillet until melted. Add the pecans and mix well.

Sauté until light brown. Remove the pecans to a bowl with a slotted spoon, reserving the pan drippings.

Add the remaining butter and onion to the reserved pan drippings. Sauté until tender. Add the rice, stirring until coated. Remove from heat.

Bring the stock, water, thyme, pepper and 2 tablespoons of the parsley to a boil in a saucepan. Add the rice mixture and mix well.

Cook, covered, over low heat for 20 minutes or until the liquid has been absorbed. Stir in the pecans and remaining parsley.

Note: This is a great dish to serve with wild game.

SERVES 6 TO 8

Rice Green Chile Casserole

Ingredients

2 cups sour cream
1 (4-ounce) can chopped green chiles, drained
1 teaspoon salt
3 cups cooked rice
8 ounces Monterey Jack cheese, shredded
1/8 teaspoon pepper
2 tablespoons butter

Method of Preparation

Combine the sour cream, chiles and salt in a bowl and mix well.

Layer the rice, sour cream mixture and cheese 1/3 at a time in a 1½-quart baking dish. Sprinkle with the pepper; dot with the butter.

Bake, covered, at 350 degrees for 20 minutes; remove the cover.

Bake for 10 minutes longer.

Note: May be prepared and frozen for future use. Thaw in the refrigerator and bake as directed.

Serves 6 to 8

Tex-Mex Rice

Ingredients

2/3 cup quick-cooking rice
1/2 cup water
2 tablespoons chopped green chile peppers
2 tablespoon sliced green onions
1 teaspoon chili powder
1/8 teaspoon salt
1/3 cup salsa
2 to 4 tablespoons shredded Monterey Jack cheese

Method of Preparation

Combine the rice, water, chile peppers, green onions, chili powder and salt in a saucepan.

Bring to a boil over medium-high heat.

Boil for 1 minute. Remove from heat.

Let stand, covered, for 5 minutes. Stir in the salsa and cheese. Serve immediately.

Variation: Use Cheddar cheese instead of Monterey Jack cheese.

Serves 4

WILD RICE AND OYSTER CASSEROLE

Ingredients

1 (6-ounce) jar oysters
1 (10-ounce) package long grain and
wild rice with seasonings
1 cup sliced fresh mushrooms
1/4 teaspoon crushed garlic
2 tablespoons margarine
3 tablespoons flour
1/2 cup half-and-half
1/2 cup chopped fresh parsley
1/4 teaspoon salt
2 tablespoons dry sherry
1/2 cup sliced celery

METHOD OF PREPARATION

Drain the oysters, reserving 2 tablespoons of the liquor.

Prepare the rice using package directions.

Sauté the mushrooms and garlic in the margarine in a saucepan for 5 minutes. Add the oysters and mix well.

Cook over medium heat for 3 minutes, stirring frequently. Add the flour and mix well. Add a mixture of the half-and-half and reserved oyster liquor and mix well.

Cook until thickened, stirring constantly. Stir in the parsley and salt. Add the sherry, rice and celery and mix well. Spoon into a greased 2-quart baking dish.

Bake at 350 degrees for 40 minutes or until heated through.

Note: May prepare in advance, store in the refrigerator, and bake just before serving.

Variation: Substitute brown rice for the long grain and wild rice mixture. Sauté 1/4 cup chopped onion with the mushrooms and sprinkle the top with finely ground cracker crumbs.

SERVES 4 TO 6

RUM-BAKED PEARS

Ingredients

3 fresh pears, peeled, cut into halves
1/2 cup packed brown sugar
1/2 cup water
1/4 cup lemon juice
1/2 teaspoon whole cloves
1 cinnamon stick
1/4 cup sugar
2 tablespoons rum
1 teaspoon grated lemon peel
Dash of cinnamon
Dash of nutmeg

METHOD OF PREPARATION

Arrange the pears cut side up in a shallow baking dish.

Bring the brown sugar, water, lemon juice, cloves and cinnamon stick to a boil in a saucepan.

Boil until of the consistency of syrup, stirring constantly. Pour over the pears.

Bake at 350 degrees for 30 minutes or until the pears are tender, basting frequently.

Spoon a mixture of the sugar, rum, lemon peel, cinnamon and nutmeg over the pears.

Broil just until the sugar begins to caramelize.

Note: Serve with chicken or turkey.

SERVES 6

DESSERTS

DESSERTS

THE BEST CHEESECAKE

Ingredients
2¹/2 cups graham cracker crumbs
¹/2 cup sugar
¹/2 cup melted butter
40 ounces cream cheese, softened
1³/4 cups sugar
3 tablespoons flour
1 teaspoon lemon juice
¹/4 teaspoon vanilla extract
5 eggs
2 egg yolks
¹/4 cup whipping cream
1 to 2 cups sour cream

METHOD OF PREPARATION
Combine the graham cracker crumbs, ¹/2 cup sugar and butter in a bowl and mix well. Press over the bottom of a 10- or 11-inch springform pan.

Beat the cream cheese, 1³/4 cups sugar, flour, lemon juice and vanilla in a mixer bowl until creamy. Add the eggs and egg yolks 1 at a time, beating well after each addition. Stir in the whipping cream. Spoon into the prepared pan.

Bake at 500 degrees for 10 minutes. Reduce the oven temperature to 250 degrees.

Bake for 1¹/2 to 2 hours. Spread the sour cream over the top while hot.

Chill until serving time.

Note: The longer baking time will result in a cheesecake with a cakelike consistency. Bake for 1¹/4 to 1¹/2 hours for a creamier texture.

SERVES 16

COOKIE MONSTER OREO CHEESECAKE

Ingredients
1 (20-ounce) package Oreo cookies
¹/4 cup butter, softened
32 ounces cream cheese, softened
1¹/4 cups sugar
2 tablespoons flour
4 eggs
3 egg yolks
1¹/2 cups sour cream
¹/4 cup sugar

METHOD OF PREPARATION
Process ³/4 of the cookies in a food processor until finely chopped. Add the butter.

Process just until mixed. Press over the bottom and up the side of an 11-inch springform pan.

Beat the cream cheese, 1¹/4 cups sugar, flour, eggs and egg yolks in a mixer bowl until smooth. Spoon ¹/2 of the mixture into the prepared pan.

Crumble the remaining oreo cookies. Sprinkle over the prepared layers. Spread with the remaining cream cheese mixture.

Bake at 425 degrees for 15 minutes. Reduce the oven temperature to 300 degrees.

Bake for 50 minutes longer or until set. Let stand until cool.

Spread the top with a mixture of the sour cream and ¹/4 cup sugar.

Note: May freeze for future use.

SERVES 12 TO 15

PUMPKIN CHEESECAKE WITH CRANBERRY GLAZE

For the crust
3/4 cup graham cracker crumbs
3 tablespoons melted butter
2 tablespoons light brown sugar
1 teaspoon cinnamon

For the filling
32 ounces cream cheese, softened
1 1/2 cups sugar
5 eggs
1 (16-ounce) can pumpkin
1/4 cup flour
2 teaspoons pumpkin pie spice
2 tablespoons rum (optional)

For the cranberry glaze
2 cups fresh cranberries
1 1/4 cups sugar
1/2 cup water
1 tablespoon cornstarch

For the topping
1 cup whipping cream
2 tablespoons sugar

TO PREPARE THE CRUST
Combine the graham cracker crumbs, butter, brown sugar and cinnamon in a bowl and mix well. Press over the bottom and up the side of a greased 9-inch springform pan.

TO PREPARE THE FILLING
Beat the cream cheese in a mixer bowl until fluffy. Add the sugar gradually, beating until blended. Add the eggs 1 at a time, beating well after each addition. Add the pumpkin, flour and pie spice gradually, beating until blended. Stir in the rum. Spoon into the prepared pan.

Bake at 325 degrees for 1 3/4 hours or until set. Cool in the pan on a wire rack.

TO PREPARE THE CRANBERRY GLAZE
Combine the cranberries, 1 cup of the sugar and water in a saucepan. Stir in a mixture of the remaining 1/4 cup sugar and the cornstarch.

Bring to a boil, stirring constantly. Let stand until cool.

TO PREPARE THE TOPPING AND ASSEMBLE
Beat the whipping cream in a mixer bowl until soft peaks form. Add the sugar and mix well.

Remove the side of the springform pan. Place the cheesecake on a serving platter.

Spoon the whipped cream into a pastry bag fitted with a star tip. Pipe the whipped cream around the edge of the cheesecake. Spread the glaze over the top of the cheesecake.

SERVES 12 TO 15

BLACKBERRY COBBLER

For the crust
1/2 cup canola oil
1/4 cup ice water
2 cups flour, sifted
1 teaspoon salt

For the filling
3/4 cup sugar
3 tablespoons flour
1/2 teaspoon cinnamon
1/2 teaspoon nutmeg
4 cups blackberries
1 teaspoon lemon juice
2 teaspoons butter
2 to 3 tablespoons (about) sugar

TO PREPARE THE CRUST

Beat the canola oil and ice water in a bowl until frothy. Stir in a mixture of the flour and salt until blended.

Divide the dough into 2 portions. Roll 1 portion of the dough between 2 sheets of waxed paper. Line the bottom and sides of a 1 1/2- to 2-quart baking dish with the dough.

Bake at 350 degrees for 20 minutes. Let stand until cool.

TO PREPARE THE FILLING

Combine 3/4 cup sugar, flour, cinnamon and nutmeg in a bowl and mix well. Stir in the blackberries and lemon juice. Spoon over the baked layer. Dot with the butter.

Roll the remaining portion of dough between 2 sheets of waxed paper to fit the top. Arrange over the filling, sealing to the edges. Sprinkle with 2 to 3 tablespoons sugar; cut vents.

Bake at 400 degrees for 45 to 50 minutes or until brown and bubbly.

SERVES 8 TO 10

CHERRY COBBLER

Ingredients
1 to 1 1/2 cups sugar
2 to 4 tablespoons cornstarch
3 to 4 cups frozen unsweetened cherries
1 tablespoon margarine or butter
1 teaspoon almond extract
2 cups sifted flour
1 cup sugar
2 teaspoons baking powder
1/4 teaspoon salt
1/2 cup shortening
1/2 cup milk
1 egg
2 tablespoons sugar

METHOD OF PREPARATION

Combine 1 to 1 1/2 cups sugar and cornstarch in a saucepan and mix well. Stir in the cherries, margarine and almond extract.

Cook over medium heat until of the desired consistency, stirring frequently. Pour into a baking dish.

Sift the flour, 1 cup sugar, baking powder and salt into a bowl and mix well. Cut in the shortening until crumbly. Beat the milk and egg in a bowl. Add to the flour mixture, stirring just until moistened.

Roll the dough on a lightly floured surface; cut into shapes.

Arrange over the cherry mixture; sprinkle with 2 tablespoons sugar.

Bake at 375 degrees for 20 to 25 minutes or until brown and bubbly.

Note: May drop the dough by spoonfuls over the hot cherry mixture.

Variation: Substitute canned cherries for the frozen cherries and decrease the amount of sugar if cherries are sweetened.

SERVES 8

FOUR-BERRY COBBLER

Ingredients
2 cups yellow cake mix
2 cups packed brown sugar
1 cup flour
1/2 cup melted butter
2 teaspoons cinnamon
2 cups sugar
1/3 cup cornstarch
2 cups frozen strawberries, thawed, drained
2 cups frozen blueberries, thawed, drained
2 cups frozen blackberries, thawed, drained
2 cups frozen raspberries, thawed, drained

METHOD OF PREPARATION
Combine the cake mix, brown sugar, flour, butter and cinnamon in a bowl, stirring until crumbly.

Combine the sugar and cornstarch in a bowl and mix well. Stir in the strawberries, blueberries, blackberries and raspberries gently. Spoon into a 9x13-inch baking dish. Sprinkle with the cake mix mixture.

Bake at 350 degrees for 45 minutes or until brown and bubbly.

Note: Serve with vanilla ice cream, whipped cream or whipped topping.

SERVES 12 TO 15

BUTTER PECAN ICE CREAM

Ingredients
2 cups pecans
5 eggs, beaten
2 cups whipping cream
1 1/2 cups sugar
1 (14-ounce) can sweetened condensed milk
2 teaspoons vanilla extract
1 teaspoon maple extract
2 teaspoons butter flavoring
Milk

METHOD OF PREPARATION
Arrange the pecans on a baking sheet.

Toast at 300 degrees for 10 minutes. Let stand until cool.

Combine the eggs, whipping cream, sugar, condensed milk and flavorings in a bowl and mix well. Stir in the pecans.

Pour into an ice cream freezer container. Add milk to the fill line and mix well.

Freeze using the manufacturer's directions.

SERVES 20

ICE CREAM BALLS WITH CHOCOLATE SAUCE

For the chocolate sauce
1 cup light corn syrup
1 cup sugar
1/2 cup baking cocoa
1/2 cup milk
2 tablespoons butter
1/4 teaspoon salt
1 teaspoon vanilla extract

For the ice cream balls
1 1/2 cups shredded coconut, toasted
1 gallon ice cream

TO PREPARE THE CHOCOLATE SAUCE

Bring the corn syrup, sugar, baking cocoa and milk to a boil over low to medium heat.

Boil for 5 minutes, stirring frequently. Remove from heat. Stir in the butter and salt.

Let stand until cool. Stir in the vanilla. Spoon into a jar with a tightfitting lid.

TO PREPARE THE ICE CREAM BALLS

Place 1/3 of the coconut in a cereal bowl. Scoop the ice cream with an ice cream scoop into a ball. Roll in the coconut. Place on a baking sheet in the freezer. Repeat the process with the remaining ice cream, adding coconut to the bowl as needed. Freeze until firm. Store in the freezer in a cookie tin or freezer container, making sure the ice cream balls do not touch.

Remove the ice cream balls from the freezer just before serving and serve with the chocolate sauce.

SERVES 16

LEFFEL'S KAHLUA ALMOND FUDGE ICE CREAM

Ingredients
8 ounces egg substitute
1 1/2 cups sugar
6 cups whipping cream
2 cups milk
1 cup Kahlúa
1 1/2 tablespoons vanilla extract
1 cup chopped almonds, frozen
1 (12-ounce) jar hot fudge ice cream topping

METHOD OF PREPARATION

Beat the egg substitute and sugar in a mixer bowl at high speed until slightly thickened. Add the whipping cream, milk, Kahlúa and vanilla.

Beat at low speed until blended. Pour into an ice cream freezer container.

Freeze using the manufacturer's directions. The freezer will slow down but may not come to a complete stop due to the presence of alcohol. Add the almonds.

Restart the freezer and let run just until the almonds are mixed. Stop the freezer; remove the dasher. Spoon into a freezer container, adding the ice cream topping in a fine stream.

Freeze in the freezer for 1 hour or until firm.

MAKES 1 GALLON

OREO COOKIES AND ICE CREAM

Ingredients

30 Oreo cookies, crushed
1/4 cup melted margarine
1/2 gallon vanilla ice cream, softened
2/3 cup sugar
1/4 cup margarine
2 ounces semisweet chocolate
2/3 cup evaporated milk
1 teaspoon vanilla extract
Whipped cream or whipped topping

METHOD OF PREPARATION

Combine the cookies and 1/4 cup melted margarine in a bowl and mix well. Press over the bottom of a 9x13-inch pan. Spread the ice cream over the prepared layer. Freeze until firm.

Combine the sugar, 1/4 cup margarine and chocolate in a saucepan.

Cook until blended, stirring constantly. Add the evaporated milk gradually. Bring to a boil, stirring constantly. Remove from heat. Stir in the vanilla.

Let stand until cool. Spread over the frozen layer. Freeze until firm. Spread with whipped cream or whipped topping.

Freeze until serving time.

SERVES 15

TOFFEE ICE CREAM PIE

Ingredients

1 1/4 cups chocolate wafer crumbs
1/4 cup melted butter
1/2 gallon vanilla ice cream, softened
6 (1-ounce) Heath bars, chilled, crushed
1/2 cup butter
2 cups semisweet chocolate chips
2 cups confectioners' sugar, sifted
1 (12-ounce) can evaporated milk
2 teaspoons vanilla extract

METHOD OF PREPARATION

Combine the wafer crumbs and 1/4 cup melted butter in a bowl and mix well. Press over the bottom of a lightly buttered 9x13-inch pan.

Chill until set.

Combine the ice cream and candy bars in a bowl and mix well. Spread over the prepared layer. Freeze for 8 to 10 hours or until firm.

Combine 1/2 cup butter and the chocolate chips in a saucepan. Cook over low heat until blended, stirring constantly. Stir in the confectioners' sugar and evaporated milk.

Cook for 8 minutes or until thickened, stirring constantly. Stir in the vanilla.

Remove the frozen dessert from the freezer 15 minutes before serving. Cut into squares. Serve with the warm chocolate sauce.

Note: May store the chocolate sauce in a covered container in the refrigerator for several days. Reheat before serving.

SERVES 8 TO 10

ORANGE CRUSH SHERBET

Ingredients

1 (2-liter) bottle orange soda
1 (20-ounce) can crushed pineapple
2 (14-ounce) cans sweetened condensed milk

METHOD OF PREPARATION

Combine the soda, pineapple and condensed milk in a bowl and mix well. Pour into an ice cream freezer container

Freeze using the manufacturer's directions.

Variation: Make pineapple sherbet by substituting pineapple soda for the orange soda.

SERVES 16

BRANDIED CHOCOLATE MOUSSE

Ingredients

2 cups semisweet chocolate chips
1/2 cup brandy
1/4 cup strong coffee
8 egg yolks
1/4 to 1/2 cup confectioners' sugar, sifted
8 egg whites
1/8 teaspoon salt
1 cup whipping cream, stiffly beaten

METHOD OF PREPARATION

Heat the chocolate chips in a double boiler over hot water until melted. Stir in the brandy and coffee. Let stand until cool.

Beat the egg yolks and confectioners' sugar in a mixer bowl until blended. Stir into the chocolate mixture.

Beat the egg whites and salt in a mixer bowl until stiff peaks form. Fold the egg whites and whipped cream into the chocolate mixture. Spoon into dessert glasses.

Chill, covered, for 8 to 10 hours. Top with additional whipped cream and/or chocolate shavings or sprinkles.

SERVES 6 TO 8

BANANA PUDDING SUPREME

Ingredients
1 (6-ounce) package vanilla instant pudding mix
2 cups milk
8 ounces cream cheese, softened
1 (14-ounce) can sweetened condensed milk
16 ounces whipped topping
1 (12-ounce) package vanilla wafers
4 to 5 bananas, sliced

METHOD OF PREPARATION
Combine the pudding mix and milk in a mixer bowl. Beat until thickened, scraping the bowl occasionally.

Beat the cream cheese in a mixer bowl until creamy. Add the condensed milk and pudding and mix well. Fold in 1/2 of the whipped topping.

Layer the vanilla wafers, bananas and pudding mixture alternately in a 9x13-inch dish until all the ingredients are used, ending with the pudding. Spread with the remaining whipped topping.

Chill, covered, until serving time.
SERVES 12 TO 15

BREAD PUDDING WITH LEMON

Ingredients
6 slices bread, cut into 1/2-inch cubes
1 tablespoon grated lemon peel
1/2 teaspoon salt
2 cups milk
1 cup sugar
3 tablespoons butter or margarine
4 egg yolks
1/3 cup lemon juice
4 egg whites, at room temperature
1/4 cup sifted confectioners' sugar

METHOD OF PREPARATION
Combine the bread cubes, lemon peel and salt in a bowl and mix well.

Combine the milk, sugar and butter in a medium saucepan.

Cook over medium heat until the butter melts, stirring occasionally. Pour over the bread cubes. Let stand until cool.

Beat the egg yolks and lemon juice in a mixer bowl until blended. Add to the bread mixture, stirring gently.

Beat the egg whites in a mixer bowl until stiff peaks form. Fold into the bread mixture. Spoon into a lightly greased 2-quart baking dish; sprinkle with the confectioners' sugar.

Bake at 325 degrees for 40 to 45 minutes or until set.
SERVES 8

PISTACHIO DELIGHT

Ingredients
1 cup flour
2 tablespoons sugar
1/2 cup melted margarine
1/4 cup chopped pecans
8 ounces light cream cheese, softened
16 ounces light whipped topping
2/3 cup confectioners' sugar
1 (6-ounce) package pistachio instant pudding mix
2 1/4 cups milk
Chopped pecans (optional)
Maraschino cherry halves (optional)

METHOD OF PREPARATION
Combine the flour and sugar in a bowl and mix well. Stir in the margarine and 1/4 cup pecans. Press over the bottom of a 9x13-inch baking dish.

Bake at 350 degrees for 15 to 20 minutes or until brown. Let stand until cool.

Beat the cream cheese, 1/2 of the whipped topping and confectioners' sugar in a mixer bowl until smooth. Spread over the baked layer.

Beat the pudding mix and milk in a mixer bowl for 2 to 3 minutes or until thickened. Spread over the prepared layers. Top with the remaining whipped topping. Sprinkle with chopped pecans and cherry halves.

SERVES 15

STRAWBERRIES ROMANOFF

Ingredients
1 cup whipping cream
1/2 cup light corn syrup
1/2 cup butter
1/2 cup sugar
1/2 cup packed brown sugar
2 teaspoons Irish cream liqueur (optional)
2 teaspoons Kahlúa (optional)
2 teaspoons brandy (optional)
3 cups whipping cream
Fresh strawberries or blueberries

METHOD OF PREPARATION
Combine 1 cup whipping cream, corn syrup, butter, sugar and brown sugar in a saucepan.

Cook to 220 degrees on a candy thermometer, stirring occasionally. Remove from heat. Add the Irish cream, Kahlúa and brandy and mix well. Let stand until cool; do not allow to harden.

Beat 3/4 cup of the caramel mixture and 3 cups whipping cream in a mixer bowl until stiff; it will not peak due to the heavy syrup content. Use remaining Romanoff mixture for additional sauce, to adjust the consistency, or save for future use.

Spoon over strawberries or blueberries in dessert goblets.

Note: Garnish with sugared slivered almonds, freshly ground nutmeg and/or freshly ground cinnamon.

SERVES 8 TO 10

STRAWBERRY FROZEN DESSERT

Ingredients
1 cup flour
1/2 cup melted margarine
1/4 cup packed brown sugar
1/2 cup chopped nuts
2/3 cup sugar
1 (10-ounce) package frozen strawberries, partially thawed
2 tablespoons lemon juice
2 egg whites
1 cup whipping cream, whipped

METHOD OF PREPARATION
Combine the flour, margarine and brown sugar in a bowl and mix well. Stir in the nuts. Spread in a 9x13-inch baking pan.

Bake at 350 degrees for 20 minutes, stirring occasionally. Let stand until cool.

Reserve 1/2 of the crumb mixture. Press the remaining crumb mixture evenly over the bottom of the baking pan.

Beat the sugar, strawberries, lemon juice and egg whites in a mixer bowl until soft peaks form. Fold in the whipped cream. Spread over the prepared layer. Sprinkle with the reserved crumb mixture. Freeze until firm.

Cut into squares. Garnish each serving with additional whipped cream and a strawberry.

SERVES 15

STRAWBERRIES IN A CLOUD

Ingredients
3 egg whites, at room temperature
1 cup sugar
10 saltine crackers, crushed
1/2 cup chopped pecans
1/2 teaspoon baking powder
2 cups sliced fresh strawberries
1 cup whipping cream
2 tablespoons sugar
1/2 teaspoon vanilla extract

METHOD OF PREPARATION
Beat the egg whites in a mixer bowl until frothy. Add 1 cup sugar.

Beat until stiff peaks form, scraping the bowl occasionally.

Combine the cracker crumbs, pecans and baking powder. Fold into the beaten egg whites. Spread in a 9-inch greased pie plate.

Bake at 300 degrees for 30 minutes. Let stand until cool.

Fill the cooled meringue with the strawberries.

Beat the whipping cream in a mixer bowl until soft peaks form. Add 2 tablespoons sugar and vanilla and mix well. Spoon over the strawberries.

Chill in the refrigerator until serving time.

Note: May pipe the meringue into small rounds on a baking sheet and bake for 15 to 20 minutes.

SERVES 8

TIRAMISU

Ingredients
1 cup hot water
2 tablespoons brandy
1 tablespoon instant coffee granules
1 1/4 cups sugar
6 egg yolks
1 1/4 cups mascarpone cheese
2 cups whipping cream
3 (3-ounce) packages ladyfingers, split
Unsweetened chocolate shavings

METHOD OF PREPARATION
Combine the hot water, brandy and coffee granules in a bowl and mix well. Let stand until cool.

Combine the sugar and egg yolks in a double boiler. Beat with a mixer until thick and pale yellow. Bring the water to a boil; reduce heat to low.

Cook for 8 to 10 minutes, stirring constantly. Remove from heat. Stir in the mascarpone cheese until blended.

Beat the whipping cream in a mixer bowl until soft peaks form. Reserve 1 cup of the whipped cream. Fold the remaining whipped cream into the cheese mixture.

Arrange a layer of the ladyfingers cut side up in a shallow glass dish. Brush with some of the coffee mixture. Spread with half the cheese mixture; smooth with a spatula. Repeat the process with the remaining ladyfingers, coffee mixture and cheese mixture. Pipe with the reserved whipped cream; sprinkle with chocolate shavings.

Chill, covered, for 8 to 12 hours.

Note: Pipe unsweetened chocolate syrup in different patterns instead of sprinkling with chocolate shavings. May use a trifle bowl for the Tiramisu, in which case you will line the side with the ladyfingers.

Variation: Substitute amaretto for the brandy for a different flavor. The mascarpone cheese has the best flavor, but the following mixture may be used as a substitute for the cheese. Combine 16 ounces cream cheese, 1/3 cup sour cream and 1/4 cup whipping cream and mix well. Use 1 1/4 cups of the mixture for this recipe, reserving the remainder for other uses.

SERVES 10 TO 12

EASY ENGLISH TRIFLE

Ingredients
8 ounces cream cheese, softened
2 cups cold milk
1 (4-ounce) package vanilla instant pudding mix
2 1/2 cups cubed pound cake
1/2 cup raspberry liqueur
3/4 cup sliced fresh strawberries
3/4 cup fresh raspberries
3/4 cup sliced fresh peaches
1 cup whipping cream
3 tablespoons sugar

METHOD OF PREPARATION
Combine the cream cheese and 1/2 cup of the milk in a mixer bowl.

Beat at medium speed until blended, scraping the bowl occasionally. Add the remaining milk and pudding mix.

Beat at low speed for 1 minute.

Layer the pound cake, liqueur, strawberries, raspberries, peaches and pudding mixture 1/2 at a time in a 1 1/2-quart trifle bowl.

Beat the whipping cream in a mixer bowl until soft peaks form. Add the sugar and mix well. Spread over the prepared layers.

Chill, covered, for 2 hours.

SERVES 6 TO 8

PEACH TORTE

For the meringues
1/2 cup egg whites
1/4 teaspoon cream of tartar
Pinch of salt
1 cup sugar

For the filling and assembly
8 ounces almond paste
3 tablespoons (or more) milk
2 cups whipping cream
1/4 cup sugar
2 cups sliced peeled peaches
1/2 teaspoon lemon juice or Fruit Fresh

TO PREPARE THE MERINGUES
Trace three 8-inch circles on waxed paper. Place the circles on a baking sheet.

Beat the egg whites, cream of tartar and salt in a mixer bowl until stiff. Add the sugar gradually, beating constantly until glossy. Spread the meringue evenly on the circles.

Bake at 275 degrees for 25 minutes. Increase the oven temperature to 300 degrees.

Bake for 25 minutes longer or until golden brown and dry to the touch.

Remove the waxed paper. Cool on a wire rack.

TO PREPARE THE FILLING AND ASSEMBLE
Process the almond paste and milk in a food processor or blender until smooth and of spreading consistency.

Beat the whipping cream in a mixer bowl until soft peaks form. Add the sugar and mix well.

Combine the peaches and lemon juice in a bowl and mix well.

Spread 1 of the meringues with 1/2 of the almond paste mixture and 1/3 of the whipped cream. Place on a serving platter. Top with 1 cup of the peaches. Arrange another meringue over the peaches.

Layer with the remaining almond paste mixture, 1/2 of the remaining whipped cream and the remaining peaches. Top with the remaining meringue. Spread with the remaining whipped cream.

Garnish with additional peach slices and almonds.

Chill for 3 hours or longer before serving.

Note: Meringues may be made the day before and left on wire racks.

SERVES 8 TO 12

FILLED CREAM CHEESE FOLDOVERS

Ingredients
1 cup butter, softened
8 ounces cream cheese, softened
2 1/2 cups flour
3/4 cup apricot or strawberry jam

METHOD OF PREPARATION
Beat the butter and cream cheese in a mixer bowl until creamy, scraping the bowl occasionally. Add the flour, beating until blended.

Chill, covered, in the refrigerator. Roll thin on a lightly floured surface. Cut into 2-inch squares.

Spoon 1/2 teaspoon jam in the center of each square. Bring 2 opposite corners together in the center, pinching to seal. Place on an ungreased baking sheet.

Bake at 350 degrees for 10 to 15 minutes or until brown.

MAKES 36 TO 48

QUICK PUFF PASTRY

Ingredients
3³/4 cups flour
1 teaspoon salt
2 cups unsalted butter, chopped
¹/2 to ³/4 cup ice water

METHOD OF PREPARATION
Combine the flour and salt in a bowl and mix well. Cut in the butter with a pastry blender until crumbly. Add the ice water 1 tablespoon at a time, stirring just until the dough clings together.

Roll into a rectangle on a lightly floured surface. Fold the dough in thirds; turn 90 degrees. Roll into a rectangle and fold in thirds; brush off excess flour.

Chill, wrapped in plastic wrap, for 30 minutes.

Repeat the rolling, folding, turning and chilling process twice.

Roll as desired. May freeze for future use.

Note: Cut the pastry into shapes with cookie cutters, sprinkle with cinnamon and sugar and bake at 350 degrees until brown. Arrange over your favorite pie filling or cobbler. Use cookie cutter shapes that correlate with your party theme or event, such as stars and longhorns for a chuck wagon party, bunnies and chicks for an Easter party, holly leaves and bells for Christmas, and hearts for Valentine's Day.

MAKES 12 FOUR-INCH-SQUARE PASTRIES

PUTTING ON THE RITZ

Ingredients
1 (14-ounce) can sweetened condensed milk
1 cup chopped dates
1 cup chopped pecans
70 to 80 Ritz crackers
1¹/2 cups confectioners' sugar
¹/2 cup margarine, softened
3 ounces cream cheese, softened
1 teaspoon vanilla extract

METHOD OF PREPARATION
Bring the condensed milk and dates to a boil in a saucepan.

Boil until thickened, stirring constantly. Remove from heat. Stir in the pecans.

Spread the date mixture on the butter crackers. Arrange on a baking sheet.

Bake at 325 degrees for 8 minutes. Let stand until cool.

Beat the confectioners' sugar, margarine, cream cheese and vanilla in a mixer bowl until blended. Spread over the top of the cooled crackers.

Note: May store in the refrigerator for 1 week or longer.

SERVES 30

RASPBERRY SAUCE

Ingredients

1 (10-ounce) package frozen raspberries, thawed
1 tablespoon cornstarch
1 tablespoon kirsch

METHOD OF PREPARATION

Press the raspberries through a sieve to purée, discarding the seeds.

Combine the purée, cornstarch and kirsch in a saucepan.

Cook over medium heat until thickened, stirring constantly.

Let stand until cool.

Note: This sauce is great for topping a cheesecake or any other dessert.

MAKES 3/4 CUP

ALMOND CREAM CONFECTIONS

Ingredients

1/2 cup butter
1/4 cup sugar
2 tablespoons baking cocoa
2 teaspoons vanilla extract
1/4 teaspoon salt
1 egg, lightly beaten
1 3/4 cups vanilla wafer crumbs
1 cup slivered almonds, toasted, chopped
1/2 cup flaked coconut
1/3 cup butter, softened
1/2 egg, beaten
1/2 teaspoon vanilla extract
2 1/2 cups sifted confectioners' sugar
2 ounces semisweet chocolate

METHOD OF PREPARATION

Combine 1/2 cup butter, sugar, baking cocoa, 2 teaspoons vanilla, salt and 1 egg in a heavy saucepan.

Cook over low heat until thickened, stirring constantly. Remove from heat. Stir in the vanilla wafer crumbs, almonds and coconut. Press onto the bottom of an ungreased 9x9-inch dish.

Chill, covered, in the refrigerator.

Beat 1/3 cup butter in a mixer bowl at high speed until creamy. Add 1/2 egg and 1/2 teaspoon vanilla.

Beat until blended. Add the confectioners' sugar gradually, beating until of spreading consistency. Spread over the chilled layer.

Chill, covered, in the refrigerator until firm. Cut into small squares. Arrange the squares 1/2 inch apart on a baking sheet.

Place the chocolate in a sealable plastic bag. Submerge the bag in hot water until the chocolate melts.

Snip 1 corner of the bag. Drizzle the chocolate over the squares. Let stand until set.

MAKES 24

CHOCOLATE-COVERED CARAMELS

Ingredients
1 cup butter
1 cup sugar
1 cup packed brown sugar
1 cup corn syrup
2 cups whipping cream
2¹/₂ cups chopped pecans
1 teaspoon vanilla extract
2 to 4 cups (or more) milk chocolate chips

METHOD OF PREPARATION

Combine the butter, sugar, brown sugar, corn syrup and 1 cup of the whipping cream in a saucepan.

Cook to 225 degrees on a candy thermometer. Add the remaining whipping cream gradually and mix well.

Cook to 240 degrees on a candy thermometer. Remove from heat. Let stand for 1 to 2 minutes. Stir in the pecans and vanilla. Pour the desired amount into disposable cookie sheets; the amount you pour into each pan will determine the thickness of the candy.

Freeze for 4 hours or longer. Thaw slightly. Cut into 1-inch squares or desired shapes. Return any candy that is not being dipped in the chocolate immediately to the freezer.

Microwave the chocolate chips 1 cup at a time in a microwave-safe dish until melted. Coat the candy squares with the chocolate. Place on a baking sheet lined with waxed paper.

Chill until firm.

Note: The caramels may be frozen for future use.

Variation: Drizzle the caramels with white chocolate or decorate with marzipan for a dramatic effect.

MAKES 24 TO 36

CREAM CARAMELS

Ingredients
2 cups sugar
1 cup light corn syrup
¹/₄ cup butter, chopped
2 cups whipping cream, heated
2 teaspoons vanilla extract
¹/₂ teaspoon salt

METHOD OF PREPARATION

Combine the sugar and corn syrup in a 4-quart saucepan, stirring with a wooden spoon to mix.

Cook over low heat until the sugar dissolves, stirring constantly. Bring to a boil, stirring constantly.

Boil over high heat to 305 degrees on a candy thermometer; do not stir. Remove from heat. Add some of the butter.

Return the saucepan to the heat source. Cook and add the remaining butter, stirring constantly; the mixture will bubble and steam.

Add the whipping cream gradually, stirring constantly; do not allow the mixture to stop boiling. Boil to 246 to 250 degrees on a candy thermometer, depending on the desired consistency. Remove from heat.

Let stand for 5 minutes. Add the vanilla and salt, stirring just until blended. Pour into a lightly greased 8x11-inch dish.

Let stand until cool. Invert onto a hard surface. Cut into squares or rectangles.

Store, wrapped individually in waxed paper or plastic wrap, in a covered tin.

Note: Caramels can be stored in a cool place for weeks and will keep well if they are not exposed to other types of candy.

MAKES 3 POUNDS

MILLION-DOLLAR FUDGE

Ingredients
3 (5-ounce) plain chocolate candy bars
2 cups chocolate chips
2 cups marshmallow creme
1 tablespoon butter or margarine
1 teaspoon vanilla extract
4 1/2 cups sugar
1 (12-ounce) can evaporated milk
1 pound pecans, chopped

METHOD OF PREPARATION

Mix the candy bars, chocolate chips, marshmallow creme, butter and vanilla in a 6- to 8-quart heatproof bowl.

Bring the sugar and evaporated milk to a boil in a 4- to 6-quart saucepan.

Boil for 6 minutes. Pour over the candy bar mixture, stirring until smooth and creamy. Fold in the pecans.

Shape by tablespoonfuls into balls. Place on a baking sheet lined with waxed paper.

Chill for 4 to 6 hours or until set.

MAKES 6 POUNDS

PRALINES

Ingredients
2 cups sugar
1 cup buttermilk
3 tablespoons light corn syrup
1 teaspoon baking soda
1 1/2 cups pecans
2 tablespoons butter
1 teaspoon vanilla extract

METHOD OF PREPARATION

Combine the sugar, buttermilk, corn syrup and baking soda in a heavy saucepan.

Cook to 236 degrees on a candy thermometer, soft-ball stage, stirring frequently. Remove from heat. Add the pecans, butter and vanilla.

Stir for 2 minutes or until the mixture loses its luster and looks creamy and opaque.

Drop by tablespoons onto parchment paper or waxed paper immediately. Let stand until cool.

MAKES 24

CARAMEL BROWNIES

Ingredients
20 light caramels
1/4 cup evaporated milk
1 (2-layer) package German chocolate cake mix
1/3 cup milk
1/4 to 1/2 cup melted butter
1 cup chopped pecans (optional)
2 cups chocolate chips

METHOD OF PREPARATION

Heat the caramels and evaporated milk in a double boiler over hot water until blended, stirring frequently.

Combine the cake mix, milk and butter in a bowl and mix well. Stir in the pecans. Spread 1/2 of the mixture in a greased 9x13-inch baking pan.

Bake at 350 degrees for 6 minutes. Sprinkle with the chocolate chips; drizzle with the caramel mixture. Top with the remaining cake mixture.

Bake for 15 minutes longer. Let stand until cool. Cut into squares.

MAKES 36

MAPLE AND BOURBON BLONDIES

Ingredients
4 cups walnut pieces
2 cups flour
4 teaspoons baking powder
1 1/2 teaspoons salt
4 cups packed light brown sugar
4 eggs
1 cup unsalted butter, softened, cut into 8 pieces
6 tablespoons bourbon
3 tablespoons maple extract
4 teaspoons vanilla extract

METHOD OF PREPARATION

Oil the sides and bottoms of two 9x13-inch baking dishes.

Combine the walnuts, flour, baking powder and salt in a food processor container fitted with a steel blade.

Process for 15 seconds or until the walnuts are coarsely chopped. Pour the mixture into a bowl.

Process the brown sugar and eggs for 30 seconds; scrape the side of the bowl. Process for 30 seconds longer. Add the butter, bourbon and flavorings. Process for 30 seconds; scrape the side of the bowl. Process for 30 seconds longer.

Add the flour mixture. Pulse for 5 or 6 times or just until mixed; do not overprocess.

Spread the batter evenly in the 2 prepared baking dishes; smooth with a spatula.

Bake at 350 degrees for 33 to 35 minutes or until the blondies test done.

Let stand until cool. Cut into 1 1/2-inch squares.
Note: This recipe may be prepared using a mixer.

MAKES 90 TO 108

ICED BUTTERSCOTCH COOKIES

For the icing
1/2 cup plus 2 tablespoons butter
21/4 cups confectioners' sugar
2 tablespoons hot water
2 teaspoons vanilla extract

For the cookies
13/4 cups packed brown sugar
1/2 cup butter
2 eggs, beaten
21/3 cups flour
1 teaspoon baking powder
1/2 teaspoon salt
1/2 teaspoon baking soda
1 cup sour cream
2/3 cup chopped nuts
2 teaspoons vanilla extract

TO PREPARE THE ICING

Heat the butter in a saucepan until golden brown. Remove from heat.

Add the confectioners' sugar, hot water and vanilla, stirring until of spreading consistency.

TO PREPARE THE COOKIES

Beat the brown sugar and butter in a mixer bowl until creamy. Add the eggs, beating until blended.

Sift the flour, baking powder, salt and baking soda together. Add to the butter mixture and mix well. Stir in the sour cream, nuts and vanilla.

Chill, covered, until firm. Drop by tablespoonfuls onto a parchment-lined cookie sheet or a cushion-air cookie sheet.

Bake at 350 degrees for 12 to 14 minutes or until brown. Remove to a wire rack to cool. Spread with the icing.

MAKES 24 TO 28

CHOCOLATE COOKIES

Ingredients
2 cups sugar
1/2 cup vegetable oil
4 ounces unsweetened chocolate, melted
4 eggs
2 cups flour
2 teaspoons vanilla extract
2 teaspoons baking powder
1/2 teaspoon salt
1 cup confectioners' sugar, sifted

METHOD OF PREPARATION

Combine the sugar, oil and chocolate in a mixer bowl, beating until blended. Add the eggs 1 at a time, beating well after each addition. Stir in the flour, vanilla, baking powder and salt.

Chill, covered, for several hours.

Shape the dough into 1-inch balls; roll in the confectioners' sugar. Place on a cookie sheet.

Bake at 350 degrees for 10 to 12 minutes.

MAKES 48

CHUNK COOKIES

Ingredients

2 cups unsalted butter, softened
2 cups sugar
1 cup packed brown sugar
4 teaspoons vanilla extract
4 eggs
4 cups flour
2 teaspoons baking powder
1/2 teaspoon salt

METHOD OF PREPARATION

Beat the butter in a mixer bowl until fluffy. Add the sugar and brown sugar, beating until creamy. Add the vanilla and mix well. Add the eggs 1 at a time, beating well after each addition.

Sift the flour, baking powder and salt together. Add to the butter mixture and mix well.

Drop by tablespoonfuls onto a greased cookie sheet.

Bake at 375 degrees for 15 to 18 minutes or until light brown.

Variation: Add 8 ounces white chocolate chunks and 2 cups macadamia nuts or 8 ounces semisweet chocolate and 2 cups pecans or walnuts. Substitute oatmeal, wheat germ or oat bran for the flour and add raisins or currants.

MAKES 48

CORNFLAKE CRISPIES

Ingredients

1 cup margarine, softened
1 cup sugar
1 teaspoon baking soda
1 teaspoon cream of tartar
1 1/2 cups flour
2 cups cornflakes
Pinch of salt

METHOD OF PREPARATION

Mix the margarine, sugar, baking soda, cream of tartar, flour, cornflakes and salt in the order listed in a bowl.

Drop by teaspoonfuls onto an ungreased cookie sheet; flatten with a fork.

Bake at 350 degrees for 10 to 15 minutes until done but not brown.

Remove to a wire rack to cool.

MAKES 24 TO 30

CREME DE MENTHE SQUARES

For the crust
1/2 cup butter or margarine
1/2 cup baking cocoa
1/2 cup confectioners' sugar
1 egg, beaten
1 teaspoon vanilla extract
2 cups graham cracker crumbs

For the filling
1/2 cup melted butter or margarine
1/4 cup green crème de menthe
3 cups confectioners' sugar

For the topping
1 1/2 cups semisweet chocolate chips
1/4 cup butter or margarine

TO PREPARE THE CRUST

Combine the butter and baking cocoa in a saucepan. Cook until blended, stirring constantly. Remove from heat.

Add the confectioners' sugar, egg and vanilla and mix well. Stir in the graham cracker crumbs. Press into an ungreased 9x13-inch dish.

Chill until firm.

TO PREPARE THE FILLING

Combine the butter and crème de menthe in a mixer bowl and mix well. Add the confectioners' sugar.

Beat at low speed until smooth, scraping the bowl occasionally. Spread over the prepared layer.

Chill for 1 hour or longer.

TO PREPARE THE TOPPING

Combine the chocolate chips and the butter in a saucepan.

Cook until blended, stirring constantly. Spread over the prepared layers.

Chill until set. Cut into squares.

Note: May be frozen for future use.

MAKES 48

LONE STAR LEMON BARS

For the crust
1 cup flour
1/2 cup butter, softened
1/4 cup confectioners' sugar, sifted

For the filling
2 eggs
1 cup sugar
2 tablespoons lemon juice
1 tablespoon flour
1 teaspoon grated lemon peel

For the glaze
1/2 cup confectioners' sugar, sifted
1 teaspoon lemon juice
1 teaspoon water
1/8 teaspoon vanilla extract
1/8 teaspoon butter flavoring
Dash of salt

TO PREPARE THE CRUST

Combine the flour, butter and confectioners' sugar in a bowl and mix well. Press into an 8x8-inch baking pan.

Bake at 325 degrees for 15 minutes.

TO PREPARE THE FILLING

Beat the eggs in a mixer bowl until frothy. Add the sugar, lemon juice, flour and lemon peel.

Beat until well mixed. Spread over the baked layer.

Bake for 25 minutes longer. Let stand until cool.

TO PREPARE THE GLAZE

Combine the confectioners' sugar, lemon juice, water, vanilla, butter flavoring and salt in a bowl and mix well.

Spread over the baked layers. Cut into bars.

Note: Do not substitute margarine for butter in this recipe.

MAKES 30

OATMEAL MOLASSES CHOCOLATE CHIP COOKIES

Ingredients

1¼ cups sifted flour
¾ teaspoon baking soda
½ teaspoon baking powder
½ teaspoon salt
1½ cups quick-cooking oats
½ cup shortening
½ cup sugar
½ cup molasses
2 eggs, beaten
1½ cups chocolate chips
1 cup chopped pecans

METHOD OF PREPARATION

Sift the flour, baking soda, baking powder and salt into a bowl and mix well. Add the oats, shortening, sugar, molasses and eggs and mix well. Stir in the chocolate chips and pecans.

Drop by heaping tablespoonfuls onto an ungreased cookie sheet.

Bake at 350 degrees for 12 to 14 minutes or until light brown. Remove to a wire rack to cool.

Note: This recipe will make approximately 18 jumbo cookies or 48 regular size cookies.

MAKES 48

SALTED PEANUT COOKIES

Ingredients
1 cup shortening
2 cups packed light brown sugar
2 eggs
2 cups flour
1 teaspoon baking powder
1 teaspoon baking soda
½ teaspoon salt
2 cups quick-cooking oats
1 cup crisp rice cereal
1 cup salted peanuts

METHOD OF PREPARATION

Beat the shortening in a mixer bowl until creamy. Add the brown sugar gradually.

Beat at medium speed until light and fluffy. Add the eggs and beat well. Add a mixture of the flour, baking powder, baking soda and salt and mix well. Stir in the oats, cereal and peanuts.

Drop by rounded teaspoonfuls onto a lightly greased cookie sheet.

Bake at 375 degrees for 10 to 12 minutes or until light brown. Remove to a wire rack to cool.

Note: These cookies may be frozen for future use.

MAKES 36 TO 48

SOUR CREAM COOKIES

Ingredients

1/2 cup butter, softened
1/3 cup shortening
2 1/2 cups flour
1 cup sugar
1/3 cup sour cream
1 egg
1 teaspoon vanilla extract
3/4 teaspoon baking powder
1/4 teaspoon baking soda
Dash of salt

METHOD OF PREPARATION

Beat the butter and shortening in a mixer bowl until creamy. Add 1 cup of the flour, beating until blended. Add the sugar, sour cream, egg, vanilla, baking powder, baking soda and salt and mix well.

Add the remaining flour gradually and mix well. Divide the dough into 2 portions.

Chill, covered, for 1 to 2 hours.

Roll each portion 1/8 to 1/4 inch thick on a lightly floured surface; cut with a cookie cutter. Place on an ungreased cookie sheet.

Bake at 375 degrees for 7 to 8 minutes or until light brown. Remove to a wire rack to cool. Spread with your favorite frosting.

Note: May wrap dough in foil and freeze for up to 3 months.

MAKES 30

SWEDISH WAFERS

For the wafers

1 cup butter, softened
1/2 teaspoon almond or lemon extract (optional)
1/3 cup half-and-half
2 cups sifted flour
Sugar

For the filling

1/4 cup butter, softened
3/4 cup sifted confectioners' sugar
1 egg yolk
1 teaspoon vanilla extract
Food coloring (optional)

TO PREPARE THE WAFERS

Beat the butter, flavoring and half-and-half in a mixer bowl until creamy. Add the flour, beating until blended. Divide the dough into 3 equal portions.

Chill, covered, for 2 hours or longer. Remove 1 portion of the dough at a time; keep the remaining dough chilled.

Roll the dough 1/8 inch thick on a lightly floured surface; cut with a 1 1/2-inch or smaller cookie cutter. Dip the side of each cookie in sugar. Place on an ungreased cookie sheet; prick with a fork several times. Repeat the process with the remaining dough.

Bake at 375 degrees for 5 to 8 minutes or just until crisp. Remove to a wire rack to cool.

TO PREPARE THE FILLING AND ASSEMBLE

Beat the butter, confectioners' sugar, egg yolk and vanilla in a mixer bowl until of spreading consistency, scraping the bowl occasionally. Add the desired amount of food coloring and mix well.

Spread the filling on half the cookies. Top with the remaining cookies, pressing gently.

Store in an airtight container in the refrigerator or freeze for future use.

Note: Do not substitute margarine for butter in this recipe.

MAKES 60

WEST VIRGINIA'S FINEST SHORTBREAD COOKIES

Ingredients
1 cup butter, softened
1 cup sugar
1 cup packed light brown sugar
1 egg
1 cup vegetable oil
1 cup rolled oats
1 cup crushed cornflakes
1/2 cup chopped nuts
3 1/2 cups sifted flour
1 teaspoon baking soda
1 teaspoon salt
1 teaspoon vanilla extract

METHOD OF PREPARATION

Beat the butter in a mixer bowl until creamy. Add the sugar and brown sugar, beating until light and fluffy. Beat in the egg and oil. Stir in the oats, cornflakes and nuts.

Add a mixture of the flour, baking soda and salt and mix well. Stir in the vanilla.

Shape into balls. Place on an ungreased cookie sheet; flatten with a fork.

Bake at 350 degrees for 12 to 14 minutes or until light brown. Remove to a wire rack to cool.

MAKES 72

WHITE CHOCOLATE CHIP COOKIES

Ingredients
1 cup butter, softened
1 cup sugar
1 cup packed brown sugar
2 eggs
2 teaspoons vanilla extract
2 3/4 cups flour
3/4 cup baking cocoa
1 teaspoon baking soda
1/2 teaspoon salt
1 2/3 cups white chocolate chips

METHOD OF PREPARATION

Beat the butter, sugar and brown sugar in a mixer bowl until creamy. Add the eggs and vanilla, beating until light and fluffy. Add a mixture of the flour, baking cocoa, baking soda and salt and mix well. Stir in the white chocolate chips.

Drop by generous spoonfuls onto an ungreased cookie sheet.

Bake at 350 degrees for 9 to 11 minutes or until puffed.

Cool on the cookie sheet for 5 to 10 minutes. Remove to a wire rack to cool completely.

MAKES 36

AUTUMN APPLE CAKE

For the cake
2 cups sugar
1 cup vegetable oil
3 eggs
1 teaspoon vanilla extract
2 cups flour
1 tablespoon cinnamon
1 teaspoon baking soda
1/2 teaspoon salt
4 cups chopped peeled tart apples
1 cup chopped pecans

For the cream cheese glaze
1 1/2 cups confectioners' sugar
3 ounces cream cheese, softened
3 tablespoons margarine, softened
2 teaspoons vanilla extract

TO PREPARE THE CAKE

Beat the sugar, oil, eggs and vanilla in a mixer bowl until light and fluffy. Add a sifted mixture of the flour, cinnamon, baking soda and salt and mix well. Fold in the apples and pecans. Spoon into a greased 9x13-inch cake pan or bundt pan.

Bake at 350 degrees for 45 to 50 minutes or until the cake tests done.

TO PREPARE THE CREAM CHEESE GLAZE

Beat the confectioners' sugar, cream cheese, margarine and vanilla in a mixer bowl until smooth, scraping the bowl occasionally.

Spread over the cake.

SERVES 15

ESPRESSO CAKE

For the cake
12 egg whites, at room temperature
1/4 cup instant espresso coffee granules
1 1/2 teaspoons cream of tartar
1/4 teaspoon salt
1 1/4 teaspoons vanilla extract
1 1/4 cups sugar
1 1/4 cups confectioners' sugar
1 cup cake flour

For the mocha icing
2 teaspoons instant espresso coffee granules
3 teaspoons baking cocoa
2 tablespoons hot water
1 1/2 cups confectioners' sugar

TO PREPARE THE CAKE

Beat the egg whites, espresso granules, cream of tartar and salt in a mixer bowl until soft peaks form. Add the vanilla, beating until blended.

Add the sugar a few tablespoons at a time, beating constantly until stiff peaks form. Fold in a sifted mixture of the confectioners' sugar and cake flour. Spoon into an ungreased 10-inch tube pan.

Bake at 375 degrees for 35 to 40 minutes or until the cake springs back when lightly touched. Cover cake with foil or place on lower oven rack if cake begins to overbrown.

Invert the pan onto a serving platter. Let stand until cool. Loosen the cake from the side of the pan with a narrow metal spatula.

TO PREPARE THE MOCHA ICING

Dissolve the espresso granules and 1 teaspoon of the baking cocoa in the hot water in a bowl and mix well. Stir in the confectioners' sugar. Add additional hot water 1 teaspoon at a time as needed for the desired consistency. Drizzle over the cake. Sprinkle with the remaining baking cocoa.

Note: The fat-conscious will be glad to learn that each serving of this cake contains less than one gram of fat.

SERVES 16

CREME DE CACAO TORTE

For the cake
1²/3 cups sugar
²/3 cup butter, softened
3 eggs
¹/2 teaspoon vanilla extract
2 cups flour
²/3 cup baking cocoa
1¹/4 teaspoons baking soda
¹/4 teaspoon baking powder
1¹/3 cups milk
2 tablespoons crème de cacao

For the crème de cacao filling
1 cup cold whipping cream
2 tablespoons crème de cacao
1 tablespoon baking cocoa

For the chocolate ganache glaze
1 (7-ounce) Hershey's Special Dark Mildly Sweet
Chocolate candy bar, broken
¹/4 cup whipping cream
1 tablespoon butter
1¹/2 teaspoons crème de cacao

TO PREPARE THE CAKE

Beat the sugar, butter, eggs and vanilla in a mixer bowl until blended. Add a mixture of the flour, baking cocoa, baking soda and baking powder alternately with the milk, blending just until mixed. Spoon into 2 greased and floured 9-inch cake pans.

Bake at 350 degrees for 30 to 35 minutes or until the layers test done.

Cool in the pans for 10 minutes. Remove to a wire rack to cool completely.

TO PREPARE THE CREME DE CACAO FILLING

Beat the whipping cream, crème de cacao and baking cocoa in a mixer bowl until stiff peaks form, scraping the bowl occasionally.

Chill, covered, in the refrigerator.

TO PREPARE THE CHOCOLATE GANACHE GLAZE

Combine the candy, whipping cream and butter in a saucepan.

Cook over low heat until smooth, stirring constantly. Stir in the crème de cacao.

Cool to lukewarm; the glaze will thicken slightly.

TO ASSEMBLE

Split each cake layer horizontally into 2 layers. Sprinkle each layer with 1¹/2 teaspoons of the crème de cacao.

Place 1 layer on a serving platter; spread with ¹/3 of the filling. Repeat the process with 2 of the remaining cake layers and the remaining filling; top with the remaining cake layer.

Chill, tightly covered, for 8 hours or longer. Spoon the lukewarm glaze over the top of the cake, allowing the glaze to drizzle down the side of the cake.

Chill, covered, until serving time.

SERVES 12 TO 14

FIVE-FLAVOR SUPREME CAKE

For the cake
3 cups sugar
1 cup shortening
6 eggs
1 teaspoon vanilla extract
1 teaspoon rum extract
1 teaspoon butter flavoring
1 teaspoon coconut extract
1 teaspoon lemon extract
3 cups flour
1/4 teaspoon baking soda
1/4 teaspoon salt
1 cup buttermilk

For the glaze
1 cup sugar
1/2 cup boiling water
1 teaspoon vanilla extract
1 teaspoon rum extract
1 teaspoon coconut extract
1 teaspoon butter flavoring
1 teaspoon lemon extract
1 teaspoon almond extract

TO PREPARE THE CAKE

Beat the sugar and shortening in a mixer bowl until creamy. Add the eggs, beating until blended. Beat in the flavorings.

Add a mixture of the flour, baking soda and salt alternately with the buttermilk, beating well after each addition. Spoon into a greased and floured bundt pan.

Bake at 350 degrees for 1 hour. Invert onto a serving platter.

TO PREPARE THE GLAZE

Combine the sugar, boiling water and flavorings in a bowl and mix well. Drizzle over the hot cake.

SERVES 16

FROSTED GINGERBREAD SQUARES

For the gingerbread
1 cup sugar
1 cup shortening
2 eggs
2/3 cup molasses
3 cups sifted flour
1 teaspoon baking soda
1 teaspoon salt
1 teaspoon ginger
1/2 teaspoon cinnamon
1/2 teaspoon ground cloves
1 cup lukewarm water

For the frosting
1/4 cup milk
1/4 cup butter
1 (1-pound) package (about) confectioners' sugar
1 teaspoon vanilla extract
Cinnamon to taste (optional)
Nutmeg to taste (optional)

TO PREPARE THE GINGERBREAD

Beat the sugar and shortening in a mixer bowl until creamy. Add the eggs, beating until blended. Beat in the molasses.

Add a mixture of the flour, baking soda, salt, ginger, cinnamon and cloves alternately with the lukewarm water, mixing well after each addition. Spoon into an ungreased 9x13-inch baking dish.

Bake at 350 degrees for 20 minutes. Remove to a wire rack.

TO PREPARE THE FROSTING

Bring the milk and butter to a boil in a saucepan. Remove from heat. Stir in just enough of the confectioners' sugar for the desired consistency. Add the vanilla, cinnamon and nutmeg and mix well.

Spread over the warm gingerbread. Cool completely before cutting into squares.

SERVES 20 TO 24

SOFT GINGERBREAD TREATS

Ingredients

1/2 teaspoon baking soda
1 cup boiling water
1/2 cup sugar
1/2 cup butter
1 cup syrup or molasses
2 eggs, beaten
2 1/2 cups flour, sifted
1 1/2 teaspoons baking powder
1/2 teaspoon salt
1/2 teaspoon ginger
1/2 teaspoon nutmeg
1/2 teaspoon allspice
1/2 teaspoon cinnamon

METHOD OF PREPARATION

Dissolve the baking soda in the boiling water and mix well.

Beat the sugar and butter in a mixer bowl until creamy. Add the syrup and eggs, beating until blended.

Add a sifted mixture of the flour, baking powder, salt, ginger, nutmeg, allspice and cinnamon alternately with the baking soda mixture, mixing after each addition. Spoon into a greased 9x9-inch baking pan.

Bake at 350 degrees for 30 to 35 minutes or until the edges pull from the sides of the pan.

Note: Serve hot with butter, ice cream or whipping cream if desired.

Variation: Bake in muffin cups for individual servings and lunch box snacks.

SERVES 9 TO 12

STICKY PECAN CAKE

Ingredients

3 cups packed brown sugar
2 cups cake flour
2 teaspoons baking powder
3 cups pecan halves, coarsely broken
6 egg whites

METHOD OF PREPARATION

Sift the brown sugar, cake flour and baking powder into a bowl and mix well.

Sprinkle a small amount of the flour mixture over the pecans in a bowl and mix well.

Add the egg whites to the brown sugar mixture and mix well. Stir in the pecans. Spoon into a greased and floured tube pan.

Place the pan in a 325-degree oven. Place a pan of water on the oven rack below the cake.

Bake for 1 1/2 to 2 hours or just until the cake tests done.

Cool in the pan on a wire rack. Invert onto a serving platter. Do not frost.

SERVES 16

APRICOT BRANDY POUND CAKE

Ingredients

3 cups sugar
2 cups butter, softened
6 eggs
3 cups flour
1/2 teaspoon salt
1/2 teaspoon baking soda
1 cup sour cream
1 teaspoon vanilla extract
1 teaspoon orange extract
1 teaspoon almond extract
1/2 teaspoon lemon extract
1/2 teaspoon rum extract
1/2 cup apricot brandy

METHOD OF PREPARATION

Cream the sugar and butter in a mixer bowl. Add the eggs 1 at a time, beating well after each addition.

Add a sifted mixture of the flour, salt and baking soda. Stir in the sour cream and flavorings. Add the apricot brandy and mix well. Spoon into a greased and floured tube pan.

Bake at 325 degrees for 1 1/4 hours.

Note: This cake is too large for a bundt pan.

SERVES 12

CREAM CHEESE POUND CAKE

Ingredients

1 1/2 cups butter or margarine, softened
8 ounces cream cheese, softened
3 cups sugar
6 eggs
3 cups cake flour
1 teaspoon vanilla extract

METHOD OF PREPARATION

Cream the butter, cream cheese and sugar in a mixer bowl until light and fluffy. Add the eggs 1 at a time alternately with the cake flour, beating well after each addition and ending with cake flour. Stir in the vanilla.

Spoon the batter into a bundt pan, tube pan or 2 loaf pans.

Bake at 325 degrees for 70 to 90 minutes or until a wooden pick inserted in the center comes out clean.

Variation: Add 1 teaspoon lemon extract for a different flavor.

SERVES 16

KAHLUA POUND CAKE

For the Kahlúa fudge
1/2 cup baking cocoa
1/4 cup sugar
1/4 cup light corn syrup
1/4 cup Kahlúa
1/4 cup water

For the cake
3/4 cup milk
1 tablespoon vanilla extract
2 1/2 cups sugar
2 cups unsalted butter, softened
6 eggs, at room temperature
4 cups flour
1/4 teaspoon baking soda

For the Kahlúa glaze
4 ounces semisweet chocolate
1/4 cup unsalted butter
2 tablespoons whipping cream
2 tablespoons Kahlúa

TO PREPARE THE KAHLUA FUDGE

Combine the baking cocoa, sugar, corn syrup, Kahlúa and water in a saucepan.

Cook over low heat until blended, stirring constantly. Bring to a boil over medium heat, stirring constantly.

Let stand until cool.

TO PREPARE THE CAKE

Combine the milk and vanilla in a bowl and mix well.

Combine the sugar and butter in a mixer bowl. Beat at high speed for 3 minutes or until light and fluffy, scraping the bowl occasionally. Add the eggs 1 at a time, beating well after each addition. Add the flour 1 cup at a time alternately with 1/4 cup of the milk mixture at a time, beating constantly and beginning and ending with the flour.

Spoon 1/3 of the batter, or about 2 1/2 cups, into a medium bowl, reserving the remaining batter. Stir the baking soda into the fudge. Stir the fudge into the medium bowl containing 1/3 of the batter.

Pour 1/2 of the reserved batter into a greased and floured 10-inch tube pan; spread with the fudge batter. Top with the remaining reserved batter.

Bake at 300 degrees for 1 hour and 40 minutes or until the cake tests done.

Cool the cake in the pan on a wire rack for 15 minutes. Invert onto a wire rack to cool completely.

TO PREPARE THE KAHLUA GLAZE

Bring the chocolate, butter, whipping cream and Kahlúa to a boil in a saucepan, stirring frequently.

Let stand until cool. Drizzle over the cake.

SERVES 16

GOLDEN POUND CAKE

For the cake
2 cups sugar
1 cup shortening
4 eggs
3 cups flour, sifted
2 teaspoons baking powder
1 cup milk
2 teaspoons vanilla extract

For the icing
1 cup confectioners' sugar
2 tablespoons melted butter
Lemon juice to taste

TO PREPARE THE CAKE

Cream the sugar and shortening in a mixer bowl until light and fluffy. Add the eggs 1 at a time, mixing well after each addition. Add a sifted mixture of the flour and baking powder. Stir in the milk and vanilla. Spoon into a tube pan or bundt pan.

Place the pan on the lower rack of the oven.

Bake at 375 degrees for 45 to 50 minutes or until the cake tests done.

Invert onto a serving platter.

TO PREPARE THE ICING

Mix the confectioners' sugar, butter and lemon juice in a bowl and mix well. Drizzle over the cake.

Note: Serve the pound cake with fresh strawberries for an added treat.

SERVES 16

PUMPKIN ROLL

For the filling
6 ounces cream cheese, softened
1 cup confectioners' sugar
1/4 cup butter, softened
1/2 teaspoon vanilla extract

For the pumpkin roll
Confectioners' sugar to taste
3 eggs
1 cup sugar
2/3 cup canned pumpkin
1 teaspoon lemon juice
3/4 cup flour
2 teaspoons cinnamon
1 teaspoon baking powder
1 teaspoon ginger
1/2 teaspoon nutmeg
1/2 teaspoon salt
1 cup finely chopped nuts

TO PREPARE THE FILLING

Beat the cream cheese, confectioners' sugar, butter and vanilla in a mixer bowl until of spreading consistency, scraping the bowl occasionally.

TO PREPARE THE PUMPKIN ROLL

Grease a jelly roll pan; sprinkle with confectioners' sugar.

Beat the eggs in a mixer bowl for 5 minutes. Add the sugar, pumpkin and lemon juice and mix well. Fold in a sifted mixture of the flour, cinnamon, baking powder, ginger, nutmeg and salt. Spoon into the prepared pan. Sprinkle with the nuts.

Bake at 375 degrees for 15 minutes.

Invert onto a towel dusted with confectioners' sugar. Roll in the towel starting with short side.

Chill for 1 hour. Unroll the cake. Spread with the filling; reroll and wrap in plastic wrap.

Chill until serving time. May freeze for future use.

SERVES 8 TO 10

STRAWBERRY CAKE WITH STRAWBERRY CREAM CHEESE FROSTING

For the cake
4 eggs
1 cup vegetable oil
1/2 cup water
1 (2-layer) package white cake mix
1 (3-ounce) package strawberry gelatin
3 tablespoons flour
2/3 cup frozen strawberries, crushed

For the strawberry cream cheese frosting
2/3 cup frozen strawberries, crushed
3 ounces cream cheese, softened
2 tablespoons plus 2 teaspoons margarine, softened
1 (1-pound) package (about) confectioners' sugar, sifted

TO PREPARE THE CAKE

Beat the eggs in a mixer bowl. Add the oil and water, beating until blended. Add the cake mix, gelatin, flour and strawberries.

Beat for 1 minute, scraping the bowl occasionally. Spoon into a greased 9x13-inch cake pan.

Bake at 350 degrees for 30 minutes or until the cake tests done.

TO PREPARE THE STRAWBERRY CREAM CHEESE FROSTING

Combine the strawberries, cream cheese and margarine in a mixer bowl, beating until mixed. Beat in just enough of the confectioners' sugar to make of spreading consistency.

Spread over the warm cake.

SERVES 15

THE CAKE THAT WILL NOT LAST

Ingredients
3 cups flour
2 cups sugar
1 teaspoon salt
1 teaspoon baking soda
1 teaspoon cinnamon
1 1/3 cups vegetable oil
2 cups chopped bananas
1 cup chopped nuts
1 cup crushed pineapple
1 teaspoon vanilla extract

METHOD OF PREPARATION

Combine the flour, sugar, salt, baking soda and cinnamon in a bowl and mix well. Stir in the oil, bananas, nuts, pineapple and vanilla; do not beat.

Spoon the batter into a greased and floured bundt pan.

Bake at 350 degrees for 1 hour and 20 minutes.

Cool in pan on a wire rack for 10 to 15 minutes. Invert onto a wire rack to cool completely.

SERVES 16

WHITE CHOCOLATE CAKE

For the cake
1¼ cups butter
¾ cup water
4 ounces white chocolate, broken
1½ cups buttermilk
4 eggs, lightly beaten
1½ teaspoons vanilla extract
3½ cups flour
1 cup chopped pecans, toasted
2¼ cups sugar
1½ teaspoons baking soda

For the white chocolate cream cheese frosting
4 ounces white chocolate, broken
11 ounces cream cheese, softened
⅓ cup butter, softened
6½ cups sifted confectioners' sugar
1½ teaspoons vanilla extract

TO PREPARE THE CAKE

Bring the butter and water to a boil in a saucepan over medium heat, stirring occasionally. Remove from heat. Add the white chocolate, stirring until the chocolate melts. Stir in the buttermilk, eggs and vanilla.

Combine ½ cup of the flour and the pecans in a bowl and mix well.

Combine the remaining flour, sugar and baking soda in a bowl and mix well. Stir in the white chocolate mixture gradually. Fold in the pecan mixture; the batter will be thin. Pour into 3 greased and floured 9-inch cake pans.

Bake at 350 degrees for 20 to 25 minutes or until the layers test done. Cool in the pans on a wire rack for 10 minutes. Invert onto a wire rack to cool completely.

TO PREPARE THE WHITE CHOCOLATE CREAM CHEESE FROSTING

Heat the white chocolate in a heavy saucepan over low heat until melted, stirring constantly. Cool for 10 minutes, stirring occasionally.

Combine the cream cheese and butter in a mixer bowl.

Beat at medium speed until creamy, scraping the bowl occasionally. Add the white chocolate gradually, beating constantly until blended. Add the confectioners' sugar gradually, beating until smooth. Stir in the vanilla.

Spread the frosting between the layers and over the top and side of the cake. Store, covered, in the refrigerator.

SERVES 16

Apple Pie with Rum Butter Sauce

For the pie
1 cup sugar
1/4 cup butter, softened
1 egg
1 cup flour
1 teaspoon salt
1 teaspoon cinnamon
2 tablespoons hot water
1 teaspoon vanilla extract
3 cups chopped peeled apples
Chopped pecans to taste

For the rum butter sauce
1/2 cup packed brown sugar
1/2 cup sugar
1/2 cup whipping cream
1/4 cup butter
1 tablespoon rum

To Prepare the Pie
Beat the sugar and butter in a mixer bowl until creamy. Add the egg, beating until light and fluffy. Beat in the flour, salt and cinnamon until blended. Stir in the hot water, vanilla, apples and pecans. Spoon into a greased and floured 9-inch pie plate.
Bake at 350 degrees for 45 minutes.

To Prepare the Rum Butter Sauce
Bring the brown sugar, sugar, whipping cream and butter to a boil in a saucepan.
Boil for 1 minute. Stir in the rum. Drizzle over each serving.

Serves 6 to 8

Brownie Pie

Ingredients
1 cup semisweet chocolate chips
1 (5-ounce) can evaporated milk
2 tablespoons margarine
1 cup sugar
2 tablespoons flour
1/4 teaspoon salt
2 eggs, beaten
1 teaspoon vanilla extract
1 cup chopped pecans
1 unbaked (9-inch) pie shell

Method of Preparation
Combine the chocolate chips, evaporated milk and margarine in a saucepan.
Cook until creamy and smooth, stirring constantly. Remove from heat.
Combine the sugar, flour and salt in a bowl and mix well. Add the eggs and vanilla and mix well. Stir in the pecans. Add to the chocolate mixture and mix well. Pour into the pie shell.
Bake at 375 degrees for 40 minutes. Cool on a wire rack before serving.
Note: Serve with whipped cream, whipped topping or vanilla ice cream.

Serves 6 to 8

197

CHERRY CHOCOLATE CHEESE PIE

Ingredients

3/4 cup sugar
11 ounces cream cheese, softened
1/4 cup baking cocoa
2 eggs
1 teaspoon vanilla extract
1/2 cup chilled whipping cream
1 (10-inch) deep-dish graham cracker pie shell
1 (21-ounce) can cherry pie filling

METHOD OF PREPARATION

Cream the sugar and cream cheese in a mixer bowl. Add the baking cocoa, beating until blended. Beat in the eggs and vanilla.

Add the whipping cream, beating until smooth. Spoon into the pie shell.

Bake at 350 degrees for 35 to 40 minutes or until a knife inserted in the center comes out clean. Spread with the pie filling.

Chill for 4 to 6 hours.

Note: Chocoholics will love this pie.

SERVES 8 TO 10

CHOCOLATE PIES

Ingredients

1 cup sugar
1/4 cup flour
2 tablespoons (heaping) baking cocoa
2 cups milk
2 egg yolks, beaten
2 tablespoons margarine
1 teaspoon vanilla extract
Pinch of salt
2 baked (9-inch) pie shells
2 egg whites
2 tablespoons sugar

METHOD OF PREPARATION

Combine 1 cup sugar, flour and baking cocoa in a saucepan and mix well. Add a mixture of the milk and egg yolks gradually and mix well.

Cook until thickened, stirring constantly. Remove from heat. Stir in the margarine, vanilla and salt until blended. Spoon into the pie shells.

Beat the egg whites in a mixer bowl until foamy. Add 2 tablespoons sugar gradually, beating constantly until stiff peaks form. Spread evenly over the filling, sealing to the edge.

Bake at 400 degrees for 5 minutes.

Note: May bake in one 10-inch deep-dish pie shell.

SERVES 12 TO 16

CHOCOLATE CHIP PIE

Ingredients
1 cup sugar
1/2 cup margarine, softened
1 teaspoon vanilla extract
2 eggs, beaten
1/2 cup flour
1 cup chocolate chips
1 cup chopped pecans
1 unbaked (9-inch) pie shell

METHOD OF PREPARATION

Cream the sugar, margarine and vanilla in a mixer bowl until smooth. Add the eggs, beating until blended. Stir in the flour, chocolate chips and pecans. Spoon into the pie shell.

Bake at 350 degrees for 35 to 40 minutes.

Variation: Delete 1/4 cup of the pecans and add 1/2 cup flaked coconut to the pie filling.

SERVES 6 TO 8

CHESS PIE

Ingredients
1 3/4 cups sugar
1/3 cup flour
1 teaspoon cornmeal
1 cup milk
1/2 cup butter or margarine, softened
4 egg yolks, beaten
1 tablespoon vanilla extract
1 unbaked (9-inch) pie shell

METHOD OF PREPARATION

Combine the sugar, flour and cornmeal in a bowl and mix well.

Stir in the milk, butter, egg yolks and vanilla. Spoon into the pie shell.

Bake at 300 degrees for 1 hour or until set.

SERVES 6 TO 8

COCONUT PIE

Ingredients

1 1/2 cups sugar
1/2 cup melted butter
3 eggs, beaten
1 tablespoon vinegar
1 teaspoon vanilla extract
1 (7-ounce) can flaked coconut
1 unbaked (9-inch) pie shell

METHOD OF PREPARATION

Combine the sugar, butter, eggs, vinegar and vanilla in a bowl and mix well.

Stir in the coconut. Spoon into the pie shell. Bake at 350 degrees for 1 hour.

SERVES 6 TO 8

MINIATURE FRUIT CHEESE TARTS

Ingredients

8 ounces cream cheese, softened
1 (14-ounce) can sweetened condensed milk
1/3 cup lemon juice
1 teaspoon vanilla extract
24 baked (2- or 3-inch) tart shells
Assorted fresh fruits
1/4 cup apple jelly, melted

METHOD OF PREPARATION

Beat the cream cheese in a mixer bowl until light and fluffy. Add the condensed milk gradually, beating constantly until blended. Stir in the lemon juice and vanilla.

Fill the tart shells with the cream cheese mixture. Top with assorted fresh fruits. Brush with the jelly.

Chill for 2 hours or until set. Store the leftovers in the refrigerator.

Note: Top the tarts with fresh strawberries, blueberries, sliced bananas, raspberries, orange sections, cherries, kiwifruit, grapes, pineapple or your favorite fruit.

SERVES 24

LEMON ICE CREAM PIES WITH RASPBERRY SAUCE

For the raspberry sauce
1 tablespoon cornstarch
1 tablespoon cold water
1 (10-ounce) package frozen raspberries, thawed
3/4 cup (or more) red currant jelly
1 tablespoon Grand Marnier (optional)

For the chocolate crust
6 tablespoons butter
1/4 cup shortening
1 1/2 cups instant cocoa mix
1 1/2 cups graham cracker crumbs
6 tablespoons sugar

For the filling and assembly
1 1/2 cups sugar
Juice of 6 lemons
1/2 gallon vanilla ice cream, softened
1 tablespoon grated lemon peel
Chocolate curls

TO PREPARE THE RASPBERRY SAUCE
Dissolve the cornstarch in the cold water in a bowl and mix well.

Press the raspberries through a sieve, reserving the juice and discarding the raspberries.

Combine the reserved juice and jelly in a saucepan. Bring to a boil. Stir in the cornstarch mixture.

Cook until thickened and clear, stirring constantly. Remove from heat.

Let stand until cool. Stir in the Grand Marnier.

TO PREPARE THE CHOCOLATE CRUST
Heat the butter and shortening in a saucepan until blended, stirring frequently.

Combine the cocoa mix, graham cracker crumbs and sugar in a bowl and mix well. Stir in the butter mixture. Press into two 9-inch pie plates sprayed with nonstick cooking spray.

Bake at 350 degrees for 8 minutes. Let stand until cool.

TO PREPARE THE FILLING AND ASSEMBLE
Combine the sugar and lemon juice in a bowl and mix well. Stir into the ice cream in a bowl. Add the lemon peel and mix well. Spoon into the prepared pie plates. Sprinkle with chocolate curls.

Freeze until set. Serve with the raspberry sauce.

SERVES 12 TO 16

PECAN PIE

Ingredients
1 cup sugar
1 cup light corn syrup
2 eggs, beaten
2 tablespoons melted butter
1 teaspoon vanilla extract
1/8 teaspoon salt
1 cup pecan pieces
1 unbaked (10-inch) deep-dish pie shell

METHOD OF PREPARATION

Combine the sugar, corn syrup, eggs, butter, vanilla and salt in a bowl and mix well. Stir in the pecans. Pour into the pie shell.

Bake at 425 degrees for 15 minutes. Reduce the oven temperature to 300 degrees.

Bake for 1 hour longer.

SERVES 8 TO 10

KAHLUA PECAN PIE

Ingredients
3/4 cup sugar
1/4 cup butter, softened
2 tablespoons flour
1 teaspoon vanilla extract
3 eggs
3/4 cup evaporated milk
1/2 cup Kahlúa
1/2 cup dark corn syrup
1 cup chopped pecans
1 unbaked (9-inch) pie shell
1/2 cup whipping cream, whipped
Pecan halves

METHOD OF PREPARATION

Beat the sugar, butter, flour and vanilla in a mixer bowl until smooth and creamy. Add the eggs 1 at a time, beating well after each addition. Stir in the evaporated milk, Kahlúa and corn syrup. Add the pecans and mix well. Spoon into the pie shell.

Bake at 400 degrees for 10 minutes. Reduce the oven temperature to 325 degrees.

Bake for 40 minutes longer or until set.

Chill until serving time. Top each serving with whipped cream and pecan halves.

SERVES 6 TO 8

UNDER
48 INCHES

UNDER 48 INCHES

INITIAL CRACKERS

Ingredients

¹/₂ cup flour
2 tablespoons sesame seeds
¹/₈ teaspoon garlic salt
3 tablespoons butter, chilled
2 tablespoons ice water

METHOD OF PREPARATION

Combine the flour, sesame seeds and garlic salt in a bowl and mix well. Cut in the butter until crumbly.

Sprinkle with the ice water and stir until the mixture forms a ball.

Roll the dough into thin ropes. Shape into your initials. Arrange on an ungreased baking sheet; flatten slightly.

Bake at 350 degrees for 15 minutes. Remove to a wire rack to cool.

SERVES 6 TO 8

COFFEE CAN ICE CREAM

Ingredients

1 cup milk
1 cup whipping cream
¹/₂ cup sugar
¹/₂ teaspoon vanilla extract
1 (1-pound) coffee can with plastic lid
Chopped fruit (optional)
Chopped nuts (optional)
1 (3-pound) coffee can with plastic lid
Ice
1 cup rock salt

METHOD OF PREPARATION

Combine the milk, whipping cream, sugar and vanilla in the 1-pound coffee can and mix well. Stir in fruit and/or nuts. Seal with the plastic lid. Place the filled can right side up in the remaining can.

Pack ice into the larger can around the filled can. Sprinkle the ice with the rock salt. Seal with the plastic lid.

Roll the can back and forth across the floor, table, driveway or patio for 10 minutes. Rinse the outside of the larger can and remove the lid. Remove the smaller can and stir the ice cream; replace the lid. Drain the water from the larger can. Place the filled can in the larger can; add additional ice and additional rock salt as needed. Replace the lid.

Roll for 10 minutes longer or until the ice cream is of the desired consistency. Rinse the outsides of the cans before removing the lids. Serve immediately.

SERVES 4 TO 6

BUBBLES

Ingredients
5 cups water
1 cup Lemon Joy dishwashing liquid
1 cup light corn syrup
1 teaspoon glycerin

METHOD OF PREPARATION
Combine the water, dishwashing liquid, corn syrup and glycerin in a bowl and mix well.

Let stand for 8 to 10 hours for the best results, but you may use immediately.

Dip bubble blowers into the soap mixture and blow bubbles or swish the blower through the air to make bubbles.

Note: Glycerine may be purchased at your local drug store.

Variation: Try blowing bubbles through a funnel, soda straw, or old thread spool.

MAKES 7 CUPS

MODELING DOUGH

Ingredients
1 cup flour
$^{1}/_{2}$ cup salt
1 teaspoon cream of tartar
1 cup water
1 tablespoon vegetable oil
Food coloring of choice

METHOD OF PREPARATION
Combine the flour, salt and cream of tartar in a saucepan and mix well. Stir in the water, oil and food coloring.

Cook over medium heat until the mixture pulls from the side of the saucepan and is doughy in consistency. Knead until cool.

Model into desired shapes.

Note: The dough is not edible. Use over and over again. Store in a covered container at room temperature for up to 3 months.

AROMATIC PLAY DOUGH

Ingredients
1 cup flour
2 tablespoons cornstarch
$^{1}/_{2}$ teaspoon salt
1 cup boiling water
1 tablespoon vegetable oil
6 drops of food coloring (optional)
2 or 3 drops of lemon or orange extract

METHOD OF PREPARATION
Combine the flour, cornstarch and salt in a bowl and mix well. Add the boiling water, oil, food coloring and lemon extract, stirring until blended.

Let stand for 3 minutes.

Note: The dough is not edible.

Variation: To make creative ornaments, roll the dough and cut into various shapes with your favorite cookie cutters. Microwave for 2 to 3 minutes or until firm.

IMITATION GAK

Ingredients
6 tablespoons warm water
1 teaspoon Borax
4 ounces Elmer's liquid school glue
$^{1}/_{2}$ cup warm water
Food coloring of choice

METHOD OF PREPARATION
Combine 6 tablespoons warm water and Borax in a bowl and mix well. Stir in the glue and $^{1}/_{2}$ cup warm water until blended. Add food coloring and mix well.

Let stand until dry and pliable. Store in an airtight container.

FINGER PAINT

Ingredients
1/2 cup Argo starch
Cold water
4 cups boiling water
1/2 cup Ivory flakes
1/4 cup talcum powder
Poster paint or food coloring of choice
Glazed shelf paper

METHOD OF PREPARATION

Soften the starch in a small amount of cold water in a saucepan and mix well. Stir in the boiling water.

Cook over medium-low heat until the mixture bubbles, stirring constantly. Remove from heat.

Cool slightly. Stir in the Ivory flakes and talcum powder until mixed. Divide into several portions and tint with poster paint or food coloring.

Moisten both sides of the shelf paper with a sponge. Lay glazed side up on a hard surface; smooth out the bubbles. Paint as desired.

Variation: Beat warm water into Ivory flakes until of the desired consistency and tint with poster paint or food coloring. Add a drop of food coloring to aerosol shaving cream and use to paint on a cookie sheet. For edible finger paint, combine instant pudding mix with water or milk and let your creative juices flow.

PASTE

Ingredients
1/2 cup flour
2 cups cold water
Oil of peppermint or wintergreen to taste

METHOD OF PREPARATION

Combine the flour and cold water in a saucepan, stirring until creamy.

Bring to a boil; reduce heat.

Simmer for 5 minutes, stirring constantly. Let stand until cool. Add additional cold water if needed for desired consistency. Stir in the oil of peppermint or wintergreen.

Store, covered, in the refrigerator.

Note: The oil of peppermint or wintergreen imparts a pleasant smell and prevents spoilage.

PICTURE TRANSFERRING

Ingredients
1 sheet waxed paper
Colored newspaper clipping or comic book page
1 spoon or wooden ice cream stick
1 sheet plain paper

METHOD OF PREPARATION

Place the waxed paper on top of the newspaper clipping or comic book page. Rub the entire surface with the spoon.

Lift the waxed paper and place on the plain sheet of paper. Rub with the spoon. The original picture will appear on the plain sheet of paper.

POTPOURRI ORNAMENTS

Ingredients
Clear Christmas tree ball ornaments
Clear tape
Scented potpourri
Hot glue gun with glue sticks
Lace, ribbon and/or flowers

METHOD OF PREPARATION

Remove the metal ring and hanger from the top of each ornament. Wrap the neck edge of the ornament with clear tape to prevent breakage.

Fill each ornament with potpourri. Remove the tape and reattach the metal ring and hanger.

Hot glue lace, ribbon and/or flowers in various designs on each ornament.

Attach a ribbon to your original ornaments and hang on your Christmas tree for an aromatic and colorful holiday.

SATIN LACE ORNAMENTS

Ingredients
Decorative lace
Fabric glue
Satin thread Christmas balls
Ribbon
Flowers

METHOD OF PREPARATION

Cut the lace into desired designs. Glue onto the Christmas balls in varying designs.

Attach ribbon to the ball for hanging. Glue flowers to the top of the ornament for a creative touch.

Note: May glue any type of decoration to the balls. Be creative and original.

LACE TRIM ORNAMENTS

Ingredients
1 (2x15-inch) strip stiff lace
Hot glue gun with glue sticks
1 (1½-inch) circle poster board
1 piece of (⅛-inch-wide) ribbon
Flowers and miniature pinecones

METHOD OF PREPARATION

Sew the ends of the 2x15-inch strip of lace together. Baste the inside edge of the lace and gather tightly to form a circle.

Hot glue the poster board circle to the lace. Attach the ribbon to the back for hanging. Decorate with flowers, pinecones and additional ribbon.

SOMETHING EXTRA

WHEN THE RECIPE CALLS FOR .... USE

Baking

$^1/_2$ cup butter	4 ounces
2 cups butter	1 pound
4 cups all-purpose flour	1 pound
$4^1/_2$ to 5 cups sifted cake flour	1 pound
1 square chocolate	1 ounce
1 cup semisweet chocolate chips	6 ounces
4 cups marshmallows	1 pound
$2^1/_4$ cups packed brown sugar	1 pound
4 cups confectioners' sugar	1 pound
2 cups granulated sugar	1 pound

Cereal-Bread

1 cup fine dry bread crumbs	4 to 5 slices
1 cup soft bread crumbs	2 slices
1 cup small bread cubes	2 slices
1 cup fine cracker crumbs	28 saltines
1 cup fine graham cracker crumbs	15 crackers
1 cup vanilla wafer crumbs	22 wafers
1 cup crushed cornflakes	3 cups uncrushed
4 cups cooked macaroni	8 ounces uncooked
$3^1/_2$ cups cooked rice	1 cup uncooked

Dairy

1 cup shredded cheese	4 ounces
1 cup cottage cheese	8 ounces
1 cup sour cream	8 ounces
1 cup whipped cream	$^1/_2$ cup whipping cream
$^2/_3$ cup evaporated milk	1 small can
$1^2/_3$ cups evaporated milk	1 (13-ounce) can

Fruit

4 cups sliced or chopped apples	4 medium
1 cup mashed bananas	3 medium
2 cups pitted cherries	4 cups unpitted
$2^1/_2$ cups shredded coconut	8 ounces
4 cups cranberries	1 pound
1 cup pitted dates	1 (8-ounce) package
1 cup candied fruit	1 (8-ounce) package
3 to 4 tablespoons lemon juice plus 1 tablespoon grated lemon peel	1 lemon
$^1/_3$ cup orange juice plus 2 teaspoons grated orange peel	1 orange
4 cups sliced peaches	8 medium
2 cups pitted prunes	1 (12-ounce) package
3 cups raisins	1 (15-ounce) package

WHEN THE RECIPE CALLS FOR USE

Meats

4 cups chopped cooked chicken . . . . 1 (5-pound) chicken
3 cups chopped cooked meat . . . . 1 pound, cooked
2 cups cooked ground meat . . . . 1 pound, cooked

Nuts

1 cup chopped nuts . . . . 4 ounces shelled or
 1 pound unshelled

Vegetables

2 cups cooked green beans . . . . $^1/_2$ pound fresh or
 1 (16-ounce) can
$2^1/_2$ cups lima beans or red beans . . . . 1 cup dried, cooked
4 cups shredded cabbage . . . . 1 pound
1 cup grated carrot . . . . 1 large
8 ounces fresh mushrooms . . . . 1 (4-ounce) can
1 cup chopped onion . . . . 1 large
4 cups sliced or chopped potatoes . . . . 4 medium
2 cups canned tomatoes . . . . 1 (16-ounce) can

MEASUREMENT EQUIVALENTS

1 tablespoon = 3 teaspoons 1 ($6^1/_2$- to 8-ounce) can = 1 cup
2 tablespoons = 1 ounce 1 ($10^1/_2$- to 12-ounce) can = $1^1/_4$ cups
4 tablespoons = $^1/_4$ cup 1 (14- to 16-ounce) can = $1^3/_4$ cups
$5^1/_3$ tablespoons = $^1/_3$ cup 1 (16- to 17-ounce) can = 2 cups
8 tablespoons = $^1/_2$ cup 1 (18- to 20-ounce) can = $2^1/_2$ cups
12 tablespoons = $^3/_4$ cup 1 (29-ounce) can = $3^1/_2$ cups
16 tablespoons = 1 cup 1 (46- to 51-ounce) can = $5^3/_4$ cups
1 cup = 8 ounces or $^1/_2$ pint 1 ($6^1/_2$- to $7^1/_2$-pound) can or
4 cups = 1 quart Number 10 = 12 to 13 cups
4 quarts = 1 gallon

METRIC EQUIVALENTS

Liquid Dry
1 teaspoon = 5 milliliters 1 quart = 1 liter
1 tablespoon = 15 milliliters 1 ounce = 30 grams
1 fluid ounce = 30 milliliters 1 pound = 450 grams
1 cup = 250 milliliters 2.2 pounds = 1 kilogram
1 pint = 500 milliliters

*NOTE: The metric measures are approximate benchmarks
for purposes of home food preparation.*

Baked beans . . . . 5 gallons

Beef . . . . 40 pounds

Beets . . . . 30 pounds

Bread . . . . 10 loaves

Butter . . . . 3 pounds

Cabbage for slaw . . . . 20 pounds

Cakes . . . . 8 cakes

Carrots . . . . 33 pounds

Cauliflower . . . . 18 pounds

Cheese . . . . 18 pounds

Chicken for chicken pie . . . . 40 pounds

Coffee . . . . 3 pounds

Cream . . . . 3 quarts

Fruit cocktail . . . . 1 gallon

Fruit juice . . . . 4 (No. 10) cans

Fruit salad . . . . 20 quarts

Ground beef . . . . 30 to 36 pounds

Ham . . . . 40 pounds

Ice cream . . . . 4 gallons

Lettuce . . . . 20 heads

Meat loaf . . . . 24 pounds

Milk . . . . 6 gallons

Nuts . . . . 3 pounds

Olives . . . . 1³/4 pounds

Oysters . . . . 18 quarts

Pickles . . . . 2 quarts

Pies . . . . 17 pies

Potatoes . . . . 35 pounds

Roast pork . . . . 40 pounds

Rolls . . . . 200 rolls

Salad dressing . . . . 3 quarts

Scalloped potatoes . . . . 5 gallons

Soup . . . . 5 gallons

Sugar cubes . . . . 3 pounds

Tomato juice . . . . 4 (No. 10) cans

Vegetables . . . . 4 (No. 20) cans

Vegetable salad . . . . 20 quarts

Whipping cream . . . . 4 pints

Wieners . . . . 25 pounds

LIQUOR

Bourbon . . . . 1 liter
Dark rum . . . . 1 (750-milliliter) bottle
Gin . . . . 1 liter
Light rum . . . . 1 liter
Scotch . . . . 2 liters
Tequila . . . . 1 liter
Vodka . . . . 2 liters (1 liter chilled)
Whiskey . . . . 1 liter

FORTIFIED WINES

Cognac . . . . 1 (750-milliliter) bottle
Courvoisier . . . . 1 (750-milliliter) bottle
Crème sherry . . . . 1 (750-milliliter) bottle
Dry sherry . . . . 1 (750-milliliter) bottle
Dry vermouth . . . . 1 (750-milliliter) bottle
Dubonnet . . . . 1 (750-milliliter) bottle
Port . . . . 1 (750-milliliter) bottle
Sweet vermouth . . . . 1 (750-milliliter) bottle

LIQUEUR

Made with a base of neutral alcohol or brandy, liqueurs get their flavor from the addition of fruit or seeds, or sometimes from whiskey that is used as a base and thereby dominates the flavor. These flavored spirits contain a higher percentage of alcohol than other spirits. Liqueurs usually are served individually in one- to two-ounce glasses. Since liqueurs and coffee complement each other's flavor, they often are served together following a meal.

ICE

Allow one pound of ice per person when serving mixed drinks.

Use fresh whole herbs when possible. When fresh herbs are not available, use whole dried herbs that can be crushed just while adding. Store herbs in airtight containers away from the heat of the stove. Fresh herbs may be layered between paper towels and dried in the microwave on HIGH for 2 minutes or until dry.

Basil . . . . Can be chopped and added to cold poultry salads. If the recipe calls for tomatoes or tomato sauce, add a touch of basil to bring out a rich flavor.

Bay leaf . . . . . . The basis of many French seasonings. It is added to soups, stews, marinades and stuffings.

Bouquet garni . . A bundle of parsley, thyme and bay leaves tied together and added to stews, soups or sauces. Other herbs and spices may be added to the basic herbs.

Chervil . . . . One of the traditional fines herbes used in French cooking. (The others are tarragon, parsley and chives.) It is good in omelets and soups.

Chives . . . . Available fresh, dried or frozen, it can be substituted for raw onion or shallot in nearly any recipe.

Garlic . . . . One of the oldest herbs in the world, it must be carefully handled. For best results, press or crush the garlic clove.

Marjoram . . . . . An aromatic herb of the mint family, it is good in soups, sauces, stuffings and stews.

Mint . . . . Use fresh, dried or ground with vegetables, desserts, fruits, jelly, lamb or tea. Fresh sprigs of mint make attractive aromatic garnishes.

Oregano . . . . . . A staple, savory herb in Italian, Spanish, Greek and Mexican cuisines. It is very good in dishes with a tomato foundation, especially in combination with basil.

Parsley . . . . Use this mild herb as fresh sprigs or dried flakes to flavor or garnish almost any dish.

Rosemary . . . . . This pungent herb is especially good in poultry and fish dishes and in such accompaniments as stuffings.

Saffron . . . . Use this deep orange herb, made from the dried stamens of a crocus, sparingly in poultry, seafood and rice dishes.

Sage . . . . This herb is a perennial favorite used with all kinds of poultry and stuffing dishes.

Tarragon . . . . . . One of the fines herbes. Goes well with all poultry dishes, whether hot or cold.

Thyme . . . . Usually used in combination with bay leaf in soups, stews and sauces.

Spices should be stored in airtight containers away from the heat of the stove or in the refrigerator. Add ground spices toward the end of the cooking time to retain maximum flavor. Whole spices may be added at the beginning but a small amount of additional spices should also be added near the end of the cooking time.

Allspice . . . . Pungent aromatic spice, whole or in powdered form. It is excellent in marinades, particularly in game marinade, or in curries.

Caraway seeds . . . Use the whole seeds in breads, especially rye, and with cheese, sauerkraut and cabbage dishes.

Celery seeds . . . . Use whole or ground in salad dressings, sauces or pickles or in meat, cheese, egg and fish dishes.

Chili powder . . . Made from dried red chile peppers, this spice ranges from mild to fiery depending on the type of chile pepper used. Used especially in Mexican cooking, it is a delicious addition to eggs, dips and sauces.

Cinnamon . . . . . Ground from the bark of the cinnamon tree, it is delicious in desserts as well as in savory dishes.

Coriander . . . . . Seeds used whole or ground, this slightly lemony spice adds an unusual flavor to soups, stews, chili dishes, curries and desserts.

Curry powder . . . A blend of several spices, this gives Indian cooking its characteristic flavor.

Cumin . . . . A staple spice in Mexican cooking. Use in meat, rice, cheese, egg and fish dishes.

Ginger . . . . The whole root used fresh, dried or ground is a sweet, pungent addition to desserts or oriental-style dishes.

Mustard (dry) . . . Ground mustard seeds bring a sharp bite to sauces or may be sprinkled sparingly over poultry or other foods.

Nutmeg . . . . Use the whole spice or a bit of freshly ground for flavor in beverages, breads and desserts. A sprinkle on top is both a flavor enhancer and an attractive garnish.

Pepper . . . . Black and white pepper from the pepperberry or peppercorn, whether whole, ground or cracked, is the most commonly used spice in or on any food.

Poppy seeds . . . . Use these tiny, nut-flavored seeds in salad dressings, breads and cakes or as a flavorful garnish for cheese, rolls or noodle dishes.

Turmeric . . . . . . Ground from a root related to ginger, this is an essential in curry powder. Also used in pickles and relishes and in cheese and egg dishes.

ACKNOWLEDGMENTS

MISSION STATEMENT

The Junior League of Abilene, Inc. is an organization of women committed to promoting voluntarism and to improving the community through the effective action and leadership of trained volunteers. Its purpose is exclusively educational and charitable.

CONTRIBUTORS

The Cookbook Committee appreciates very much those who contributed recipes and those who graciously volunteered to assist with kitchen testing.

Leslie Alford
Leah Andrews
Jeanne Angel
Joann Angel
Aloma Asbury
Patsy Bagley
Paige Baker
Kay Berry
Jill Bishop
Leigh Black
Lisa Bloomer
Vicki Brady
The Briarstone Group
Susie Bridges
Gina Bridwell
Charnell Brown
Cindy Brown
Sherry Burchell
Cathy Burgess
Pauline Burke
Silvetta Burns
Barbara Cameron
Grace C. Carroll
Joleen Carson
Catherine Cathey
Martha Chambers
Debbie Cole
Mary Cooksey
Jana Crawford
Jolene Crow
Carol Davis
Kathy Denton
Jody DePriest
Joy De Shazo
Joann Dickey
Lynn Dickey
Sharon Dickey
Sylvia Dickey
Betty Diller
Shari Dozier
Laura Dyer
Joy Ellinger
Molly England
Mrs. Mack Eplen
Lale Estes
Cheryl Etter
Barbara Fahrlender

Adrianne Fergus
Anita Fergus
Mary Ann Fergus
Mrs. Dan Fergus, Sr.
Margaret Flowers
Jayne Ford
Jill Forehand
Margaret Forrester
Holly Frizzell
Lori Frymire
Mary Gee
Stacey Geisler
Sally Goldsmith
Terri Goldsmith
Cindy Gossett
Melanie Gray
Nancy Green
Jackie Hamp
Maryana Harrell
Jill Harris
Laura Beth Hawkinson
Lois Haynes
Gretchen Henson
Tommie Holley
Leta Holmes
Mary Clark Holt
Barbara House
Cindy Howard
LeAnne Huff
Kim Huggins
Glynell Hughes
Shelley Hughes
Carol King Hutcheson
Mitzi Jackson
Jolyn Johnson
Denise Jones
Mrs. Jon Rex Jones
Lisa Jones
Margaret B. Jones
Marilyn Jordan
Gail Kaiser
Kathryn Keathley
Beth Kellar
Beverly Kimbrough
Dorothy Kiser
Roxanne Klump
Patty Knight

Lisa Kuntz
Debbie Langford
Delores Lawhon
Sharon Lawler
Diane Leggett
Lera Lewis
Terry Lindley
Lisa Linn
Sheila Lloyd
Wilma Lucas
Connie Mann
Chesley Martin
Jan McCaslin
Pat McCleskey
Diana McMillan
Emily Meador
Kathy Merrill
Geraldine Metcalf
Marsha Mickler
Jaynne Middleton
Mary Minter
Portia Moore
Lisa Morgan
Carol Morris
Kim Munden
Patti Musgrave
Cheryl Niblo
Susan Odom
Alison Otis
Jacki Cutbirth Parker
Martha Pearson
Connie Petross
Pam Porter
Dottie Preston
Billye Proctor-Shaw
Catherine Quainton
Sonya Quinn
Betty Ray
Mrs. Travis Robinson
Lynn Roeder
Sheila Rollins
Karen Roper
Pam Rosenbaum
Jim Roskopf
Brenda Sandifer
Jerita Sayre
Norma Schaffer

Donna Schnitman
Elizabeth Schumacher
Melissa Scott
Cristy Seago
Melinda Seale
Kelli Secord
Sandra Self
Debbie Senter
Kimberly Shahan
Paula Shahan
Jayree Shaw
Judy Shaw
Carolyn Shelburn
Sue Shields
Karon Shira
Jean Shoultz
Sharon Sibert
Liz Sinclair
Wanda Singer
Judy Rose Sivley
Rachel Smith
Charlene Stanley
Sherri Statler
Becky Stewart
Carolyn Strain
Patty Taliaferro
Regina Taylor
Gail Thames
Lori Thiry
Doris Thompson
Dr. Carl Trusler
Jane Voss
Laura Wardroup
Patty Wenetschlaeger
Kathryn White
Judy Wilson
Mrs. Stanley P. Wilson
Russell Ann Wilson
Joni Wood
Marilyn Woolly
Alice Wright
Bev Wright
De Ann Yeilding
Lanita Zachry
Vanessa Zientek

Abilene Convention and Visitors Bureau: Abilene, Texas: Abilene Cultural Affairs Council: Abilene, Texas Historical Walking Tour Brochure: 1991.

Alternative Learning Program for Gifted Students and Taylor County Historical Commission: Insights to The Past Central Downtown Walking Tour Pamphlet: Abilene, Texas: R & R Printing, 1990.

Corbitt, Helen. *Helen Corbitt's Cookbook*: Boston, Massachusetts: Houghton Mifflin Co., 1957.

Zachry, Juanita Daniel. *Abilene: The Key City*: Northridge, California: Windsor Publications, Inc.—History Book Division, 1986.

Hendrick Home Hunt Committee: Abilene, Texas: Mary Ann Fergus, Hendrick Ranch Pamphlet, 1993.

Morgan, Sara. *Dining With the Cattle Barrons Yesterday and Today*: Texian Press, 1981.

INDEX

COOKBOOK COMMITTEE

Jill Forehand, Chairman
Laura Dyer
Mary Ann Fergus
Donna Schnitman
Elizabeth Schumacher
Rachel Smith

MARKETING COMMITTEE

Jill Forehand, Chairman
Nanci Perini, Assistant Chairman
Leta Holmes, Internal Marketing Chairman
Jackie Love, External Marketing Chairman
Linda Stanley, Treasurer
Elizabeth Schumacher, Sustaining Advisor
Lisa Bloomer
Stacey Geisler
Christy Macon
Pam Percival
Jena Price
Rachel Smith
Linda Sullivan
Stephanie Taylor
Elizabeth Wagstaff

Additional copies of *Landmark Entertaining* may be obtained by writing or calling:
The Junior League of Abilene
774 Butternut Street
Abilene, Texas 79602
(915) 677-1879
WATS (888) 626-6000
FAX (915) 677-1870